3/93

Cinematic Vampires

Cinematic Vampires

The Living Dead on
Film and Television, from
The Devil's Castle (1896) to
Bram Stoker's Dracula (1992)

by
John L. Flynn

McFarland & Company, Inc., Publishers
Jefferson, North Carolina, and London

To the memory of Angeline Gertsen,
my grandmother and mentor,
who always believed in my dreams.

To Susan, who believed in me
and helped me to dream again.

To my family—Norma Jean, James, Norman,
Robert, Edna, Bobbie, and Timmie—
who supported me with their faith.

And to Bela Lugosi, John Carradine,
Frank Langella, and Christopher Lee—
who will always be Dracula to me.

British Library Cataloguing-in-Publication data are available

Library of Congress Cataloguing-in-Publication Data

Flynn, John, 1954–
 Cinematic vampires : the living dead on film and television, from
The devil's castle (1896) to Bram Stoker's Dracula (1992) / by
John Flynn.
  p. cm.
 Includes bibliographical references and index.
 ISBN 0-89950-659-3 (lib. bdg. : 50# acid-free paper) ∞
 1. Vampire films—Catalogs. I. Title.
PN1995.9.V3F58 1992
016.79143′675—dc20
                                                                92-53578
                                                                CIP

Manufactured in the United States of America

McFarland & Company, Inc., Publishers
 Box 611, Jefferson, North Carolina 28640

Contents

About the Filmographies

The filmography entries throughout the book are meant to provide a complete listing of the vampire film from 1896 to the present. Only films about or related to vampires are included, although there may be some crossover to other horror subjects. The entries have been arranged chronologically (whenever possible) to accompany the text. Titles of foreign films have been translated into English with careful precision, the original title appearing in parentheses. Certain films, most notably those from independent producers, which were rereleased under different titles are noted by their alternate titles whenever possible.

Each listing gives the year of the film's general release (rather than its production). Although the credits have been exhaustively researched and compiled, some are missing, particularly in the early period. Since some records identifying the director, producer, writer, and stars were poorly kept, the filmography lists all the known information. (In some cases, the film itself has been lost.) Producer credits for films from countries where the film industry is a national asset are meaningless and have been omitted. And in many other countries, where directors are true *auteurs*, there is only a single entry of their work.

To die! To be really dead! That must be glorious!
— Dracula, in *Dracula*

The strength of the vampire is that no one will believe in him!
— Dr. Van Helsing, in *Dracula*

Mad? I, who have solved the secret of life, you call me mad?
— Dr. Otto Von Niemann,
in *The Vampire Bat*

Introduction

For over ninety-five years, from *The Devil's Castle* (1896) to *Bram Stoker's Dracula* (1992), the vampire has freely stalked movie theaters and preyed upon the willing patrons of over three hundred films. Though his origins may have been lost in the cave etchings of primeval mythology, obscured by the superstitions of folklore, or exploited by the "penny dreadfuls" of Victorian melodrama, the vampire has remained a popular subject for motion pictures and television. The novel *Dracula*, for example, has been adapted for the silver screen more times than any other book and has inspired countless imitations, sequels, parodies, and spoofs. The words *vampire* and *Dracula* have become synonymous with sexual seduction, power, and domination, and are an integral part of our daily vocabulary. The vampire film continues to be a lively and prominent form of entertainment—fifteen or so were in production at the beginning of 1992. Perhaps the reason for its longevity and prolificacy is a message that is universal; or perhaps it has something to do with myth and our collective unconscious. In either case, many media students, film critics, historians (this author among them), and filmgoers contend that the vampire film has been largely responsible for popularizing the horror genre. This seems like an enormous claim, but there may be some validity to that contention, considering its humble beginnings and progenitors as well as its worldwide acclaim. The purpose of this study, then, is to examine the role of the vampire in the cinema and discover why this particular motif continues to be a ubiquitous part of our popular culture.

1

The vampire or Dracula image is one that has instant recognition throughout most of the world in both print and media forms, and it is an icon which we become familiar with from the time we are old enough to color in a coloring book, watch a television show, or read. Almost any first- or second-grade child (as well as many preschoolers) can identify the vampiric characters of Count Count from "Sesame Street," Count Duckula from the noted British cartoon series (of the same name), or Count Chocula from their favorite General Mills cereal. As they grow older and become consumers, adolescents (as well as many adults) are attracted to print advertisements and radio-television commercials which feature Count Dracula as a spokesman for products as diverse as men's toiletries (from Gillette Industries), sugarless gum (Trident), and copper-top batteries (Duracell). (The product line doesn't stop there either; over the years, the vampire image has been associated with mouthwash, cat food, alcohol, fruit juice, pizza, security systems, and two dozen other items. During the Halloween season, the product line nearly doubles with the large variety of greeting cards, party favors, candy, centerpieces, napkins, and paper plates that feature Count Dracula or some other noted vampire [Vampirella, Vampira, Elvira, to name a few].) Children of all ages dress in the traditional black cape and fangs and gain instant identification of character while celebrating the curious holiday of demons, witches, and other creatures of the night. Throughout the rest of the year, contributors to more than a dozen scholarly journals (including a special newsletter from MENSA) regularly discuss the psychological, sociological, anthropological, and literary merits of the most famous creature who never lived. It is quite obvious that the vampire image has had a major impact on as many levels of contemporary society as cultures of the past.

Superstitions, myths, and legends about the vampire can be found, with divergent variations, in almost every culture in the world. Most of the stories date back thousands of years and have been handed down orally from generation to generation. The single element which seems to unite the most diverse traditions is the belief that the vampire is a dead person who returns from the grave to suck the life (blood) from living persons. This conception of the vampire, known as *nosferatu* (the "undead"), is probably the most common among mid–European Slavonic peoples, particularly in the Balkan countries and Hungary, Bohemia, Moravia, and Silesia. (Besides stories in folklore, actual documentation of historical vampires dates from the late seventeenth century.) In White Russia and parts of Ukraine, the vampire is also identified as a wizard, or sorcerer, who seeks to destroy the living. In Greece, the *broncolaia* or *bourkabakos,* a curious crossing of the vampire and werewolf legends, steals the heart of the living during certain lunar phases. The traditions are not, however, exclusively European. The Polynesians' *tii,* the Malayans' *hantu penyardin,* and the Karens' *kephn* are vampires who devour not only blood but also human souls. They appear as dog-headed water demons from the sea. In Africa, the vampire is a demonic servant who steals the souls of the unfaithful.

Many obvious ties link this tradition to zombie and voodoo worship. In China, vampires are mischievous shapechangers who, much like the *jinn*, attack babies and other helpless individuals. The United States, Britain, and other English-speaking countries have no established traditions of their own (beyond certain legends of the American Indian) and have borrowed many of the familiar precepts from their European forebears. But regardless of the origins of their diversity, the various beliefs all suggest that there is much more to the vampire myth than superstition.

Thematically, the modern vampire story deals with the disturbing survival of romantic ideals (represented by the vampire) in an era of industrialism or scientific rationalism (contemporary society). That presupposition, while it may have taken on different forms in the last ninety-five years, lies at the very core of the vampire film. Magic, or any force of the supernatural, no longer has a place in a world where Edison's light bulb has replaced the gas lamp, yet the vampire does attempt to survive, challenging the new order with his antiquated methods. Those roots of discontentment lie not only in the classic stories of *Carmilla,* by Joseph Sheridan Le Fanu; *The Vampyre,* by John Polidori; and *Dracula,* which for many vampire films are source materials, but also in older literary conventions and attitudes from Judeo-Christian mythology and the medieval morality play. Both the legend of Lilith and the story of Satan are parables of human presumption, man (or demigod) playing God, that predate the Dracula story by some five thousand years. Lilith, the first wife to Adam, according to the Talmud and other Semitic writings, refused to concede her husband's superiority and was damned to walk the earth in search of human blood forever. Satan, the most beautiful angel in Judeo-Christian mythology, tried to become like God, at the cost of great suffering and eternal damnation. Both acts challenge the natural order of things, and both individuals suffer similar punishment for their arrogance. Similarly, the medieval story of Dr. Faustus (though not strictly a vampire tale) portrays a man who is willing to sell his soul to the devil for an eternal life of pleasure. Faust, like Lilith and Satan, openly defies God and must be destroyed to preserve the spiritual foundations of the Judeo-Christian faith. This common theme is also central to our understanding of the vampire mythos.

Because it also draws from such a rich literary heritage, questions about the nature of life and death, good and evil, science and faith can also be found in most well-written vampire stories. Joseph Campbell, in his treatise on the power of myth in literature (*The Hero with a Thousand Faces*), recognized that man chose certain archetypes and symbols to deal with those universal questions. The vampire, as the embodiment of romantic ideas, is the ultimate Byronic hero, an outcast who like Milton's Satan or Goethe's Faust has rejected God's salvation in favor of his own version of immortality or life after death. Clearly, the "gothic" romances of the last two hundred years have provided a wealth of mythopoetic characters who are no more than archetypes or symbols that fit this pattern.

Carmilla, the seductive beauty of Joseph Sheridan Le Fanu's novella of the same name, is the archetype for the first female vampire and a symbol of sexual deviance (inherent in many vampire stories). When her carriage is overturned in a highway accident, Carmilla is taken to a wealthy Austrian estate. There she meets and eventually seduces Laura, the innocent daughter of the household. What she fails to realize is that the lesbian relationship calls attention to herself and reveals the age-old vampire Mircalla, Countess Karnstein. Lord Ruthven, the first great fictional vampire from John Polidori's *The Vampyre,* dresses, speaks, and in general performs like a nobleman, but there is a dark, mysterious (even dangerous) side to his nature that his traveling companion, Aubrey, eventually notices. Ruthven represents beauty and power, both seductive, as well as a tragic side which echoes Satan's sentiments in Milton's epic poem: "Better to rule in Hell than serve in Heaven." Unfortunately, Aubrey fails to recognize his friend as evil until it is too late: the vampire has already seduced and destroyed his innocent sister.

Count Dracula is the quintessential vampire and symbol of romanticism, immortality, sexuality, aggression, and power. Having dominated his Transylvanian homeland for centuries, he moves into Carfax Abbey and instantly attempts to impose his values and way of life upon the citizenry of England. At first he is welcomed into the finest homes and quickly establishes himself as a visiting nobleman, a man of great importance. His Old World charms and mysterious sexual allure cause heart flutters in Mina Murray, Lucy Westenra, and other women he encounters. However, the charm and sexual allure are merely illusionary. Dracula intends to feed upon his female conquests, and to satisfy his needs fully, he must dominate them completely, body and soul. Unfortunately for Dracula, his control becomes unraveled with the appearance of a man of science. Dr. Abraham Van Helsing recognizes Dracula for what he is, and soon his first victim, Lucy, is staked, his servant Renfield imprisoned, and Mina placed under protective care. The vampire is forced to flee to his homeland to reestablish his world and power base. Bram Stoker's novel brilliantly explores that unknown territory of the soul where love, imagination, and mutual satisfaction become sex, fantasy, dominance, submission, and degradation of spirit—all central to our understanding of the vampire mythos.

Literary scholar James Twitchell, in his landmark article "The Vampire Myth," wrote that Dracula (along with his counterpart Frankenstein) was the most important archetype from Victorian literature and that his presence in our popular culture was significant. Besides being "the stranger in a strange land," the outsider, Dracula is a constant reminder of the many Old World traditions that never quite made the transition to contemporary society. He is the romantic hero, like many of us, lost in an unfamiliar world of microchips and computer technology. Whereas we might stumble around in ignorance or allow ourselves to be intimidated, Dracula refuses to acknowledge such reproaches, surviving at all costs. He also represents the symbol of eternal life. Like Peter Pan, the boy who refused to grow up, Dracula remains unchanged in a changing society with no conscience or remorse for his actions. He knows only what he wants and satisfies those desires without any consideration for the consequences. He is the embodiment of evil without guilt, power without restraint, and sexuality without conscience. And in essence we secretly admire his ability to resolve or ignore problems with which we have difficulty in dealing.

Similarly, the act of drinking blood works on many different levels. The most obvious is food and nourishment. Traditional Christian mythology views blood as the life force which Jesus Christ sacrificed to grant his followers eternal life. Since the vampire myth is a perversion of that belief, Dracula drinks the blood of the living as a shortcut to immortality. Less obvious reasons concern sexual deviance and the need for power or dominance over another. Dracula has total control over Lucy Westenra and Renfield through his manipulation of blood; for Lucy, the control is somewhat sexual, and for his servant, a bizarre sadomasochism. They can be free only after his control is broken. Finally, at the heart of the vampire myth is the desire for reunion with deceased loved ones. How many of us would leap at the opportunity to see our long-dead mother, father, or spouse? When Lucy appears from the grave, her fiancé, Arthur Holmwood, is relieved to discover that she is not dead, but he soon realizes that she is part of the "undead" and must be destroyed in order to free her soul. Romanticism, power, sexuality, and visions of immortality, all key elements of the vampire myth, have provided (and continue to provide) endless fascination for the general public.

Like many mythological or literary stories, the vampire film relies heavily upon a set of traditions which have been handed down from generation to generation. For example, vampires are creatures of the night, afraid of the purifying rays of the sun. They must sleep in the earth of their native land, and they must drink the blood of willing victims to survive. They fear the cross (of Jesus) or other Holy implements and can be destroyed by a stake through the heart. Like the morality play, which shares much of its ritual nature, plots of most vampire films deal with the struggle of ideals, good versus evil, in terms which provide *katharsis* ("cleansing" in Aristotelean tragedy) and good entertainment. Countless times, characters like David Gray, Dr. Van Helsing, and Carl Kolchak have ventured forth into darkness, or hell, as a symbol of good to defeat Dracula, Carmilla, Count Yorga, or other symbols of evil. The story is a most familiar one, and each time it is replayed, audiences thrill to the ageless conflict.

The continued use of these common elements, set symbols, and ageless traditions has not diminished the interest in, nor hampered the development of, the vampire film but has provided an arena for ingenuity and imagination to examine old themes and to explore new ones. Early in its history, the vampire film became not only a contemporary morality play but also a social and aesthetic reflection of its popular culture. And we can learn much about the attitudes of the period in which each film was made. For example, in *Nosferatu* (1922), *Dracula* (1931), and other early films, the nocturnal blood lust equated to a necrophilic passion in which a demon or vampire preyed at night upon sleeping innocence. Prior to World War II, America pictured itself as a sleeping innocent being preyed upon by the pestilences of poverty, injustice, and war. In films like *The Horror of Dracula* (1958), *The Vampire Lovers* (1970), and others, the vampire was still cloaked in ritual and superstition but had taken on an air of sadism and erotic sensationalism, much in keeping with our changing attitudes toward free love, drugs, campus revolt, the generation gap, and Vietnam. For the seventies and eighties, in an age which had rejected most religious and supernatural beliefs in favor of science and technology, the vampire was no longer simply a night stalker. In films like *Martin* (1978), *The Keep* (1983), and *Lifeforce— The Space Vampires* (1985), he had become a maniacal psychotic looking to drain not only blood but the entire soul from his victims.

By implication, then, the vampire film is a subject of established ritual and shifting and variable emphasis. It is also a unique art form which has contributed much to the evolution of the modern "horror" film. But in all fairness to the form, the words *horror* and *monster*, when used in conjunction with *film*, are really misnomers and largely inappropriate to our study of the vampire mythos. *Horror*, by definition, suggests an intense, painful feeling of revulsion or loathing, and *monster* conjures images of an offensive grotesque who commits perverse acts of random violence. These terms might more amply describe the splatter films of Herschel Gordon Lewis or the highly successful *Friday the 13th* series (in which a maniac in a hockey mask indiscriminately murders teenagers) but certainly not any in the scope of this study. Vampire films transcend those common labels; they belong to the *cinéfantastique*, the cinema of the fantastic, which combines the literature of imagination with the mystique of motion picture technology.

Although the stories may be largely interchangeable, the films are distinguishable from one another through differences in visual styles, characterization, and approach. There are five different types of vampire films, and even though any attempt at definitive classification is impossible, they may be roughly divided into the following categories:

1. The *traditional vampire film:* A human, through sympathetic magic, a curse, or the evil of another vampire, has been forced to seek blood as nourishment. Most *Dracula* movies fit into this category, particularly the ones which attempt to establish a historical lineage for the noted vampire. Other films, like *Vampyr* (1932), *The Vampire Lovers* (1970), *The Night Stalker* (1972), *Vampire* (1978), *Salem's Lot* (1979), *Fright Night* 1 and 2 (1985, 1989), and many others fit nicely into this category.

2. The *alternate species film:* The premise holds that somewhere at the beginning of our human history, there may have been another race like humans, a species which found immediate sustenance in the blood of its human cattle. What became of that race has been lost in antiquity, and it has purposely existed apart from its human counterparts. Although a relatively new concept, it has permeated most contemporary vampire novels and is typified in films like *Nightwing* (1979), *The Hunger* (1983), *The Keep* (1983), and *Near Dark* (1987). (For his classic vampire film *Nosferatu* [1922], F. W. Murnau, who envisioned his vampire as an offshoot of another species, deserves the credit for this recent, cinematic conceit.)

3. The *deranged, psychotic film:* Twisted humans think they are vampires and act out their fantasies in horrifyingly real ways. The concept, however deplorable it might seem, has its historic antecedents, such as the "Dusseldorf vampire," who believed himself to be a real vampire and committed a series of bizarre and grotesque murders. Films like *The Tenderness of Wolves* (1978), *Martin* (1978), and *Fade to Black* (1980) fit into this category.

4. The *man-made vampire film:* A man, through accident of design, creates a vampire. This is a broad category and encompasses films like *The Unholy Love* (1929), *The Bat Whispers* (1930), *The Return of Dr. X* (1939), *The Last Man on Earth* (1964), and *The Omega Man* (1971). The key to most of these films is that man, by tinkering with the natural order of the universe, unleashes a horrible pestilence (vampires) upon those around him. (Conceptually, these films also fall into the study of the Frankenstein mythos.)

5. The *alien vampire film:* The vampire is part of a race of beings from another planet. Although this borders on science fiction, there are a number of notable exceptions. *Demon Planet* (1965), *Queen of Blood* (1966), *Horror of the Blood Creatures* (1971), and *Lifeforce — The Space Vampires* (1985) all belong to this category.

Whatever the category or sociological importance, the vampire film does have a legitimate place in the cinema as in every other art form and is an integral part of our popular culture. It provides worthy entertainment, challenges the creative imagination, and utilizes the best in motion-picture technology. We all know that not a single vampire stalks the streets of our cities, but through the vampire film and our willing suspension of disbelief, he still haunts our theaters and television parlors.

Silent Beginnings

From *The Devil's Castle* (1896) to *London After Midnight* (1927)

The years between 1896 and 1927 witnessed the first appearances on film of the famous monsters of literature—Quasimodo, Mephistopheles, the phantom of the opera, Dr. Jekyll and Mr. Hyde, the Frankenstein monster, and Count Dracula—and paid deference to the form which would help develop, and ultimately popularize, the adolescent motion picture industry. That form was known as the cinema of the fantastic, but unlike its many progenitors, the *cinéfantastique* offered a photographic image that was both real and illusionary and urged audiences to join Alice on a magical journey through the looking glass. That form also produced many true *auteurs* whose revolutionary ideas and approaches helped produce what French film critic Ado Kyrou called *le nouveau mythe de l'homme* (man's new myth, or mythos).

Progressive and internationally renowned directors like the great Georges Méliès of France, Walter Booth and Robert Paul of England, Edwin S. Porter and Tod Browning of the United States, and F. W. Murnau and Henrik Galeen of Germany recognized the power of the cinema's illusions and created films that would mystify and astonish audiences with the extraordinary. Their superior efforts dominated the early cinema and established notable movie companies like Pathé, Gaumont, UFA, Edison, Nordisk, and Cines. But more significantly, their early silent experiments with the vampire film created the visual blueprint for future horror fantasies.

Without sound-tracking as a crutch, the directors had to be visually oriented from the start. And although it would take some time before cinema techniques were universally recognized and established, these cinematic pioneers demonstrated great freedom with their ingenious and creative use of the new photographic equipment. Through stop-motion photography, double exposures, masking, dissolves, point-of-view shots, and other camera tricks, they produced classic silent movies which filmmakers today still copy in style and content.

For the general public, the earliest photographs—those static images reproduced in sepia-tone or dark olive tint—seemed miraculous yet rather staged. But when Etienne-Juley Marey used the photographic gun, which he had invented to record the flight of birds, to create *La Marche de l'Homme* (*The March of Man*, 1888), he gave audiences the illusion of movement through a careful sequencing of those still photographs, and cinema was born.

A few short years later, at a popular nightclub of mystery and prestidigitation known as the Théâtre Robert-Houdín, the proprietor and principal performer introduced elements of fantasy in his first film, *The Vanishing Lady* (1896) and stunned that same audience. Georges Méliès had turned the camera lens away from reality and with sleight of hand displayed his talents as a magician and a budding filmmaker. By "artifically arranging scenes" (what we accept today as common editing), he made a woman vanish and reappear as a skeleton. The photographic images were so "real" that audiences didn't quite know what to make of them, but they did hunger for more.

The great Georges Méliès first learned about "moving pictures" at the historic film exhibition of the brothers Lumiere in a Paris basement café on December 27, 1895. He was astounded by their invention and immediately recognized the potential of *le cinématographe* to communicate ideas of the fantastic. Less than eighteen months later, Méliès had eclipsed many of his contemporaries, including the brothers Lumiere, and had built his own studio at Montreuil. He had also achieved many cinematic firsts, including the first Faust film (*The Laboratory of Mephistopheles*, 1897), the first literary adaptation (*Faust and Marguerite*, 1897), the first robot movie (*Gugusse and the Automaton*, 1897), and the first vampire movie (*The Devil's Castle*, 1896).

Méliès's aim, much like his former ambitions as a magician, was to mystify and astonish his audiences through the miracles of photography and his macabre imagination. By the turn of the century, Méliès had achieved that by producing more than 244 short films and establishing a reputation as a true *auteur*.

1896 *The Devil's Castle* (*Le Manoir du Diable*)
French, b/w, 2 min. Director-Producer-Writer: Georges Méliès.

Although Méliès's masterpiece *Un Voyage dans la Lune* (*A Trip to the Moon*, 1902) made him famous in the United States, a large part of his cinematic output which dealt with the supernatural and the fantastic never made it to this country until years later. *Le Manoir du Diable* (*The Devil's Castle*, 1896), which actually predates Bram Stoker's classic by a year, was the first vampire film but arrived years after the novel *Dracula* and French and German films had made the subject of vampires passé. This is somewhat unfortunate because it may well be the most significant film of his early career. Not only is it, historically speaking, the first horror film, but *The Devil's Castle* also demonstrates Méliès's raw talent as a filmmaker. Through the invention of several dissolving effects, Méliès relates the struggle between the vampire (and demon) Mephistopheles, who has transformed himself into a huge bat, and the Cavalier, who, armed only with a crucifix, must fight him to the death. Méliès further demonstrates his talents by photographing each scene with bold panache in creating an atmosphere that is both ambitiously conceived and visually realized. The imaginative climax occurs when the bat is vaporized in a puff of smoke, and from that puff of smoke, the vampire film was born. Méliès would continue to make films for another twenty-five years, but he would never eclipse the creative, raw energy seen in his earliest efforts, notably *The Devil's Castle*. Tragically, Méliès's fortunes dwindled during World War I and the two decades that followed, and he died after a long illness at the French film industry's Home for the Destitute and Aging in 1938. But there are few who would debate Georges Méliès's contribution to the newly evolving art form.

The year 1901 ushered in not only a new century but a new epoch of the cinema. Thomas Edison, the modern Prometheus who had harnessed the power of electricity and channeled it through a light bulb, created one of the first film companies. And even though his invention of the kinetoscope (in 1891) was quickly supplanted by Auguste and Louis Lumiere's *le cinématographe*, Edison's many other contributions to film influenced a whole new generation of filmmakers. Most of them were cinematic storytellers, not magicians like Méliès; but they all recognized the cinema's power of illusion. In England, Robert Paul, a visionary and futurist, and Walter Booth, a cartoonist and former magician (!), joined forces to create a series of fantastic films, including *The ? Motorist* (1905), *The Aerocab and Vacuum Provider* (1909), *The Aerial Submarine* (1910), and *The Aerial Anarchists* (1911), that would thrust audiences into a new age of filmmaking. In France, Ferdinand Zecca made *La Machine Volante* (*The Flying Machine*, 1901) and other cautionary tales about the dangers of that new technology. Early Faust and Satan films (of which Michael Laclos lists twelve between

1896 and 1911 in *Le Fantastique au Cinéma*) dominated Germany's cinema
of the fantastic. But for the most part, American filmmakers, with the exception of D. W. Griffith, Robert Vignola, and Edwin Porter, remained detached from the *cinéfantastique* until the 1930s. Griffith, who would later
become one of the most influential silent filmmakers, experimented briefly
with adaptations of Edgar Allan Poe stories before creating epics like *Birth
of a Nation* (1915) and *Intolerance* (1916), but the honor of creating the first
American vampire film belonged to a relative unknown.

1913 *The Vampire*
b/w, 15 min. (?) Director-Writer: Robert Vignola.

Robert Vignola, an obscure director with no other cinematic efforts to
his credit, introduced the vampire legend to American audiences in 1913
with *The Vampire*, but it was not very popular compared to those being
offered by European filmmakers. One explanation suggests that customers
of the penny arcades may have associated the word *vampire* with "vamp"
(a woman who uses her charms to seduce men) and were disappointed.
Although no copies of this film exist today, early records indicate that
Vignola's story follows a familiar path and represents, like other motion pictures of the period, an experiment in filmmaking techniques. Several deaths
occur in a small town (or village), and the local constable must hunt down
the vile creature responsible. This movie, which had a running time of
about fifteen minutes, is often confused with Porter's *A Village Vampire*
(1916), but the two seem to share only the most superficial similarities.
Porter, the man singularly responsible for the creation of the first Frankenstein film, was much more skilled with the camera and produced a far
superior effort.

1916 *A Village Vampire*
Edison Films, b/w, 16 min. Director-Writer: Edwin S. Porter.

Edwin S. Porter was intrigued with Méliès's methods and studied the
Frenchman's films, sometimes literally frame by frame on Edison's
kinetoscope, to learn his secrets. Porter joined the Edison Company in 1899
after having toured throughout America showing films in fairgrounds. He
also recognized the power of film to create illusion. While working as a
director and scenarist there, he made a number of lackluster projects that
were really derivative of Méliès. *Faust and Marguerite* (1900) was little more
than a remake of the earlier film, and *Fun in a Butcher Shop* (1901) was no
more than a copy of any one of a number of "sausage machine" movies.

Then Porter made *The Great Train Robbery* (1903) and forever changed the course of filmmaking by introducing the "point-of-view" shot. (Prior to that, movie cameras remained stationary and simply recorded events as they occurred in front of the lens. Porter felt that this form of filmmaking was much too limited and static, and chose to involve the audience in the action by selecting shots that would establish perspective and point of view. His close-ups of the bandit firing at the camera have become indelible for cinema audiences.) *The Great Train Robbery* became the most popular film of its day and caused audiences and critics alike to reexamine the work of the young American filmmaker.

Edwin Porter went on to make *Frankenstein* in 1910 and *A Village Vampire* in 1916. Unfortunately, while a few key sequences remain of his first horror film, not one frame or still has survived to this day of his vampire film. The plot synopsis in Edison's catalog reveals a familiar story line (similar in many ways to Vignola's *The Vampire*, 1913). The aristocratic prince of a small Eastern European village is discovered to be a vampire by the sheriff after several deaths occur. Contemporaries of Porter (including some of his harshest critics) complained that both films suffered from too much reliance on camera tricks and were really pale copies of early Méliès efforts. It was clear that Porter had fallen into the trap of his French predecessor, even though he believed just the opposite.

By 1915, the era of the magician as filmmaker had really come to an end. Cinema audiences had become much more sophisticated. Too many of the current films depended upon the impact of camera techniques and special effects (made popular by Méliès), and viewers were bored, looking beyond the camera tricks for realism and drama. They found little to be excited with in the early horror and science fiction movies, which dominated the period, and the threat of diminishing returns on a cinematic release was real. However, the rich inventions of plotting, pace, and characterization of Louis Fevillade's serials brought audiences back into the cinema week after week hungering for more. Though most of his films were primarily thrillers, he did create one strange nightmare vision of the world, *Les Vampires.*

1915–16 *The Vampires (Les Vampires)*
French, b/w, 12-part serial. Director-Producer: Louis Fevillade. Writers: Marcel Allain, Pierre Souvestre. Starring Musidora, Jean Ayme, Edouard Mate, Larcel Levesque.

Les Vampires (*The Vampires*, 1915–16) was a "series film" of ten episodes produced, directed, and improvised by Fevillade during an eight-month shooting schedule. Unlike many of his other serials, the episodes did not appear weekly but at intervals of two to five weeks. The first and second parts ("La Tete Coupee" [The Decapitated Head] and "La Bague qui tue" [The Killing Ring"]) premiered on November 13, 1915, and the last episode ("Les Noces sanglantes" [Bloody Wedding]) appeared on June 30, 1916. (After their initial screenings in France, they appeared in the United States as weekly episodes.) The plot concerns a band of vampires who, led by the Grand Vampire (Jean Ayme) and Irma Vep (Musidora), commit a series of brilliant crimes. They are tracked down by journalist Guerande (Edouard Mate) and his assistant (Marcel Levesque). And after many chases in cars and over rooftops, kidnappings, gassings, and bodies in trunks, the vampires are discovered in their hideout during an orgy and are killed by the police.

Stylistically, *Les Vampires* is less ambitious than *The Devil's Castle* with its blend of realism, fantasy, and comedy. Fevillade did not envision himself as a magician performing tricks but as a storyteller. Even though he made use of the technology available to him, his first concern was to entertain his audience. And it was that spirit which produced many of the great vampire films and resulted, indirectly, in much of the genre's cinematic quality.

While Fevillade was making his imaginative thrillers in France, silent experiments in the *cinéfantastique* continued in England, Russia, and Denmark, but it was the work then being done in Germany that advanced the vampire's mythic themes and shaped future efforts in the genre. Heavily influenced by the visionary writings of Hoffman, Kafka, Buchner, and Nietzsche, German directors chose to distort the established conventions of cinema to draw viewers into a world where the normal perceptions of reality were no longer valid. Through the ingenious use of special camera lenses, mirrors, and out-of-focus photography, they totally transformed film into surreal visions, dreams, and nightmares. Controversial, avant garde, and expressionistic, these efforts redefined the term *cinéfantastique*. (Patterns and ideas from this rich cinematic epoch would later be brought to the United States in the thirties and forties to produce some of the great horror films.)

Many film scholars contend that the first great horror cycle began in Germany and ascended to its greatest heights just after World War I in films as diverse as *Satanus* (1919), *Nosferatu: A Symphony of Terror* (1922), and *Metropolis* (1926). The popularity of these fantastic films is not surprising in view of Germany's cultural interest in myth, fantasy, and mysticism. One film in particular, *Das Kabinett von Dr. Caligari (The Cabinet of Dr. Caligari*, 1919), is commonly identified as having single-handedly remade cinema design. Siegfried Kracauer wrote in his famous study *From Caligari to Hitler* (Dobson, 1947) that the film's preoccupation with psychosis and psychological horror signified the course German cinema (and German history) was to follow. *Dr. Caligari*, the forerunner of the Frankenstein film, was responsible for preparing the way for the success of two notable vampire films and inspired the style later known as expressionism.

The roots of expressionism can be traced directly to Swedish playwright August Strindberg, who in *The Dream Play* (1902) and *The Ghost Sonata* (1907) introduced characters who change their identities at will and constantly wander through dreamlike landscapes. In these two plays as well as several others, Strindberg laid the foundation for the movement that German filmmakers would embrace as their own. This movement, eventually called expressionism, was a reaction to realism, the tendency of contemporary playwrights (and filmmakers) to reduce drama to its most common or basic elements. Strindberg, who earlier had won critical acclaim as a realist, rejected most of its trappings, reasoning that art should be a reflection of a much larger world of wonders and nightmares invisible to the average audience. By making use of bizarre sets, exaggerated makeup, and overstated costumes, German directors and scenarists chose to explore that larger world. The intense emotional crises of their central characters would often be portrayed through odd shapes, textures, and colors glimpsed in the background. Dreams would often become confused with reality, and insanity was objectified to depict the world through lunatic eyes. Motion pictures of the period were so filled with such rich, visual images, clues, and portents that the traditional limitations and conventions of storytelling were thrown off in favor of artistic eloquence. Accordingly, German filmmakers like Arthur Robison, Henrick Galeen, and F. W. Murnau came the closest to capturing a real nightmare on film and making cinema a truly interactive medium.

1916 *A Night of Horror*
German, b/w, 55 min. Director: Arthur Robison. Starring Werner Krauss, Emil Jennings.

A Night of Horror (1916) marked not only the directorial debut of Arthur Robison but the first German vampire film. Starring Werner Krauss (destined to be remembered as the first mad scientist in *Das Kabinett von Dr. Caligari*, 1919) and Emil Jennings, the story focuses on a protagonist who must spend a night of horror among the "Grey People" (or vampires) of superstition. For one of the earliest of the German films, the background and lighting are very expressionistic and help to suggest Krauss's confused state of mind. A split-screen technique, created by Méliès as a camera trick, is used quite effectively by Robison as a storytelling device. Innovative, the film also established the pattern for future successes and is clearly a precursor to *Homunkulus der Fuhrer* (*Homunculus the Leader*, 1916), *Das Kabinett von Dr. Caligari* (*The Cabinet of Dr. Caligari*, 1919), and *Nosferatu* (1922) —

all three of which virtually revolutionized the struggling young industry. Following the war, Germany would emerge as the predominant producer of imaginative cinematic nightmares.

1918 *Alraune*
German-Neutral Films, b/w, 88 min. Director-Writer: Eugen Illes, based on the novel by Hanns Heinz Ewers. Starring Hilde Wolter, Gustav Adolf Semler, Friedrich Kuehne, May Auzinger, Ernst Rennspies.

1918 *Alraune*
Austrian-Hungarian, b/w, 80 min. Director: Mihaly Kertesz (Michael Curtiz). Screenwriter: Richard Falk, based on the novel by Hanns Heinz Ewers. Starring Guyla Gal, Rozsi Scollosi, Jeno Torzs, Margit Lux, Kalman Kormendy.

Two competing versions of Hanns Heinz Ewers's popular gothic story *Alraune* (1913) were produced in the same year by German and Austrian filmmakers. (The novel would be filmed three additional times, in 1928, 1930, and 1952.) No copies of either film appear to have survived the onslaught of war, and that is truly unfortunate, even though critical accounts suggest that they were both poor adaptations. The story, which appears to be a retelling of the familiar Frankenstein legend, concerns a mad scientist, Ted Brinken, who artificially inseminates a prostitute to create a beautiful but demonic woman. Alraune drinks human blood, then consumes the souls of the victims she encounters. Eventually she desires a sexual relation with her spiritual father, Brinken, but he wants nothing to do with her. Rejected by her creator, she turns against the mad doctor and destroys him. For the first time on film, sexual perversity is linked to vampirism, a common theme that will be repeated again and again. Director Eugen Illes would fall into obscurity; Mihaly Kertesz would travel to America and become a famous action director (as Michael Curtiz).

1919 *Lilith and Ly (Lilith und Ly)*
Austrian, Fiat Films, b/w, 65 min. Director: Drich Kober. Writer: Fritz Lang. Starring Elga Beck, Hans Marschall, Ernest Escherich, Fritz Kammauf.

One year after World War I, Germany began to rebuild its film industry with the help of its three undisputed masters—Fritz Lang, F. W. Murnau, and Henrick Galeen. Lang, a Viennese architect and cartoonist, had been wounded in the war and while recuperating in a veteran's hospital, had written numerous film scripts. Although no print of this movie appears to have survived, the first of his many motion pictures was *Lilith und Ly* (*Lilith and Ly*, 1919), premiering a few months before *Caligari*. Directed (in his absence) by Drich Kober, Lang's script combines the legend of the Golem with vampire themes in a shadowy, expressionist vision. Frank Landow (Hans Marschall) has discovered a way to create life, by means of a special ruby, in a sort of television screen. He animates a statue of Lilith (Elga Beck), whose image comes to life, and falls madly in love with her. Unfortunately, his old love, Ly (Beck, in a dual role), begins to fade away, her life force becoming weaker and weaker. Distressed, he confides in Lilith and discovers that she is a vampire who is increasing in strength as Ly gets weaker. By casting the blood-red ruby in a stream, Landow destroys Lilith and restores his real love. Even though the story is somewhat predictable, it provides a wonderful analysis of "true love" and "desire." Lang later met Thea Von Harbou and collaborated on numerous projects, including the classic science fiction film *Metropolis* (1926).

By 1922, Germany had developed two important production companies, DeclaBioskop and UFA, and F. W. Murnau, one of Germany's eminent directors, had produced the classic vampire film — *Nosferatu: Eine Symphonie des Gravens* (*Nosferatu: A Symphony of Terror*). Born Friederich Wilhelm Plumpe in 1889, Murnau was fascinated by the literature of the imagination. His first film, *Satanus* (1919), drew heavily from Goethe's *Faust*, and his second picture, *Janus-Faced* (1920), which starred horror greats Bela Lugosi and Conrad Veidt, was based on Robert Louis Stevenson's *Dr. Jekyll and Mr. Hyde*. When he approached his third project, he chose Bram Stoker's *Dracula* as source material. However, Stoker had died, and the copyright had passed to a stubborn widow who wished to maintain the integrity of the book by keeping it from being filmed. (She did allow actor-manager Hamilton Deane to produce an early stage version in 1925, but Mrs. Stoker did not believe film was the right medium for her late husband's work.) Murnau remained undaunted and proceeded to film the classic vampire story anyway.

1922 *Nosferatu: A Symphony of Terror* (*Nosferatu: Eine Symphonie des Gravens*)

German, Prana Films, b/w, 95 min. Director: F. W. Murnau. Screenwriter: Henrich Galeen, based on the novel *Dracula* by Bram Stoker. Starring Max Schreck, Alexander Granach, Gustav von Wangerheim, Greta Schroder, John Gottowt, Ruth Lanshoff, G. H. Schell, Gustav Botz.

Written for the screen by Henrik Galeen, the film version of *Nosferatu: A Symphony of Terror* made several departures from the Stoker novel. Murnau envisioned the vampire, as portrayed by Max Schreck, as part of a reptilian race apart from humanity with claws, pointed ears, deep-set eyes, and a pale, cadaverlike complexion. The vampire is named Count Orlock instead of Dracula, and his presence in the film gradually emerges as the incarnation of an evil pestilence. The setting of Transylvania is moved to the Baltic area, and many of the central characters' names are changed to German-sounding ones. And the hero is not Dr. Van Helsing, who is portrayed as a feeble old man, but Nina, the Count's female prey. When, instead of fleeing from the vampire, Nina, the clerk's innocent daughter, welcomes him into her room, she sacrifices her virtue to destroy Orlock with the morning sun.

The film opens, much like the novel *Dracula*, with Count Orlock renting a home in Brennen, a port city in the northern part of Germany. After dispatching Jonathan (Gustav Von Wangerheim), the man who has rented him the property, he travels aboard the cargo ship *Empusa* with his dreadful shipment of coffins. When the ship arrives in Brennen with its dead crew, the people fear a deadly pestilence has come to their city. It is really the curse of the vampire. Orlock takes residence across the street from the beautiful fiancée of the land agent (whom he has already killed). The story is climaxed when Nina (Greta Schroeder) plots the demise of the vampire. No longer the virginal, idealized bride that she was when she met Orlock, she now "knows" the dark side of sexuality and uses it to her advantage. She gives herself to him, and in a major departure from the book, the vampire awakes to be destroyed by the purifying rays of the sun as it engulfs Nina's room.

Nosferatu: A Symphony of Terror is a masterpiece of the German cinema and the first great horror school with its innovative camera techniques, atmospheric sets, and Schreck's grotesque makeup. Although the acting is stilted and crude by today's standards, Fritz Arno Wagner's eerie camerawork surrounds the film with great mystery. Like most cinematic nightmares of the period, *Nosferatu* was filmed on a limited budget and features photographic tricks (worthy of Méliès) that now appear rather commonplace. Irises introduce and close scenes; slow-motion, blurred photography gives the vampire a supernatural existence; and negative printing gives the woods and skies an uncanny, ghastly appearance. Its suspense-filled ending, though overly melodramatic, is an interesting variation

Opposite: Nosferatu: A Symphony of Terror (1922) — Max Schreck as Count Orlock. F. W. Murnau envisioned his vampire as an offshoot of another race and portrayed him bald with pointed ears and elongated fingernails. Photo courtesy of Prana-Films.

of the Beauty-Beast theme, and Max Schreck's excellent characterization of the vampire would later provide a model for several other stalkers of the night.

Shortly after *Nosferatu* debuted in 1922, Florence Stoker (Bram's widow) brought a lawsuit against Murnau for copyright infringement, alleging that his film was an unauthorized version of *Dracula*. The court recognized the similarities and ordered that the film be destroyed. Less than a month later, Murnau's film company folded, and it seemed that his classic would be forever lost. Fortunately, prints of the film survived, and Murnau's later success with *The Last Laugh* (1925) and *Sunrise* (1927) created a demand for *Nosferatu* in the United States, where it was eventually released in 1929. (*Nosferatu* was remade as *Nosferatu the Vampire* in 1979 by Werner Herzog for Twentieth Century–Fox, starring Klaus Kinski in the role of Count Orlock.)

1922 *Drakula*
b/w. Hungarian. Additional information unknown.

Similar in style and content, the Hungarian-made *Drakula* (1922) was completed a year before Murnau's *Nosferatu* but inexplicably held for release until after the Prana Films classic. This supposedly first unauthorized adaptation of Stoker's work had very limited exposure (outside Hungary) and was lost during World War II. Since most of the records from the time were also lost, it is really impossible to determine which film was actually first. None of the legal action that seemed to plague Murnau's classic affected this production in any way, although it is entirely possible that Florence Stoker never saw or had any knowledge of its existence. Since legends about Vlad Dracul (the Impaler) and vampires were fairly common in Hungary, this lost film could simply tell another story.

1925 *The Vampires of Warsaw*
Polish, b/w. Director-Writer: Wiktor Bieganski.

Reputedly the best of all the films that have been lost, *The Vampires of Warsaw* (1925) was adapted by Wiktor Bieganski from his own stage play about a visitor to Poland who takes up residence at a house haunted by vampires. As with all Grand Guignol productions of the time, the protagonist

Opposite: **Count Orlock (Max Schreck) emerges from the cargo hold of the *Empusa* to unleash his horrible plague of vampirism in Murnau's *Nosferatu: A Symphony of Terror* (1922). Photo courtesy of Prana-Films.**

Klaus Kinski was inspired by Schreck in the 1979 remake. Note the similarity in makeup. Photo courtesy of Twentieth Century–Fox.

must endure all manner of brutality before escaping the clutches of his hosts. The motion picture regrettably disappeared during the German assault on Warsaw in the opening days of World War II, and not much else is known. It was never released in Britain or the United States and had very limited play in Poland and the rest of Eastern Europe. Contemporaries said that the motion picture shared the Germans' creative potential for innovative photography, special effects, and unusual set design, but regrettably we'll never know.

1928 *The Unholy Love* (aka *Alraune*)

German, AMA Films, b/w, 140 min. Director: Henrich Galeen. Producer: Helmut Schreiber. Screenwriters: Hanns Heinz Ewers, Henrich Galeen, based on the novel by Ewers. Starring Paul Wegener, Ivan Petrovich, Brigitte Helm, Georg John, Valeska Gert, John Lader, Hans Trautner, Louis Ralph, Mia Pankau.

Although hardly in the same class as *Nosferatu, The Unholy Love* (also known as *Alraune,* completed in 1927 and released in 1928) was another noteworthy vampire film produced during the German gothic period. Based on the immensely popular German novel *Alraune* by Hanns Heinz Ewers, the material was hardly unique or fresh. The book had already been made into two motion pictures in 1918 (one by Michael Curtiz and one by Eugen Illes), and was destined to be remade in 1930 and 1952. However, as directed by Henrik Galeen (the screenwriter of *Nosferatu*) and starring his longtime collaborator Paul Wegener (*Der Golem,* 1914), the film combined the themes of *Dracula* and *Frankenstein* into an interesting hybrid fantasy.

Wegener plays Ted Brinken, a scientist who artificially inseminates a prostitute with the semen of a hanged criminal. The experiment produces an incredibly beautiful but cold woman named Alraune (Brigitte Helm, riding a wave of success following her portrayal of Maria in *Metropolis*). She seeks out young men, then drains them of their loving essence, much like a vampire. She is also attracted in an incestuous way to her "father," who is fascinated, appalled, and seduced by his creation. But when she learns of her unholy origins and that she has no soul, Alraune deliberately takes her own life. Strong on plot and atmosphere, masterly in its trick photography, this film, for all its shortcomings, was a powerful fantasy. The experience by which the artificial woman is brought back to life is treated with great skill and innovation. (Along with the creation of the Robotrix in *Metropolis,* this film would influence James Whale's vision in the 1931 *Frankenstein.*) Though not up to *Nosferatu, The Unholy Love* is remembered as the last important feature of the first great horror school.

1930 *Alraune* (aka *Daughter of Evil*)

German, UFA, b/w, 103 min. Director: Richard Oswald. Producer: Erich Pommer. Screenwriters: Charlie Roellinghaff, Richard Weisbach. Starring Brigitte Helm, Albert Basserman, Agnes Straub, Kaethe Haack, Harold Paulsen.

The 1930 version of *Alraune* was little more than a talkie remake of the 1928 version, also starring Brigette Helm.

Murnau's *Faust* (1928) and a fourth version of *Alraune* (1930) followed Galeen's *The Unholy Love* to the screen and came and went with very little fanfare. Expressionism, Germany's indisputable contribution to world cinema, had nearly run its course and by 1933 would be totally suppressed by the Nazi movement. Ironically, films like *Homunculus the Leader* (1916), *The Cabinet of Dr. Caligari* (1919), and *Nosferatu* (1922) appealed to Adolf Hitler. He and his minister of propaganda, Joseph Goebbels, sought out many of the creative geniuses behind expressionism (including Wegener, Galeen, Murnau, Riefenstahl, Lang, Von Harbou, and Robison) to make prestige films for the Third Reich. A large number of them declined and on the same day left for the safety of the production studios in England and Hollywood. Many, like Murnau, would eventually reach the summit of their film careers, while others, like Galeen, would disappear into obscurity. (Still others, like Riefenstahl and Von Harbou, would produce some of the most powerful propaganda films in cinema history, including *Triumph of the Will* [1934].) But their influence and early efforts would have a much longer, more far-reaching effect on cinema, as the ghosts of Count Orlock and the mad doctors of Germany's UFA would continue to haunt horror films for years to come and inspire the future talents of Tod Browning, Orson Welles, Alfred Hitchcock, Steven Spielberg, and many others.

Two and a half years after *Nosferatu,* the famous stage version of *Dracula* opened in Scotland. Written by actor-manager Hamilton Deane, the play was actually the second theatrical version of *Dracula.* (Bram Stoker had written a version in 1898 which he had hoped to produce prior to his death.) Deane tried to capture the essence of the German expressionist movement, and on stage he appeared as Dr. Van Helsing to Edmund Blake's Schreck-like Dracula. After a successful run in Scotland, the drama premiered at the Grand Theatre, Derby, on August 5, 1925. During the summer of 1926, the production toured the provinces, and on Valentine's Day 1927 opened in London at the Little Theatre, with Raymond Huntley as Dracula and Bernard Jukes as Renfield. Later, collaborating with American playwright John L. Balderston, Deane revised his work for New York. The newly written *Dracula* opened on Broadway in October 1927 and starred a Hungarian immigrant named Bela Lugosi in the title role. The play received rave reviews in New York and broke box-office records during its U.S. tour, but film audiences would have to wait nearly four years for the first screen adaptation of *Dracula.*

While France and Germany were furthering their film industries and the stage version of *Dracula* was touring the United States, Hollywood tried with little success to imitate its European competitors. The great American director D. W. Griffith produced a number of psychological fantasies based on the works of Edgar Allan Poe, but his *The Avenging Conscience* (1914) was the only film to come close.

1926 *The Bat*

United Artists, b/w, 77 min. Director: Roland West. Writers: Mary Robert Reinhart, Avery Hopwood. Starring Emily Fitzroy, Claudette Colbert, Lillian Gish.

United Artists, attempting to imitate European success formulas, released *The Bat* in 1926, but it was pale in comparison to *Les Vampires* and *Nosferatu*. Directed by Roland West and featuring photographic effects by Arthur Edeson, the story tells of a mysterious thief who disguises himself as a giant vampire bat to terrorize an unsuspecting household. The film was moderately successful in the United States and was remade by West in 1930 (as *The Bat Whispers*) using sound, but it suffered greatly from uninspired camerawork and poor scripting. Eventually Hollywood magnates and producers, including German-born Carl Laemmle, decided to import talent from abroad, offering incentives and American dollars. They hoped to attract the expertise of Murnau, Lang, and others to engender originality and vision, sadly lacking in American films.

1927 *London After Midnight* (aka *The Hypnotist*)

MGM, b/w, 63 min. (?) Director: Tod Browning. Screenwriters: Tod Browning, Waldemar Young, based on an original idea by Browning. Starring Lon Chaney, Marceline Day, Henry Walthall, Percy Williams, Conrad Nagel, Polly Moran.

The singular exception, which rekindled the American public's imagination, was Tod Browning's *London After Midnight* (1927). The film marked the first and only appearance of Lon Chaney, Sr., as a vampire, and it was an unqualified success due in large part to Chaney's unusual characterization. Each decade would have its stock menace, an expert in contortion and makeup, who became the cinema's resident monster and mad psychotic. In the thirties and forties, it was Boris Karloff; in the fifties, Vincent Price; in the sixties, Christopher Lee; and in the eighties, Robert Englund; but Chaney dominated the twenties with a series of brilliant characterizations. In real life Lon Chaney was rather ordinary-looking, slightly middle-aged, with horn-rimmed glasses and a face that made him look like a business manager. He spent more than ten years altering that image (by twisting his body or distorting his face) and established the fashion for movie monsters to come.

Born on April Fool's Day 1883, Lon Chaney began his career as a stage actor (in 1901), playing a variety of roles from the hero to the villain to the speak carrier. "It was purely by chance," he explained in an article written shortly before his death, that he became associated with screen characterizations which required the use of grotesque makeup. "All during that time, the thing that interested me most was makeup," he revealed, "but not merely grease-paint and putty noses but mental makeup as well. If I played the role of an old man, I tried to crawl into the old man's mind." His first screen appearance was twelve years later in *Poor Jake's Demise* (1913).

London After Midnight (1927). The great Lon Chaney played an imaginary vampire in Tod Browning's silent classic. (It is unfortunate that no complete prints of the film survive today.) Photo courtesy of MGM.

Executives at Universal Pictures saw great potential in Chaney's work and signed him to an exclusive contract for $5 a day. *The False Faces* (1919), one of his earlier makeup jobs, virtually launched his film career. After playing a gallery of tortured grotesques like Fagin in *Oliver Twist* (1922), Quasimodo in *The Hunchback of Notre Dame* (1923), and Erik, the disfigured composer, in *The Phantom of the Opera* (1925), Chaney reached the summit of his career as the vampire in *London After Midnight*. His bone-white face and bulging eyes demonstrated a mastery of the art of theatrical makeup, and his performance was a triumph of the macabre. (To create his most effective monster, Chaney used a thin wire which went around each eye socket and when tightened made his eyes bulge horrifyingly.) Black-clad with a top hat, his eerie figure glided, half creeping through the dark shadows, into movie history.

Tod Browning shared Chaney's propensity for warped minds and twisted bodies, and collaborated with the "Man of a Thousand Faces" on many superior films, including *The Unholy Three* (1925), *The Unknown* (1926), and *London After Midnight*. For what he hoped would be the ultimate vampire film, Browning gave Chaney free rein with his character. Regrettably, all that remains today of this classic are a handful of still photographs which merely suggest the film's greatness. (Forrest J. Ackerman, former editor of *Famous Monsters of Filmland* and the curator of science fiction's only museum, recently assembled a photo-novel of *London After Midnight* which gives a somewhat accurate record of the film.)

When viewed in still life, however, the story for *London After Midnight* appears rather simpleminded. A murder has been committed in a creepy haunted house. Five years later, Detective-Inspector Burke of Scotland Yard (Chaney) is convinced that the murder was no accident or suicide and sets in motion a scheme to expose the real murderer. First he suggests that the murder was committed by a vampire, then shows his two suspects—the dead man's friend (Henry Walthall) and his nephew (Conrad Nagel)—the empty coffin. Finally, utilizing an elaborate masquerade as a vampire, Chaney forces the real murderer to confess. His vampire, as it turns out, is not even real. Remade eight years later as *Mark of the Vampire* by Browning, the original remains an unquestionable classic.

Browning and studio executives were so impressed with Chaney that they offered him the role of Dracula in the film being mounted. Unfortunately, Lon Chaney died of throat cancer on August 26, 1930, having spoken only once on the sound screen. (In fact, he spoke in four different voices as a sideshow ventriloquist in the talkie remake of *The Unholy Three*, 1930.) With his passing the silent era came to a close, heralding a new epoch of technology and collaboration between American and European film-makers. Chaney's fine work in *London After Midnight*, coupled with the landmark success of *Les Vampires* and *Nosferatu*, firmly established the

Dashing young Bela Lugosi as Dracula. This publicity still was taken during the Broadway stage version of *Dracula* (1927) four years prior to the famous film.

vampire film as a legitimate art form, and the technical skill, vision, and expertise of the new era would produce worthy (as well as unworthy) successors to the legacy of its silent beginnings.

2

Foul Things
of the Night
From *Dracula* (1931)
to *Return of the Vampire* (1943)

The early 1930s saw the development of the second great horror school in America and the production of the first sound classics of the genre. Following the immediate and enormous success of *Dracula* and *Frankenstein* in 1931, Universal Pictures launched several highly profitable series, including the *Dracula* film cycle as well as numerous others which fall outside the scope of this study; and, like the UFA before it, the studio became known as the "House of Horror." Prior to that, Universal Pictures had been distinguished by only a few films, little more than a twenty-first birthday present given to Carl Laemmle, Jr., by his wealthy father. But the junior Laemmle worked very hard to build up his studio, notably by luring some of the finest talents of the silent period from Germany and France. However, it should be noted that in spite of what many film scholars contend, Laemmle did not "create" the second great horror school; rather, he and his counterparts at Paramount Pictures, Metro-Goldwyn-Mayer (MGM), Twentieth Century–Fox, Radio-Keith-Orpheum (RKO), and Warner Brothers were merely the beneficiaries of a long and carefully cultivated cinematic tradition that had been transplanted from Europe to the United States. Outside this country, the horror tradition died out, with very few exceptions (notably Carl

Dreyer's *Vampyr* [1932] and several Mexican films), as European film-makers turned their attention to more immediate problems.

Directors F. W. Murnau, Fritz Lang, Michael Curtiz; cinematographers Karl Freund, Rudolph Maté, Karl Struss; and actors Bela Lugosi and Conrad Veidt came to Hollywood in the late twenties and early thirties to escape the oppressive rule of Hitler and the Nazi party and brought with them superior technical skills and a richness of vision which greatly influenced American cinema. That richness of vision in turn sparked the imagination and creativity of *auteurs* like Tod Browning, James Whale, Rouben Mamoulian, and others. Their films and motion pictures like *Murders in the Rue Morgue* (1932), *Mystery of the Wax Museum* (1933), *Dracula's Daughter* (1936), and *The Return of the Vampire* (1943) are still remarkable from an artistic point of view and represent milestones of the Golden Age of the American horror film.

The horror film had also finally achieved a degree of respectability in the thirties before plummeting to its lowest depths in the forties. During the early part of the decade, the ravages of the depression (in this country) and the winds of war in Europe caused many people to seek out the simple escapist fare of fantasy films. But the motion pictures were so much more than that, as many of the Dracula films proved to audiences to be a popular indictment of America's financial institutions and Nazi Germany's totalitarian regime. The monolith of our economic systems, a bloodsucking vampire created by wealthy industrialists, had collapsed under its own veight, leaving millions literally destitute. The wealthy, aristocratic Dracula represented one (or more) of those industrialists and was destroyed (in film after film) by the common man for exploiting the innocent.

Later in the decade, the image of the bloodsucking aristocrat had been replaced by a much more obscene one. The advent of fascism and the rise of Nazi Germany presented a superior race of social vampires content to exterminate all those that didn't fit their Aryan ideals. It was certainly no accident, then, that Count (Vlad Tepes) Dracula had assumed a distinctive German flavor and that Dr. *Abraham* Van Helsing was a learned scholar with a Hebrew name and Judeo-Christian roots. (In fact, several American war posters portrayed the Nazis as bloodsucking vampires.) Audiences couldn't get enough of these pictures, and the studios cranked them out in large numbers. This gave rise to low-budget second features, known as "B" movies, that were generally not very good and largely exploitative. By the end of the period, the horror genre in America had run its course, deteriorating into a slapdash of sequels, parodies, and monster team-ups. Most filmmakers had forgotten that it was the innocence of theme and the sincerity of pure artistry that had made the early efforts so endearing.

Dracula (1931). Bela Lugosi as the Transylvanian Count eavesdropping on Renfield at Castle Dracula. Photo courtesy of Universal Pictures.

1931 *Dracula*

Universal, b/w, 85 min. Director: Tod Browning. Producer: Carl Laemmle, Jr. Screenwriters: Garret Fort, Dudley Murphy, from the play by Hamilton Deane and John Balderston, based on the novel by Bram Stoker. Starring Bela Lugosi, David Manners, Dwight Frye, Helen Chandler, Edward Van Sloan.

One of the most enduring and influential genre films of the period, and the first one chronologically in this study, was the 1931 version of *Dracula*. In the wake of the immense commercial and unexpected success of the stage play, Carl Laemmle, Jr., acquired the film rights in 1930 from Bram Stoker's estate. He had already initiated several other genre productions, including adaptations of Edgar Allan Poe's *Murders in the Rue Morgue* and Mary Shelley's *Frankenstein*, but he decided that the vampire classic, which had already been filmed by Murnau, would be the first in a series of high-quality, moderately budgeted horror films. Junior Laemmle further announced that the team that had made the very successful *London After Midnight*, Tod Browning and Lon Chaney, Sr., would direct and star (respectively) in his feature. Unfortunately, Chaney had become ill (and later died from throat cancer), and many of the studio's top executives urged Laemmle to begin production as soon as possible to capitalize on the hot word-of-mouth publicity from the play. The part of Dracula was then offered to Bela Lugosi, the actor who had originated the role on Broadway.

Born Bela Ferenc Blasko in Lugos, Hungary, in 1882, he had starred in several European films, including Murnau's *Janus-Faced* (1920), and had also appeared as Ariztid Olt in numerous stage productions prior to emigrating to America. Lugosi was the ideal choice for many silent films as the suave European lover or the smooth European villain and was cast to type in *The Silent Command* (1923), *The Rejected Woman* (1924), *Renegades* (1930), and *Oh, For a Man* (1930). His chilling stage presence and Hungarian accent instantly established him in the stage role of the Transylvanian Count and brought him to the attention of Carl Laemmle, Jr. Ironically, his accent became a handicap in later films as sound revolutionized the cinema, and he became typecast in many inferior horror films. Lugosi was often paired with Boris Karloff, another alumnus of Universal Pictures. Disappointed in the direction his career was going, he turned to drugs and died in 1956. (Two biographies, *The Count*, by Arthur Lennig, and *Lugosi: The Man Behind the Cape*, by Robert Cremer, recount the life and films of Bela Lugosi in much greater detail than this survey.) No one will dispute the contribution he made to the genre, starring in over fifty horror and science-fiction films, but he will always be remembered as Count Dracula.

Tod Browning had worked with Lugosi once before, on *The Thirteenth Chair* (1929) when he cast him in the role of Inspector Delzante, and he was familiar with his accomplishments on stage. (*Dracula* was the fifth Broadway play Lugosi had worked on.) He found Lugosi's acting range limited, but he felt that with the proper direction he would do fine in the lead role.

Opposite: *Dracula* (1931). **Bela Lugosi as the charismatic vampire in Tod Browning's classic, pictured here with Helen Chandler. Photo courtesy of Universal Pictures.**

Using Garrett Fort's screenplay (based on the original play by Hamilton Deane and John Balderston), Browning wanted to avoid the melodrama of Murnau's *Nosferatu* and went back to Stoker's original conception. (Sometimes the film's development is too literal.) Dracula would be played as a Transylvania nobleman (instead of the embodiment of plague and pestilence) who travels to London to satisfy his vampiric craving for blood. He would be dressed in the finest suits (updating the time to the present) and, like a wealthy aristocrat, would attend the symphony, opera, and exclusive dinner parties. And only after the stroke of midnight would his Count become a night stalker. Browning was able to achieve this through Lugosi's presence and the memorable photography of Karl Freund, which is hypnotic and chilling.

The film story of *Dracula* is much the same as Stoker's novel and the play by Hamilton Deane and John Balderston, and this might account for the film's stagy quality. Little has been changed except the combining of the roles of Harker and Renfield. When the film opens, Renfield, portrayed by Dwight Frye, has traveled into the Carpathians to discuss several rental properties in England with a mysterious count. He refuses to heed the warnings of the local townspeople and soon falls under the spell of Dracula. After a short sea journey to Whitby in which the vampire destroys all but the captain of the ship, Dracula emerges as the new resident of Carfax Abbey. Count Dracula quickly becomes the toast of London by posing as a wealthy displaced aristocrat. He attends the theater, recitals, and other local cultural events. He is also a frequent guest of Dr. Seward and is introduced to many women there, including Lucy Westenra and Mina Murray, who all find him quite charming. However, when Lucy dies and Mina becomes ill, Dr. Abraham Van Helsing is called in to help. The learned professor believes that she is suffering from the bite of a vampire, and that to cure her, they must take steps to find and destroy the evil creature. Dr. Seward and Arthur Holmwood are skeptical but follow his instructions. Van Helsing soon unmasks Dracula as a vampire by accidentally discovering that the Count casts no reflection in the mirror lid of his cigarette case. The two adversaries recognize each other for the first time. Outnumbered and exposed, Dracula attempts to make off with Mina, but he is too late. Van Helsing traps the vampire in his Hampstead cellar and drives a stake through his heart.

Although the film was highly regarded in its time and is viewed today as a classic, it must be pointed out that the pacing is very slow and pedantic and the horror kept to a minimum. Contemporary audiences, who are used

Opposite: Dracula (1931). **When land agent Renfield (Dwight Frye) cuts his finger on the corner of the deed to Carfax Abbey, Dracula (Bela Lugosi) is unable to move his attention from the dripping blood. Photo courtesy of Universal Pictures.**

Dracula (played by Lugosi) strangles Renfield (Dwight Frye) when he learns that his servant has betrayed him—from the 1931 version of *Dracula*. Photo courtesy of Universal Pictures.

Bela Lugosi, as the Transylvanian Count, puts the bite on leading lady Helen Chandler in Tod Browning's *Dracula* (1931). Photo courtesy of Universal Pictures.

Rare publicity still of Lugosi with long-time rival, costar, and friend Boris Karloff.

to the graphic violence of the *Nightmare on Elm Street* films, *Hellraiser* (1987), or *Hellbound: Hellraiser II* (1988), will find this material very tame. Much of the action of the film takes place offscreen, leaving things to the imagination. Even the climax, which is glimpsed in silhouette, is handled so that Dracula's death is merely suggested and not shown. Perhaps this is a fault of the Deane-Balderston play rather than the film, but it is nevertheless a major blunder because it robs the audience of the much needed catharsis. Tod Browning also insisted on having the period transposed to present (rather than Victorian) London, and this too is a mistake. The story works best by contrasting the repressed sexual urges of Victorian morality with Dracula's irresistible sexuality. However, Browning avoids this question entirely and in doing so takes away much of the vampire's potency. Perhaps his reasoning was to minimize any controversy about the film, but unfortunately it achieves the opposite effect by removing one of the central conflicts in the novel.

Dracula premiered on Friday, February 13, 1931, and in spite of its many flaws, was a major box-office success for Carl Laemmle and Universal Pictures. The motion picture grossed over $25 million from its original $441,984 investment in its initial release. During the next dozen years, Dracula would appear in five more films, only one of which was a direct sequel, *Dracula's Daughter* (1936). Lugosi became an overnight success and played Dracula, or a relative vampire, six more times until his death in 1956. Although he became typecast as a heavy in a series of inferior horror movies, Lugosi remarked a few years before his death that he "wanted the public to scream with terror, as on a rollercoaster. . . . I might have grown angry with the vampire putting me forever in the evil mold, but it was a living — or — a dying in its own way." Tod Browning went on making horror films for another ten years, including *Mark of the Vampire* (1935) with Lugosi, but he was never able to eclipse the success of *London After Midnight* (1927) and *Dracula*.

1931 *Dracula*

Universal, b/w, 85 min. Director: George Melford. Producers: Carl Laemmle, Jr., Paul Kohner. Screenwriters: Garret Fort, Dudley Murphy, from the play by Hamilton Deane and John Balderston, based on the novel by Bram Stoker. Starring Carlos Villarias, Barry Norton, Eduardo Arozamena, Pablo Alvarez Rudio, Lupita Tovar, Carmen Guerrero.

Filmed back-to-back with the Tod Browning version, using the same sets and whole scenes, the Spanish-language *Dracula* was also an enormous success critically and financially. Universal Pictures and Junior Laemmle wisely recognized that half their revenues came from foreign countries, many of which were Latin. Since dubbing was years away, they decided to produce a simultaneous foreign-language version at an extremely low cost ($70,000 total). Principal photography was shot at night on the Universal lots by George Melford, cinematographer George Robinson, and a crew of Mexican actors and technicians after the American crew had gone home, and other scenes were lifted in tact from the negative print.

Carlos Villarias essayed the Lugosi role as Dracula; Barry Norton appeared as "Juan" Harker; Eduardo Arozamena as Dr. Van Helsing; and Pablo Alvarez Rudio as "Rendfield" (not Renfield). Noted actress Lupita Tovar played Eva (not Mina), and Carmen Guerrero completed the cast as Lucia (not Lucy). Ironically, Melford's version was completed first and released in Mexico weeks before the Browning picture. Critics were very enthusiastic about the foreign-language film (more so than the earlier Spanish-language adaptation of Rupert Julian's *The Cat Creeps*), and *Dracula* played for many years in Spanish-speaking countries. The film was lost during the forties, but an archival copy was shown in 1977 at the Library of Congress.

There are numerous differences between the Browning and Melford versions, but the most striking difference is the lack of a flat stage play in the foreign-language film. George Melford apparently studied Browning's version shot for shot on a moviola and chose to revise certain scenes, creating more of an atmospheric chiller like *Nosferatu* (1922) than a filmed play. Personal tastes differ, and ultimately the audience must decide which is the better version.

1932 *Vampyr* (aka *The Strange Adventure of David Gray, Not Against the Flesh,* and *Castle of Doom*)

German-French, Carl Theodor Dreyer Film Produktion, b/w, 82 min. Director-Producer: Carl Theodor Dreyer. Screenwriters: Carl Dreyer, Christen Jul, based on *Carmilla* by Joseph Sheridan Le Fanu. Starring Julien West, Henriette Gerard, Rena Mandel, Sybille Schmitz, Albert Bras, Jan Hieronimko.

The year after Browning's *Dracula*, Carl Theodor Dreyer produced and directed a macabre fantasy known as *Vampyr* (released in England and the United States as *The Strange Adventure of David Gray*, 1932). Handsomely photographed by Rudolph Maté, the film is superior to *Dracula* in almost every way. The Danish filmmaker's vision is most striking and recalls to mind the earlier works of Méliès, Fevillade, and Murnau.

Freely adapted from Joseph Sheridan Le Fanu's *Carmilla*, the script borrows from other stories contained in his collection, *In a Glass Darkly*. David Gray (Allan Grey in the German version), a young traveler in Eastern Europe (possibly Transylvania), arrives at a lonely inn for dinner and a good night's rest. Awakened from a sound sleep, he is given a package by a mysterious stranger, who warns him to open it if the stranger should die. On the following day, he meets several other strange characters, including

Opposite: Dr. Van Helsing (Edward Van Sloan) uses a mirror in the lid of a box to reveal the true nature of the vampire in *Dracula* (1931). Photo courtesy of Universal Pictures.

a doctor (Jan Hieronimko) and an old woman named Marguerite Chopin (Henriette Gerard). He also stumbles upon an old château (something eerie like Castle Dracula) whose owner turns out to be his mysterious night visitor. He is introduced to the man's daughters: Leone (Sybille Schmitz), who seems to be suffering from a strange illness, and Giselle (Rena Mandel), who appears to be held captive. The château owner dies, and in keeping with his request, Gray opens the package. He discovers a book on vampires (and how to destroy them) and learns that the old woman is a vampire. She has apparently enslaved (with her doctor's help) the elder daughter, Leone, and is draining her dry. Gray and a servant stake Chopin. Then he attempts to save Leone with a blood transfusion, but unfortunately she too has become a vampire. Gray becomes psychically linked to her through the transfusion, and in the celebrated sequence envisions being buried alive. He soon realizes that she is beyond hope and runs away with the younger sister, Giselle.

The film opened in England and the United States with little fanfare and was commercially unsuccessful. However, when viewed in retrospect, *Vampyr* is virtually a textbook piece on creative cinematography, making use of many techniques that filmmakers today view as commonplace. Instead of the stark contrast of black and white, the images are hazy, dissolving into many shades of gray. There is also a play of mists and shadows on the camera lens, which according to film history, occurred quite by accident. (Years later, this style would be known as *film noir*.) Utilizing natural settings and Hermann Warm's celebrated designs, cinematographer Rudolph Mate plunges audiences into a dreamworld of shadows, coffins, and vampires. Carl Dreyer explained that he deliberately wanted "to create a nightmare on the screen and to show that the horrific is not to be found around us but in our own subconscious mind." *Vampyr* may be a pale film stylistically, but it succeeds most effectively by capturing a true cinematic nightmare.

Although critics of the period were quick to dismiss *Vampyr* as a "museum piece," the film has come into its own over the years. Starring the famous European actress Sybille Schmitz as Leone, the motion picture featured all nonactors in the other roles, including Baron Nicholas de Gunzburg (under the alias Julian West), a principal backer, in the lead as David Gray. The lack of professional skill made the cast unrecognizable and lent an air of believability to the piece. Dreyer, disappointed in the poor showing of his film, did not make another movie for twelve years, and when he returned to filmmaking, his project was a cruel, angry piece on institutionalized religions entitled *Vredens Dag* (1943). Happily, time has

Opposite: Dracula (1931). **Held at bay by a crucifix, Dracula (Bela Lugosi) curses Dr. Van Helsing's exceptional knowledge of vampires. Photo courtesy of Universal Pictures.**

vindicated his true masterpiece. *Vampyr* remains one of the finest examples of the vampire film.

1933 *The Vampire Bat*

Majestic Pictures, b/w, 67 min. Director: Frank R. Strayer. Producer: Phil Goldstone. Writer: Edward T. Lowe. Starring Lionel Atwill, Fay Wray, Melvyn Douglas, Maude Eburne, George E. Stone, Dwight Frye, Lionel Belmore.

At about the same time Dreyer's *Vampyr* was being released in the United States (as *The Strange Adventures of David Gray*), the primitive low-budget chiller *The Vampire Bat* (1933) was exciting audiences on both coasts. Dealing with a similar subject and setting, the two films have such vastly different styles that comparisons are pointless. *The Vampire Bat* was Majestic Pictures' attempt to cash in on the success of Universal's *Dracula* and *Frankenstein* (1931). Shot at Universal Studios and starring Lionel Atwill, Fay Wray, and Melvyn Douglas, the film is a strange mix of vampires and mad scientists. In fact, the material is so derivative that it appears to be outtakes from many of the efforts under way at Universal.

The story (written for the screen by Edward T. Lowe) involves a series of murders in the central European village of Klein Schloss. Several townspeople have been found dead, drained of blood. The police inspector (portrayed by leading man Melvyn Douglas) is unable to convince the villagers that the deaths are the work of a human monster, not a vampire, and they set off on a witch-hunt. Dr. Otto Von Neimann (devilishly played by Atwill) assures the townspeople that vampires do exist, and when an elderly villager dies, he leads them to the village idiot. Because he is retarded and shows affection for bats, the townsfolk drive Herman Glieb (Dwight Frye) to his death and put a stake through his heart. But the real nemesis is Dr. Neimann, who has been experimenting with test-tube creations of life. Terrorizing the village with his illusionary vampire, he has enslaved the townspeople with hypnotism. When he is discovered by his assistant, Ruth (Fay Wray, fresh from her role in *King Kong*, 1933), he must kill her. But, in typical Hollywood melodrama, when the heroine is threatened, the hero, in the guise of the police inspector, rescues her and destroys the mad scientist.

The Vampire Bat was one of Majestic Pictures' big successes in 1933, but it has been largely forgotten today. Part of the reason for that is the film's derivative nature. The superior projects from Universal, RKO, Paramount, and others simply dwarf Frank R. Strayer's directorial debut. Unfortunately, the film is an uninspired jumble of bloodletting, stake driving, and general mayhem. (Dwight Frye might as well be playing Renfield or Igor, or rather a caricature of those characters, which are themselves caricatures.) The motion picture's single redeeming quality was that it made audiences thirst for *Mark of the Vampire* (1935) and *Dracula's Daughter* (1936).

1935 *Condemned to Live*

Invincible, b/w, 65 min. Director: Frank R. Strayer. Producer: Muary M. Cohen. Writer: Karen Dewolf. Starring Ralph Morgan, Maxine Joyce, Mischa Aver, Russell Gleason, Pedro De Cordova.

Like *The Vampire Bat* (1933), Invincible Pictures' *Condemned to Live* gave director Frank Strayer a second chance to investigate vampiric attacks on another central European village. But this time he approached his material more seriously and produced a worthy effort that is both thought-provoking and thoroughly entertaining.

Middle-aged Ralph Morgan (brother of Frank Morgan of *The Wizard of Oz*, 1939) portrays a kindly old professor, unaware that he's a vampire. Apparently, he has blackouts when he turns into the night creature and awakens in the arms of his loyal hunchback servant (Mischa Aver). When the deaths begin to mount, Dr. Bizet (Pedro de Cordova), the village physician, uncovers evidence that links Morgan to the vampire attacks. (Years before, the story goes, the professor's mother was bitten by a giant bat in Africa just prior to his birth.) Bizet tries to help him with a scientific cure, but he is too late to prevent another murder. Local villagers mistake the hunchback for the vampire and pursue him to the professor's study. Distraught, attempting to save his servant's life, Morgan confesses his guilt, then commits suicide. The hunchback is heartbroken and follows him to his death.

Filmed entirely at Universal Studios (using existing sets from *The Bride of Frankenstein*, 1935), the motion picture has the look of a low-budget second feature. But that is more than made up with expressive camerawork, an above-average story, and the outstanding performance of Morgan. (Interestingly, the movie linked several legends about the werewolf to vampire legends and advanced the confusion of the two myths which still exists in many films.)

1935 *Mark of the Vampire*

MGM, b/w, 60 min. Director: Tod Browning. Producer: E. J. Mannix. Screenwriters: Guy Endore, Bernard Schubert, based on *London After Midnight*, by Tod Browning. Starring Bela Lugosi, Lionel Barrymore, Carol Borland, Jean Hersholt, Elizabeth Allen, Lionel Atwill, Henry Wadsworth, Donald Meek, Holmes Herbert.

Eight years after *London After Midnight* and four years after *Dracula*, Tod Browning began production on his last great horror film. Having worked in the business for more than twenty years, he had painstakingly fine-tuned his filmmaking into an art and had produced some fine motion pictures. Little had he known when he was growing up in Louisville, Kentucky, that he would be singularly responsible for the start of the Hollywood horror cycle of the early thirties. Born in 1882, he ran away from home at the age of sixteen to join the circus. He later toured as a vaudeville comic and became an actor at Biograph Studios. When D. W. Griffith recognized his raw talent, Browning was engaged as a film assistant on *Intolerance* (1916). Following the totally unexpected success of his first film, *Jim Blusco* (1917), he built up a considerable reputation as a producer of highly atmospheric and imaginative low-budget films, mainly in the cinema of the fantastic. He met Lon Chaney while directing program films for Universal and later worked with him on eight films. His horror movies, particularly the vampire films, were directed and photographed with an imaginative dignity that established him as a true *auteur*.

Even though *Freaks* (1932) was neither a financial nor a critical success (and was banned in the United States until 1963), MGM was still banking on Browning's solid reputation when they decided to back his remake of *London After Midnight*. Vampires were still big business, and *Mark of the Vampire* (1935) boasted the reteaming (from *Dracula* fame) of Lugosi and Browning. Tod Browning looked upon the project as a vindication of his previous failure and approached the film cautiously. The result was a semispoof horror film, which was in some ways both a triumph and defeat for him.

Set in Czechoslovakia, the film features Bela Lugosi as Count Mora, a wealthy aristocrat suspected of being a vampire. Together with his vampire daughter, Luna (played by Carol Borland), they haunt a derelict castle. But they are not real vampires, merely actors and vaudeville performers who have been hired by a police detective (Lionel Atwill) to solve an old murder. (The plot deviates somewhat from the original Lon Chaney film.) The trumped-up scheme to force a murderer to reenact his crimes provides a wonderful backdrop for the talents of Lugosi, Atwill, Lionel Barrymore (in a Van Helsing–type role), and Jean Hersholt (as the murderer). And James Wong Howe's excellent lighting creates a compelling mood piece. However, the edge present in so many of Browning's other motion pictures is somehow missing here. Or perhaps the story was simply not strong enough for the more sophisticated audience of the thirties. In either case, *Mark of the Vampire* was certainly a disappointment for Browning. He would make two more films before retiring in 1939 and dying in 1962 at the age of eighty.

The box-office success of *Dracula* in 1931, and its subsequent reissues in 1933 and 1934, caused Carl Laemmle, Jr., and other executives at

Universal Pictures to ponder a sequel, but they all realized that it would be at least four years before the principals, Browning and Lugosi, would be available again. Lugosi had suddenly become a hot property (in spite of losing the role of the Frankenstein monster to Karloff) and would make at least seven genre films during the four-year period, including *The Murders in the Rue Morgue* (1931), *White Zombie* (1932), *Chandu the Magician* (1932), *Island of Lost Souls* (1933), and *The Black Cat* (1934, with Karloff). Browning was also in demand, directing *The Iron Man* (1931), *Freaks* (1932), and the aforementioned *Mark of the Vampire*. He had also worked out an enclusive contract with MGM, and his availability was in question. And besides, there was the problem of the film's ending. Dracula *dies* at the end of the movie, and there was no contigency plan to bring the most popular character of the film back to life. Undaunted, Laemmle announced preproduction of *The Bride of Dracula* (later changed to *Dracula's Daughter* to avoid conflict with Universal's *Bride of Frankenstein*, 1935) and commissioned Garret Fort (who wrote the screenplay to the original) to begin work on a sequel.

1936 *Dracula's Daughter*

Universal, b/w, 72 min. Director: Lambert Hillyer. Producer: E. M. Asher. Screenwriter: Garret Fort, based on a short story by Bram Stoker. Starring Otto Kruger, Gloria Holden, Marguerite Churchill, Edward Van Sloan, Irving Pichel, Nan Grey, Hedda Hopper, Gilbart Emery, Calud Allister, E. E. Clive, Halliwell Hobbes, Billy Bevan.

Dracula's Daughter (1936), the first of many sequels that would be made from the Bram Stoker classic, was actually based on a leftover chapter from *Dracula* entitled "Dracula's Guest." The movie bears little resemblance to its source material but does pick up (right as Browning left it) with Van Helsing being charged with Dracula's murder. Apparently no one believes the good doctor has really disposed of a vampire. The daughter of Dracula, Countess Marya Zaleska, travels to London to burn her father's body and avenge herself on Van Helsing and the others. From there, the sequel develops into a complex Sherlock Holmes mystery, with the chief of police, Van Helsing, and others in pursuit of another vampire.

Gloria Holden played the titular character with a chilling vitality that the publicists proclaimed: "More sensational than her unforgettable father!" But other than her superb characterization and Edward Van Sloan's reprise of the famous vampire hunter, the film was largely forgettable, a mere answer to a Trivial Pursuit question. The direction by Lambert Hillyer was uninspired, and the photography by George Robinson was purely pedestrian. One wonders what Tod Browning would have done with the material.

However, the film made money and inspired Laemmle to produce a second sequel.

1942 *Son of Dracula*

Universal, b/w, 79 min. Director: Robert Siodmak. Producer: Ford Beebe. Writer: Eric Taylor. Starring Lon Chaney, Jr., Louise Albritton, Frank Carven, J. Edward Bromberg, Robert Paige, Samuel Hinds, Evelyn Ankers.

Son of Dracula (1942) was a further digression in the series of *Dracula* sequels. Budgeted at nearly twice what the original had cost, this film was proof of the old axiom that "bigger isn't necessarily better." Carl Laemmle, Jr., had become ill, and a group of executives had taken control of (what would become) Universal Studios. By the end of the 1930s, box-office returns on horror films had begun to dry up, but the 1938 rerelease of *Dracula* and *Frankenstein* on a double bill demonstrated to the businessmen, who were now in charge, that there was still a market for those types of films. The decision was made to introduce another vampire sibling, and production was begun on the "biggest and most exciting" monster movie yet. In fact, the studio's original intention was to make the film in color, but tests proved that the vampire's makeup would not hold up under the intensity of the hot light. Unfortunately, the film was strictly a formula piece generated by a committee, and the use of color would not have been able to raise it above mediocrity.

A mysterious stranger named Count Alucard (Dracula spelled backwards), travels to the United States and takes up residence at a Southern plantation. He soon becomes entranced with a Southern belle (played by Louise Albritton) and draws her hypnotically into his world of vampirism. Their relationship becomes strangely erotic as she gladly embraces the world of the "undead" to share immortality with him. He desires her position of power and wealth and hopes to use it to gain world domination. Fortunately, several locals who are familiar with the extermination of vampires rescue the girl and destroy the mysterious Count.

Son of Dracula featured a few nice moments and some good trick photography in which the Count disappears in puffs of smoke. But the casting is all wrong. Lon Chaney, Jr., (not half the actor his father was) is totally unbelievable as a vampire, in spite of the great makeup by Jack

Opposite: Dracula's Daughter (1936). Above-average sequel to *Dracula* was based on Bram Stoker's leftover chapter entitled "Dracula's Guest." Here, Countess Marya Zaleska (Gloria Holden) confides her desire to be free of the vampiric curse to Dr. Garth (Otto Kruger), a sympathetic psychologist. Photo courtesy of Universal Pictures.

Son of Dracula (1942). Lon Chaney, Jr., appears as Count Alucard (Dracula spelled backward) in this second sequel to the original 1931 *Dracula*. Count Alucard wasn't the son of Dracula but the old Count himself. Photo courtesy of Universal Pictures.

Pierce. He is simply not suave or menacing enough and should have continued to play werewolves, as in *The Wolf Man* (1941). Also, the title cheats. Count Alucard isn't the son of Dracula but the old Count himself. The Universal series of *Dracula* (and *Frankenstein*) films would continue into the forties, but they would never again engender the respect of the originals.

In this publicity still from *Son of Dracula* (1943), Lon Chaney, Jr., sporting a suave mustache and powdered temples, takes on the role his father was never able to play, Dracula. Photo courtesy of Universal Pictures.

1939 *Return of Dr. X*

Warner Bros., b/w, 62 min. Director: Vincent Sherman. Producer: Bryan Foy. Screenwriter: Lee Kathy, based on the novel *The Doctor's Secret,* by William Makin. Starring Humphrey Bogart, Dennis Horgan, Rosemary Lane, Wayne Morris, John Litel.

Warner Bros.'s *The Return of Dr. X* (1939) was more imaginative than any of those sequels. Though not a direct sequel to Michael Curtiz's *Dr. X* (1932), the film owes much of its vision and style to that earlier film. Directed by Vincent Sherman (his first motion picture), this minor thriller focuses on a modern vampire (played by Humphrey Bogart) who terrorizes a major metropolis. Bogart, his hair white-streaked and complexion grisly, becomes a scientific vampire who when resurrected from the dead by a mad doctor (John Litel) must feed on living blood in order to survive. Although the film resembles plots taken from *Dracula* and *Frankenstein,* it was able to transcend the mad scientist motif to stand on its own merit. The film was produced on a low budget and featured Bogart in his only horror movie but failed in its initial release. However, after Bogart's successes in *The Maltese Falcon* (1941) and *Casablanca* (1942), the motion picture was reissued by Warners as a second feature and became moderately successful.

1940 *The Devil Bat* (aka *Killer Bats*)

PRC, b/w, 69 min. Director: Jean Yarborough. Producer: Jack Gallagher. Screenwriter: John Thomas Neville, based on a story by George Bricher. Starring Bela Lugosi, Dave O'Brien, Suzzane Karen, Hal Price, Donald Kerr, Guy Usher.

The Devil Bat (1940) (and its sequel, *Devil Bat's Daughter,* 1943) was also designed to cash in on the success of Universal's horror series and followed roughly a similar plot as *The Vampire Bat* and *The Return of Dr. X.* Produced by PRC (a low-budget movie house), the film starred Bela Lugosi as Dr. Paul Caruthers, a crazed scientist who trains vampire bats to attack at the scent of a certain perfume. The movie, like its sequel and its companion film *Dead Men Walk,* is largely unintelligible by today's standards. They were basically incompetent chillers from the bottom of the crypt.

Opposite: Son of Dracula (1942). Southern belle Louise Albritton restrains Count Alucard (Lon Chaney, Jr.) from attacking a new victim. Photo courtesy of Universal Pictures.

1943 *Dead Men Walk* (aka *Creature of the Devil*)

PRC, b/w, 64 min. Director: Sam Newfield. Producer: Sigmund Neufield. Writer: Fred Myton. Starring George Zucco, Mary Carlisle, Nedrick Young, Dwight Frye, Fern Emmett, Robert Strange.

An almost unwatchable vanity vehicle for George Zucco, essaying a dual role. Dr. Harold Clayton (Zucco), a distinguished man of science, has been unable to solve the mystery of existence. Determined to live beyond his years, he turns to the black arts to create a vampiric twin, Elwyn (also Zucco). Predictably, Elwyn becomes jealous of Harold's attraction for a young woman (Mary Carlisle) and enlists Zolarr, a hunchback assistant played by Dwight Frye (his last role), to destroy him. This quickie film, predictable and incompetent, is worthy of no further comment.

1943 *Return of the Vampire*

Columbia, b/w, 69 min. Director: Lew Landers. Producer: Sam White. Writer: Griffen Jay. Starring Bela Lugosi, Nina Foch, Frieda Inescort, Miles Mander, Roland Varno, Gilbert Emery, Otala Nesmith, Matt Willis.

The last great vampire film of the period was Columbia's *The Return of the Vampire* (1943). Originally written by Griffin Jay as a direct sequel to *Dracula*, Carl Laemmle and Universal turned down the screenplay, claiming that their own series was in no need of assistance. Jay rewrote the story, changing the vampire's name from Dracula to Armand Tesla, and submitted the story to Columbia. Producer Sam White was impressed and immediately hired Lugosi to play the title role, knowing that the public would recognize it as a true sequel to *Dracula* and purchase those valuable theater tickets. Regrettably, Columbia Pictures insisted that White include a werewolf in the film after they learned that Universal was working on a monster team-up entitled *Frankenstein Meets the Wolf Man* (1943).

In a precredits sequence (worthy of the Bond films), Armand Tesla (Lugosi), a Romanian vampire, is hunted down and destroyed in London in 1918. (The sequence is reminiscent of the climactic battle in Browning's *Dracula*, 1931.) Twenty-five years later, during the London blitz, a German bomb upsets the Count's resting place, and workmen remove the stake from his heart, assuming it to be a chunk of shrapnel. Tesla is immediately revived and kills the men who brought him back to life. His first thought is to seek revenge upon those who first tried to destroy him. Thereafter, alternating between shadowy graveyards and aristocratic drawing rooms, the vampire stalks his prey. Eventually, Frieda Inescourt (as a Van Helsing–like detective) exposes Tesla as a vampire and with the help of the wolf man

Poster art from Columbia's sequel to *Dracula, Return of the Vampire* (1943). The Count returns to "life" during the German blitz of London. Poster art courtesy of Columbia.

(Matt Willis) exposes him to the sun as he sleeps. The final shot of Lugosi's face melting (cut by a censor in Britain) is most unforgettable, as is the rest of the film. *The Return of the Vampire* is a surprisingly well-made nightmare, the single drawback being the intrusion of the wolf man.

The second great horror school had flourished in America for almost twelve years and was now quickly withering away. The Germanic influence had resulted in a number of excellent horror fantasies. Many critics contend that Hollywood in the thirties was one of the richest cinematic periods of all time. This is completely understandable with such marvelous efforts as *Dracula* (1931), *Vampyr* (1932), and *The Return of the Vampire* (1943). But with the advent of war, the public became disinterested in horror films and more interested in light, escapist fare. Producers attempted to comply, and the horror film sank to its lowest level. For nearly fifteen years, parodies, featuring the likes of Abbott and Costello, Martin and Lewis, Bob Hope, and the Bowery Boys, dominated the field until the middle fifties when the boom of the science-fiction film and the production of Hammer's first motion picture would once again establish credibility for the genre.

3

Spooks and Spoofs
From *House of Frankenstein* (1944)
to *Dragstrip Dracula* (1962)

The innovative richness of the thirties was followed by fourteen years of disintegration and decline wherein the horror film descended to its lowest level. The old Hollywood which, distinguished by the second great horror school, had produced such cinematic gems as *Dracula* (1931), *Vampyr* (1932), and *The Return of the Vampire* (1943) had passed away into legend, and what remained was an industry in which the values and foundations of the past had been muted and corrupted into something that was largely unrecognizable. Carl Laemmle, Jr., was dead, and his eagerness to experiment with bold, original ideas and concepts had been replaced by an attitude of conservatism and a general lack of vision. Wild-eyed *auteurs* like Browning and Dreyer were supplanted by business-suited executives with accounting ledgers and corporate mentalities. Productions became a matter of dollars and cents rather than creativity, and the cinematic nightmares of the period were rather routine, with very few exceptions. The deteriorating rip-offs of *Dracula*, dimwitted and threadbare, contributed much to the decline. And soon the staples of the horror genre, which had kept many studios afloat during the depression, were no longer respectable. They were simply (with apologies to Bogart) "the stuff of which" B movies were made.

Parodies, remakes, and team-ups dominated the period from 1944 to

1958 (from roughly the outbreak of World War II to the middle of the cold war and *Sputnik*). Films like *House of Frankenstein* (1944), *House of Dracula* (1945), *Abbott and Costello Meet Frankenstein* (1948), and *The Bowery Boys Meet the Monsters* (1954) replaced the darker expressionist visions of the previous period. One reason for this change was the corporate takeover of the studio system, and another had to do with the psychological makeup of the film audience. America had been scared by monsters far more terrifying than Count Dracula. The technological horrors imposed by Nazi Germany, the atom-bombings of Hiroshima and Nagasaki, and the threat of nuclear war with the Soviets were all very real terrors, much worse than any imaginary monster that the screen could produce. Audiences had simply reached a burnout point and wanted to see films that made them laugh. Hollywood executives complied with the demands of the audience and concocted every known way to have the famous monsters of filmland play straight men to the comic talents of Abbott and Costello, Martin and Lewis, Bob Hope, and the Bowery Boys. The results were tragic and the degradation complete, as the character of Dracula, the Frankenstein monster, the wolf man, the invisible man, Dr. Jekyll and Mr. Hyde (and others), became stooges and mere shadows of their original selves.

Insult was added to injury when horror films came under attack for decency in the forties and early fifties. During World War II, horror films were banned in England, parts of Europe, and North Africa because governments thought these motion pictures had a negative effect on morale. After the war, stricter regulations dealing with theme and content were initiated throughout the world; in particular, the United Kingdom established the British Board of Film Censors. That organization became the watchdog of the Eastern Hemisphere, creating the first rating system for movies. A U rating meant that a film was suitable for general audiences (today, the equivalent of a G rating). An A rating meant that the film was mature and suggested parental guidance (much like the PG or PG-13 rating). The kiss of death for most movies in that era of repression was the H rating, which meant that the film was graphic in its portrayal of horror (equivalent to an R or X today). The Motion Picture Association of America (MPAA) followed suit in 1946. Many horror films, except for the light, comic spoofs, were classified under that rating and came under the attack of religious and civic groups. That threat translated to fewer markets and even less take at the box office, and studio executives became very cautious. Thankfully, by the middle fifties, restrictions had been relaxed on certain types of horror films.

During the fourteen-year period, Hollywood's use of the vampire mythos was distinguished by its propensity to remake subjects again and again, a reflection of the cautious nature of the business. It was certainly easier (and safer) to make use of proven formulas and well-established characters than to create new ones, and the producers of horror films (notably at Universal Pictures) were constantly reviving monsters who had died in previous movies for further adventures. Since the plots of the time leaned more on comedy and parody rather than horror, no attempt was ever made to explain how the monsters came back to life. Following his demise in *Dracula* (1931), the Transylvanian Count returned (in one guise or another) in four other motion pictures, leading ultimately to supporting roles opposite Abbott and Costello. The quality of these films was generally poor, varying in direct proportion to the ingenuity of the scripts and the skill of their direction. Films like *Vampire's Ghost* (1945), *House of Dracula* (1945), *Valley of the Zombies* (1946), and *Abbott and Costello Meet Frankenstein* (1948) were pale copies of the great horror films. Unfortunately, these parodies and remakes were quickly joined by another "safe" format, the monster team-up. The idea of pairing monsters was dreamed up by an executive at Universal Pictures in 1942 on the pretense that two monsters would make a film twice as terrifying. The first team-up was *Frankenstein Meets the Wolf Man* (1943) (even though Columbia beat Universal by a few weeks with the release of *The Return of the Vampire*), and over the next few years Count Dracula met the likes of the Frankenstein monster, the wolf man, the hunchback, and a score of mad doctors (as well as the previously noted comics) with varying degrees of success.

By the end of the period, Hollywood had many other problems to contend with. The introduction of television in 1947 meant that fewer people would be going to the movies. Even though great technological strides were being made in color processing, the development of a celluloid lacquer for black-and-white prints, and gimmicks like Cinerama and 3-D, the studios remained very cautious. They began to limit budgets and cut back on the number of productions yearly. And when antitrust laws ended the studio's "block-booking" system (thus giving theater owners the right to select what films they would exhibit without being forced to take the good with the bad), it seemed to spell certain doom for lower-budget films. (The Big Five studios—Paramount, Loew's [MGM], Fox, Warners, and RKO—owned most of the theaters in the United States, ones which consistently delivered three-fourths of the revenue. The ten-year antitrust suit broke this domination and greatly crippled the industry. The "studio era" literally came to an end and eliminated the need for B second features.) McCarthyism and the threat of nuclear war in the fifties were the final nails in the coffin for many cinematic nightmares.

Only three films of the period offered anything that was genuinely new and imaginative to the vampire mythos, and each achieved a certain level of success by giving audiences something above the common fare. *The Man in Half Moon Street* (1944), based on a popular stage play, refused identification with the horror genre and produced a dark, *film noir* look strongly reminiscent of the mainstream thrillers of the era. *House of Frankenstein,* the first of the monster team-ups, offered an interesting premise, which regrettably was carried further in lackluster sequels. *Return of Dracula* (1958), though derivative of *Dracula* (1931) and *Son of Dracula* (1942), was actually a taunt, literate chiller produced on a low budget. Each of the films was highly atmospheric and original and demonstrated a sincere and uncompromising approach to the material. They were also written, directed, photographed, and edited with such imagination and feeling for the medium that each motion picture (almost) has stood the test of time remarkably well. Part of the secret of that longevity was the filmmaker's determination to treat the material fairly. And while other horror films continued the downward spiral, at least two of the three films pointed in the direction that future efforts would take.

1944 *The Man in Half Moon Street*

Paramount, b/w, 92 min. Director: Ralph M. Murphy. Producer: Walter MacEwen. Screenwriter: Charles Kenyon, based on the stage play by Barré Lyndon. Starring Nils Asther, Helen Walker, Reinhold Schuenzel, Paul Cavanagh, Edmund Brown.

The Man in Half Moon Street (1944) is an apt symbol of the rich expressionist movement which preceded its release and the horror renaissance which would follow thirteen years later, and it provides a valuable link in a period of utter desolation between the two horror traditions. Adapted by Charles Kenyon from Barré Lyndon's play, the screen version concerns a 104-year-old surgeon who has learned to prolong life by using the blood of his murdered victims. At a social reception, the title character (Nils Asther) meets an old woman who comments on his striking resemblance to someone she once knew. What she does not realize is that he is that man. He gives her hints by teasingly recounting details of their past relationship, which his grandfather has supposedly confided to him, but she fails to see his real identity. A former friend and colleague from his student days (Reinhold Schuenzel) who actually discovered the life-extension process does recognize him.

The two scientists exchange greetings that are somewhat chilly, and Schuenzel then demands to know how Asther corrected the flaw in the glandular transplantation process. Asther confesses that he hasn't and that he must commit murder every six years to secure the vital blood for his continued longevity, but he trusts, with the European doctor's aid, that they can reach a permanent solution. Unfortunately, as the next six-year cycle ends, he must kill again, and this time it is a young medical student (Morton Lowry). Learning of the murder, Schuenzel is outraged: "We are no longer scientists; now we are murderers!" Chillingly, Asther replies: "What is one life to science—or a dozen?" Like Dr. Frankenstein, he has become a mad doctor tampering with God's universal plan. Like Dracula, he must feed upon humans for his existence, and after much soul-searching he realizes that he is wrong. But before he can confront his fiancée (Helen Walker) with the truth, he suddenly begins to age. Stumbling from their private train coach, his body withers and dies on the station platform.

Less horrific but probably more compelling than most of its American counterparts, *The Man in Half Moon Street* (coproduced by Paramount Pictures) represented one of Britain's earliest excursions into the field. The atmosphere of terror and tension in the film is conveyed through a very literate, well-acted screenplay and the dark, moody photography of Henry Sharp. Each of the scenes, which are bound tightly together by Miklos Rozza's clever score, purposely downplays visual horror in favor of psychological horror and avoids many of the standard pitfalls of the genre. An unskilled director might have been tempted to show each murder in grisly detail, but Ralph Murphy shrewdly turns our attention to something else while the horrific events occur in silhouette or offscreen. This "misdirection" actually heightens suspense and produces in the audience imaginings far worse than any screen terror. Predictably, further experiments in the genre would give rise to the third great horror school in England and lead to its dominance of the field. In fact, Hammer Films, the British company largely responsible for that takeover, would remake *The Man in Half Moon Street* fifteen years later as *The Man Who Could Cheat Death* (1959). (The 1973 made-for-television *Night Strangler* covered the same thematic ground by introducing Richard Anderson as a centuries-old surgeon who must commit murder every sixty-six years to rejuvenate himself.)

1944 *House of Frankenstein*

Universal, b/w, 71 min. Director: Erle Kenton. Producer: Paul Malvern. Writer: Edward T. Lowe. Starring Boris Karloff, Lon Chaney, Jr., Martha Driscoll, John Carradine, Lionel Atwill, Onslow Stevens, Jane Addams, Glenn Strange.

House of Frankenstein (1944) followed a few months later. Even though it features an all-star cast of villains (Lon Chaney, Jr., as the wolf man, Boris Karloff as a mad scientist, and John Carradine as Count Dracula), the film bears little resemblance to *Dracula* (1931), *Frankenstein* (1931), *The Wolf Man* (1941), or any of the Universal monster classics. The story concerns an evil scientist and his obsession to destroy those who (he believes) wronged him. When the film opens, the mad doctor has just taken over Zucco's traveling circus, a freak show which tours the European countryside giving patrons a chance to witness unspeakable horrors. The prize exhibit is

John Carradine, a contemporary of Lugosi, took over the role of Dracula in *House of Frankenstein* (1944) and continued playing the Transylvanian Count, or a relative vampire, into the seventies.

Dracula (!), and Karloff briefly frees him before letting him die in the sunlight. Once he has dispatched Dracula, he sets off in search of Frankenstein's diary, hoping to learn the secret of eternal life. He finds instead the preserved bodies of Frankenstein's creature (portrayed by Glenn Strange, a Western movie stuntman) and the wolf man. Reviving them, he plans to use the creatures to do his bidding, but plans go awry, and he and the monsters disappear forever (?).

Flawed and faded by today's standards, *House of Frankenstein* was perhaps the best of the monster rallies. Scripted by Edward T. Lowe from a story treatment by Curt Siodmak, the film provides an excellent starring vehicle for Boris Karloff. After having played so many gentle mad scientists (and, of course, the misunderstood Frankenstein creature), Karloff has a field day with the darkly sinister carnival owner; in fact, the role is strongly reminiscent of Werner Krauss's Dr. Caligari. When combined with the slick direction of Larry Kenton and the outstanding support of Carradine (in his first appearance as Dracula), Chaney, and George Zucco, the motion picture was a box-office success. Unfortunately, the studio believed the success formula could work again and again and produced two ludicrous follow-ups: *House of Dracula* (1945) and *Abbott and Costello Meet Frankenstein* (1948). They would have been far better off to leave it alone because the last two films represent such a sad ending to an era that started so promisingly with the expressionistic *Dracula*. (Years later, Taft/Barish Productions tried unsuccessfully to gather the famous monsters of filmland for yet another go-round, in *The Monster Squad* [1987]. But instead of thrills and chills, the audience found the monsters laughable.)

1945 *House of Dracula*
Universal, b/w, 71 min. Director: Erle Kenton. Producer: Paul Malvern. Writer: Edward T. Lowe. Starring Lon Chaney, Jr., Martha Driscoll, John Carradine, Lionel Atwill, Onslow Stevens, Jane Addams, Glenn Strange.

Thankfully forgotten today, *House of Dracula* was a further descent of the vampire film into mediocrity. Attempting to discover a scientific explanation for vampirism and lycanthropy, the concept was an interesting one; however, Lowe's script mishandles every possible avenue with unintentionally humorous dialogue and clichéd characters. It is difficult to sit through the film straight-faced, particularly with Kenton's uninspired direction compounding the problem.

Clearly played for laughs rather than chills, the story opens bizarrely with Carradine's Dracula (actually Baron Latos) arriving at the clifftop home of a mad scientist in search of a cure. Dr. Edelman (Onslow Stevens)

is sympathetic to the vampire's plight and believes that he can find "an antibody that will consume the parasites of vampirism to affect a complete cure." In the midst of their conversation, Chaney's wolf man, Lawrence Talbot, shows up looking for a cure. The doctor accepts him as a patient, working under the dubious assumption that Talbot's problem is due to pressure on the brain and that a softening drug will cure him. (The film makes it quite clear that the executives at Universal Pictures took the softening drug prior to approving this effort.) Meanwhile, Edelman's hunchback nurse is growing special flowers in a foggy dungeon with the hopes they will revive the Frankenstein monster (once again played by Strange). The film reaches a shattering climax when the mad doctor becomes infected with the vampire's blood and goes on a rampage, releasing the Frankenstein monster. Villagers of Vasaria, led by Lionel Atwill's Inspector Holtz (whose character was wonderfully spoofed by Kenneth Mars in Mel Brooks's *Young Frankenstein*, 1974), fight him back with torches and burn the house to the ground. Only Lawrence Talbot survives the conflagration and discovers, much to his amazement, that he is forever cured as the wolf man (that is, until the next movie).

House of Dracula has only two saving graces that have kept the film from obscurity—Jack B. Pierce and John Carradine. Pierce, who had created the makeup for the wolf man, the mummy, Dracula, and the Frankenstein monster, worked on his last monster in this movie. Having served the industry for more than twenty-two years, he had been responsible for a number of innovations in makeup. But with all the new advances in plastic and foam rubber, Pierce was unwilling to change and found his services no longer needed at Universal Pictures. (Ironically, Pierce's designs for the Frankenstein monster would become the standard for the next thirty years.) Carradine, on the other hand, was very much in demand.

Born Richmond Reed Carradine in 1906, he has been featured or starred in over 230 films since his debut in *Tol'able David* (1930) and holds the Guinness record for the most screen credits. This gaunt character actor, who had scored critical praise in such films as *Stagecoach* (1939) and *The Grapes of Wrath* (1940), made a big impression as Dracula to the American public. His two performances as the Transylvanian Count in *House of Frankenstein* and *House of Dracula* established him as Lugosi's successor to the role. Until his death in 1988, he had played Dracula, or a relative vampire, nine times on screen, with occasional stage and television performances. When Universal was casting *Abbott and Costello Meet Franken-*

Opposite: House of Frankenstein (1944). **Mad doctor (Boris Karloff) attempts to revive the Frankenstein monster (Glenn Strange) after having disposed of Dracula (John Carradine). Both the Frankenstein monster and Dracula, forever linked in the cinema, make their first appearance together in this film. Photo courtesy of Universal Pictures.**

stein, he was, fortunately, touring with his one-man Shakespeare readings and was unavailable. Executives at Universal cast Lugosi, in spite of his drug habit, in that horrible film instead. (In 1989, John Carradine's son David played a vampire in the Western *Sundown: The Vampire in Retreat.*)

1944 *Crime Doctor's Courage*

Columbia, b/w, 66 min. Director: William Castle. Writers: Graham Baker, Louise Lantz, based on the popular radio serial "Crime Doctor." Starring Warner Baxter, Margaret Lindsay, John Litel, Ray Collins.

Warner Baxter starred in this third film about an amnesiac who becomes a successful psychiatrist and crime fighter. The two previous films had been straight detective stories (relying on the gimmick of the locked-door mystery for suspense). In *Crime Doctor's Courage* (1944), an element of the supernatural (notably the vampire) was added to spice up the series. Baxter uncovers an unusual number of deaths which have the same modus operandi (extreme blood loss). Further investigation leads him to a strange vampire cult which abducts and drains its victims of blood. Unfortunately, most devout horror fans will guess the proper sequence of events before fifteen minutes have passed, and the film achieves very little suspense. Columbia Pictures produced ten *Crime Doctor* films in all between 1943 and 1949, based on the popular radio series. This motion picture stands head-and-shoulders above the other second features.

1945 *Vampire's Ghost*

Republic, b/w, 59 min. Director: Lesley Selander. Producer: Armand Schaefer. Writers: Leigh Brackett, John Butler, based loosely on *The Vampyre,* by John Polidori. Starring John Abbott, Peggy Stewart, Roy Barcroft, Grant Withers, Charles Gordon.

While Universal was in preproduction of *Abbott and Costello Meet Frankenstein,* Republic Pictures and the PRC rushed out low-budget vampire films, and the French industry, struggling to rebuild itself after the war, made one also. Of the four, *Vampire's Ghost* (1945), from Republic, was a near miss, while the other three—*The Spider Woman Strikes Back* (1946) from Universal, *Devil Bat's Daughter* (1946) from PRC, and *Valley of the*

Opposite: House of Dracula (1945). Dracula (John Carradine) is held at bay by mad scientist (Onslow Stevens), who specializes in curing the abnormalities of the famous monsters of filmland. Photo courtesy of Universal Pictures.

The Spider Woman Strikes Back (1946). Gale Sondergaard portrays a blind woman who raises vampire plants in this low-budget thriller. Photo courtesy of Universal Pictures.

Zombies (1946), also from Republic—were retreads of previously covered material. *Vampire's Ghost*, scripted by science-fiction great Leigh Brackett (who also cowrote *The Empire Strikes Back* in 1980), suggests that vampirism can be traced back to an ancient African tribe. When explorers arrive at a West African village, they meet Webb Fallon (John Abbott), a white man who has been cursed with vampirism and has been living among the natives for over one hundred years. The production values are low, but in imagination it far exceeded those being lensed at Universal.

Opposite: The Spider Woman Strikes Back (1946). Gale Sondergaard and her hideous deaf-mute servant (Rondo Hatton) raise vampire plants. Photo courtesy of Universal Pictures.

1946 *The Spider Woman Strikes Back*

Universal, b/w, 59 min. Director: Arthur Lubin. Producer: Howard Welsch. Writer: Eric Taylor. Starring Gale Sondergaard, Rondo Hatton, Milburn Stone, Brenda Joyce, Hobart Cavanah.

Inspired by Universal's *Sherlock Holmes and the Spider Woman* (1944) though not a direct sequel, this film reintroduces Gale Sondergaard as the "spider woman." This time she is a blind woman who is raising carnivorous plants. Assisted by her deaf-mute servant (Rondo Hatton), she lures young women into her service only to kill them for blood. Brenda Joyce comes to work for her, and her fiancé, Milburn Stone, begins to suspect that something is not quite right in the household. The two villains attempt to feed Joyce to the plant but perish in a less than convincing fire (leaving plenty of room for future sequels). The motion picture was not a very effective chiller, but the concept of vampire plants would be satirized several years later by Roger Corman's *Little Shop of Horrors* (1960).

1946 *Valley of the Zombies*

Republic, b/w, 56 min. Director: Philip Ford. Producers-Writers: Dorell McGowan, Stuart McGowan. Starring Robert Livingston, Adrian Booth, Ian Keith, Thomas Jackson.

Ormand Murks (Ian Keith), a low-rent undertaker, returns from the dead after having found (in [surprise] the valley of the zombies) a formula for immortality. The problem with the formula is that it requires fresh blood. Kidnapping, then hypnotizing the heroine (Adrian Booth), he enlists her aid to acquire new victims. Predictably, her fiancé (Robert Livingston) comes to the rescue and destroys the vampire. Like *The Spiderwoman Strikes Back* and many other pictures of the period, *Valley of the Zombies* offered little that was fresh to the vampire myth. In fact, if combined with that other feature, the casual moviegoer would have much difficulty determining where one film ended and the other began.

1948 *Abbott and Costello Meet Frankenstein*

Universal, b/w, 92 min. Director: Charles T. Barton. Producer: Robert Arthur. Writers: John Grant, Frederic Renaldo, Robert Lees. Starring Bud Abbott, Lou Costello, Bela Lugosi, Lon Chaney, Jr., Glenn Strange, Leonore Aubert, Jane Randolph.

Opposite: Abbott and Costello Meet Frankenstein (1948). Dracula (Bela Lugosi) and the other famous monsters of filmland corner weak-willed Bud Abbott and his companion Lou Costello. Who's on first? Photo courtesy of Universal Pictures.

Three years after *Vampire's Ghost*, Universal Pictures released a comedy spoof which would put an end to its cycle of horror films. *Abbott and Costello Meet Frankenstein* (1948) had been produced to showcase the talents of the two vaudevillian comics and to feature Universal classic monsters. However, the film only succeeded in further contributing to the decline of the horror film. It also assisted in the continued decay and degradation of the Hollywood vampire.

The loosely devised plot follows Bud Abbott and Lou Costello, as two railway porters, through a series of mishaps in a haunted house. After delivering two crates—containing the Frankenstein monster (Strange) and the wolf man (Chaney)—the comics are welcomed by Dracula (Lugosi) to his home and invited to spend the night. The Count is anxious to revive the Frankenstein monster, and Lou's brain is slated for the creature. The film then degenerates into a moving comic strip (barely watchable today) with the monsters chasing Bud and Lou through the usual shenanigans.

Lacking any originality or imagination, the film was nonetheless a success and paved the way for more entries in the series; subsequently, Abbott and Costello would meet *The Killer, Boris Karloff* (1949), *The Invisible Man* (1951), *Captain Kidd* (1952), and *Dr. Jekyll and Mr. Hyde* (1953), among others. However, Universal's release of *Abbott and Costello Meet Frankenstein* marked the end of America's domination of the vampire film. The ritualized nature and the mystique had slipped away, and what remained was a caricature of the form, with Chaney and Lugosi appearing foolishly awkward. Although United Artists and American International Pictures attempted to breathe new life into the vampire film, it would remain dead until a British production company made *The Horror of Dracula* (1958).

1952 *My Son, the Vampire* (aka *Old Mother Riley Meets the Vampire, Vampires Over London*, and *Dracula's Desire*)

b/w, 74 min. Director: John Gilling. Writer: Dudley Lovell. Starring Bela Lugosi, Arthur Lucan, Kitty McShane, Dora Bryan, Hattie Jacques, Dandy Nicholls, Richard Wattis, Charles Lloyd-Pack, Graham Moffatt.

Lugosi followed his lurid performance as Dracula in *Abbott and Costello Meet Frankenstein* with an equally embarrassing role in *Old Mother*

Opposite: Abbott and Costello Meet Frankenstein (1948). Dracula (Bela Lugosi, in his only appearance in the role apart from *Dracula*) seeks a new brain for the Frankenstein monster and selects Lou Costello as the donor in this routine haunted-house comedy. Photo courtesy of Universal Pictures.

Riley Meets the Vampire (aka *My Son, the Vampire*, 1952). Teaming with British comedian Arthur Lucan, who specialized in portraying drag dames, Bela Lugosi plays himself. The plot, which was paper thin, concerns Old Mother Riley's attempt to convince her daughter, Kitty, and the police that she has seen a vampire. The vociferous Irish washerwoman (played by Lucan) believes that Lugosi is Dracula because he is dressed in the regalia and sleeps in a coffin, but no one will believe her! Originally entitled *Vampires Over London*, the film was cheaply made, and the padding is difficult to sit through; however, it made a sizable profit from British provincial showings, presumably because of Lugosi. That same year, he starred in *Vampire*, another low-budget English production, which was critically panned but moderately successful.

Even though he had fallen on hard times and was forced into playing a parody of his former roles, Lugosi's name on a horror film could still pull in some box-office cash and add respectability to the picture. The Hungarian stage actor, who had become famous as Dracula and had starred in some of the greatest horror-film classics, had declined steadily, both personally and professionally, since the late thirties. (In fact, his decline paralleled the decline of the horror industry.) His accent and his addiction to morphine were handicaps for normal roles, and he became typecast as a heavy in horror and science-fiction films, eventually descending through B-movies to lurid, exploitative Z pictures like *Old Mother Riley Meets the Vampire* (1952), *Glen or Glenda* (1953), and *Bride of the Monster* (1955). When notorious film producer Edward D. Wood, Jr., offered him the starring role in *Tomb of the Vampire*, Lugosi jumped at the opportunity, convinced that it would restore his image. Unfortunately, he died (at the age of seventy-three) a couple of days into the shooting, having completed only a few scattered silent shots (of Dracula stalking a cemetery). According to the wishes of his last will and testament, Lugosi was buried in 1956 in the suit and black cloak of his famous vampire. Later, capitalizing on Lugosi's death, Wood included the existing footage from *Tomb of the Vampire* in his science-fiction epic *Grave Robbers from Outer Space* (1959, better known as *Plan Nine from Outer Space*, one of the worst films ever made), and he publicized the movie as "the great Bela Lugosi's last film." What a sad end to a great but flawed career!

1953 *Dracula in Istanbul (Drakula Istanbula)*

Turkish, b/w, ? min. Director and Writer: Mehmet Muhtar. Starring Atif Kaptan (as Count Dracula).

Drakula Istanbula (1953) was a Turkish-made version of *Dracula* which combined the familiar Stoker tale with the historical material about Vlad

Abbott and Costello Meet Frankenstein (1948). Mad lady doctor (Leonore Aubert) and Dracula (Bela Lugosi) examine the Frankenstein monster (Glenn Strange) and determine he needs a brain transplant. Photo courtesy of Universal Pictures.

the Impaler. Not much information about this version exists, as the film was never shown in Britain or the United States and had limited showing in cold war Turkey. Records indicate that large sections of dialogue were apparently lifted from the original novel in an effort to produce a truly faithful production. The connection to Vlad the Impaler is probably the first attempt to link the two myths (beyond possibly an earlier Hungarian silent). Later films, notably in the early seventies, would routinely reference that infamous Transylvanian prince.

1954 *The Bowery Boys Meet the Monsters*
Universal, b/w, 73 min. Director: Edward Bernds. Producer: Ben Schwalb. Writers: Edward Bernds, Elwood Ullman. Starring Leo Gorcey, Huntz Hall, Lloyd Corrigan, Ellen Corby, John Dehner.

Despite triumphs like *The Man in Half Moon Street* and *House of Frankenstein*, the horror film continued its decline, reaching an all-time low

in the late fifties. *The Bowery Boys Meet the Monsters* (1954) represented the lowest point in the history of the vampire film and was really nothing more than a continuation of the nonsense started in the forties with efforts like *The Ghost Breakers* (1940), *Spooks Run Wild* (1941), *Spook Busters* (1946), *Abbott and Costello Meet Frankenstein* (1948), and *Scared Stiff* (1952). Not even the latest gimmicks, such as 3-D, emergo, hypnovision, perceptovision, psychorama, or Cinerama, were enough to keep theater-goers from defecting in large numbers for the little black box. In Edward Bernds's very inept film, the Bowery Boys must contend with Ellen Corby's man-eating trees and Laura Mason's vampiric charms. To mention just one of the many unbelievable plot contrivances, Huntz Hall is turned into a werewolf. How convenient!

Eighteen months after Lugosi's death, American International Pictures, United Artists, and several independent filmmakers tried, with little success, to resurrect the vampire by releasing a number of low-budget horror cheapies. Aimed primarily at the youth market, films like *Blood of Dracula* (1957), *Revenge of Dracula* (1957), *Mark of the Vampire* (1957), and *I Was a Teenage Vampire* (1959) were popular as double-billed entertainment at the local drive-in, but they never really reached a critical audience.

1957 *Blood of Dracula* (aka *Blood Is My Heritage, Blood of the Demon*)

AIP, b/w, 69 min. Director: Herbert L. Strock. Producer: Herman Cohen. Writer: Ralph Thornton. Starring Sandra Harrison, Louise Lewis, Jerry Baline, Gail Gauley, Malcom Atterbury.

Blood of Dracula (not to be confused with *I Was a Teenage Vampire*, 1959) was probably the weakest link in Herman Cohen's trend-setting teenage horror series (which included *I Was a Teenage Werewolf*, 1957, *I Was a Teenage Frankenstein*, 1958, and others). Wicked chemistry teacher (Louise Lewis) hypnotizes an unhappy and unpopular "teen angel" (Sandra Harrison) with a powerful amulet, then transforms her into a blood-sucking vampire. Harrison suddenly becomes popular as she begins stalking around campus in her vampire cape, bobby socks, and letter sweater. She heartlessly seduces several young jocks (Jerry Blaine, Malcolm Atterbury) and raises the ire of her female friends (Gail Ganley, Heather Ames). Her

Opposite: **A few years before his death, Lugosi parodied his famous role as Dracula in the lowbrow comedy** *My Son, the Vampire* **(1952, aka** *Old Mother Riley Meets the Vampire***).**

vampire powers are ultimately discovered, and her evil fairy godmother is destroyed. Surprised? Produced specifically for a drive-in double feature, the movie rarely rises above the commonplace.

1957 *Mark of the Vampire* (aka *Vampire*)

United Artists, b/w, 75 min. Director: Paul Landres. Producers: Arthur Gardner, Jules Levy. Writer: Pat Fielder. Starring John Beall, Colleen Gray, Kenneth Tobey, Paul Brinegar, Lynda Reed.

Mark of the Vampire (1957) was the first of two films in which Paul Landres and Pat Fielder attempted to inject new life into the familiar legend. (*Return of Dracula,* which followed one year later, is the better of the two efforts.) A brilliant doctor (John Beall) accidentally swallows bat-serum pills that a colleague has developed as part of a research project on vampire bats. The pills slowly begin to alter his personality (in a variation of the Jekyll-Hyde story) and eventually turn him into a blood-addicted junkie. Several murder and vampire attacks later, he faces the horrifying truth, but it is too late to reverse the process. Near the end of the film, Kenneth Tobey turns to the audience and explains that there are certain mysteries that man is not meant to understand. His message is hardly a new one, and unfortunately, neither is the plot. *Mark of the Vampire* anticipates the later trend to mix horror and science fiction, but the film's lame science-fantasy excuse is not strong enough to save it.

1958 *Blood of the Vampire*

Eros Films, 85 min. Director: Henry Cass. Producers: Robert S. Baker, Monty Berman. Writer: Jimmy Sangster. Starring Sir Donald Wolfit, Barbara Shelley, Victor Ball, Victor Maddern, William Devlin.

Often confused with Herman Cohen's magnum opus, *Blood of the Vampire* represented the last vestiges of British horror before Hammer Films revolutionized the genre. In a story by Jimmy Sangster, Dr. Callistratus (Donald Wolfit), a physician afflicted with vampirism, dies, returns from the dead, and takes administrative control of a mental hospital. There he uses inmates to satisfy his blood lust. Victor Maddern, the great English character actor, plays his one-eyed, hunchback assistant, and Victor Ball the young, idealistic medical student who must stop the mad doctor. In the shattering climax, worthy of any Hammer film, both Ball and his girlfriend (Barbara Shelley) are chained to the dungeon walls of the asylum and tortured by Callistratus. Angered by his master's evil deeds, the

Poster art from *Blood of the Vampire* (1958) features the tag line "He begins where Dracula left off." Photo courtesy of Universal Pictures.

hunchback rescues the girl, and Ball is able to drive the mad doctor to his death.

Blood of the Vampire is rarely seen on television or in film retrospectives, and some historians believe that all the prints have vanished or been destroyed. The film is noteworthy because of the talents of Jimmy Sangster and Barbara Shelley. That same year, Sangster would script the famous *Horror of Dracula* for Hammer Films and forever change the face of modern horror films. Shelley made her second appearance in this motion picture as a heroine in distress, a role she would play many times. Otherwise, the film is yet another variation of the mad-scientist-as-vampire plot, which dates back to Bogart's *Return of Dr. X* (1939).

1958 *Return of Dracula* (aka *Curse of Dracula, The Fantastic Disappearing Man*)

United Artists, b/w and color, 77 min. Director: Paul Landres. Producers: Arthur Gardner, Jules Levy. Writer: Pat Fielder. Starring Francis Lederer, Norma Ebehardt, Ray Striklan, Jimmie Baird, John Wengraf.

Landres and Fielder's *Return of Dracula* (1958) was far superior to their first collaborative effort. Released in England as *The Fantastic Disappearing Man*, the film takes full advantage of its limited budget and delivers an interesting horror movie. Count Bellac (played convincingly by Francis Lederer, who would play a vampire in several films), a vampire of Eastern European origins, makes his way to a small American town under the guise of a refugee iron curtain painter. He sets up shop in a small boardinghouse and begins to feed upon the townspeople. Even though the direction is slow and detached, the motion picture has a certain atmosphere which recalls the great vampire films of the past and provides a valuable link between traditions.

1959 *The Teenage Frankenstein*

Independent Productions, b/w, 65 min. Director-Writer-Star: Gene Gronemeyer.

1959 *Slave of the Vampire*

Independent Productions, b/w, 65 min. Director-Writer-Star: Gene Gronemeyer.

1959 *I Was a Teenage Vampire*
Independent Productions, b/w, 70 min. Director-Writer-Star: Donald Glut.

1961 *Monster Rumble*
Independent Productions, b/w, 71 min. Director-Writer-Star: Donald Glut.

1962 *Dragstrip Dracula*
Independent Productions, b/w, 70 min. Director-Writer-Star: Donald Glut.

As the titles might indicate, *The Teenage Frankenstein* (1959), *Slave of the Vampire* (1959), *I Was a Teenage Vampire* (1959), *Monster Rumble* (1961), and *Dragstrip Dracula* (1962) were several more entries which equated adolescent sexual drives with monsterhood in the lucrative teenage market. All five films were produced on a shoestring budget, utilizing amateur actors and local settings to tell a familiar story. All five films also had sporatic showings as seconds (or sometimes thirds) on a double bill or were viewed on college campuses. Today they have completely disappeared from sight, since all the negatives and prints were destroyed. Like Herman Cohen's far superior series (though that is not saying much about quality), these films investigated the cultural mores of the teenagers of the late fifties and early sixties. References to "make-out" parties, "rumbles," and drag racing (watchwords of the young) were specifically made to exclude older viewers. If they were shown as part of a retrospective today, they would appear as quaint time capsules of a more innocent time. Frankie and Annette, where are you now?

Donald Glut, who appears in three films as the discontented and unpopular son of Count Dracula, distinguished himself in the seventies with the definitive biography of Dracula and a book about historical vampires.

By the time *Dragstrip Dracula* debuted in 1962, America had already lost its lead in the market. The dominance of Universal's House of Horror had ended and would never again reclaim its past glories. The many mistakes of the period, however, would have two long-range positive effects—the resurgence of other film studios in England, Europe, and Mexico with the production of horror films, and the science-fiction boom. The vampire film would enter a new period of sophistication where ideas became more important than gimmicks and psychological terror, gothic horror, and symbolic sexuality replaced comedy and parody. And though television would continue to draw viewers away, the new forms would offer audiences something they couldn't see at home.

4

Hammer's Vampires

From *The Horror of Dracula* (1958)
to *Legend of the Seven Golden Vampires* (1974)

Although largely undistinguished until 1945, the British cinema developed independently of its American counterpart, producing four notable fantasy classics: Menzies's *Things to Come* (1936), Korda's *Thief of Bagdad* (1940), Murphy's *Man in Half Moon Street* (1944), and Balcon's *Dead of Night* (1945). Its late entry into the field of horror films, however, was a propitious one. Whereas Hollywood had exhausted its creative avenues as well as box-office potential, by 1957, Britain's fresh, imaginative approach quickly established it as the third great horror school. One of the most prodigious studios, largely responsible for that distinction was Hammer Films.

Founded by Will Hammer (1887–196?), a noted British producer, the Hammer Company began producing films shortly after the Second World War. Its early efforts were in the field of science-fiction, including the excellent *Four-Sided Triangle* (1952) and Terence Fisher's *Spaceways* (1953). The motion pictures were moderate successes in their own right, but it was the critical and financial triumph of Fisher's *Curse of Frankenstein* (aka *Frankenstein* in Britain, 1957) that determined the path the studio would take. Like Carl Laemmle, Jr., before him, Hammer was a shrewd movie mogul. He recognized the potential and popularity of certain American properties, and virtually any idea filmed in black-and-white by Universal in the thirties and forties was presented in large-screen color in the fifties and sixties. *Frankenstein* was followed by *The Horror of Dracula* (1958) and in subsequent years *The Hound of the Baskervilles* (1959), *The Mummy* (1959), *The Two Faces of Dr. Jekyll* (1960), *Curse of the Werewolf* (1961), and many others.

Hammer Films also produced sixteen vampire films between 1958 and 1974, and was working on a seventeenth when the company developed financial problems and folded in 1975. Eight of those films were in the Dracula cycle, three in the Karnstein saga, and five largely independent efforts. Their production values were generally of a high quality, extravagant by Hollywood standards, and the studio employed some of the finest talents of the British cinema. Directors Freddie Francis, Roy Ward Baker, Terence Fisher; writers Anthony Hinds, Don Houghton, Jimmy Sangster; and stars Peter Cushing, Christopher Lee, and Sir Donald Wolfit enriched and elevated the vampire movie above (and beyond) its B-film level. And with the fresh approach, which made use of the new technologies of color and special effects, Hammer competed directly with the American market (and the open European one). Although the films were not always classics, they made money. They also gave the vampire film a new lease on life, restoring dignity to the monster that in Universal's hands had degenerated into a stooge for Abbott and Costello.

1958 *The Horror of Dracula* (aka *Dracula*)

Hammer Films, 82 min. Director: Terence Fisher. Producer: Anthony Hinds. Writer: Jimmy Sangster, based on the novel by Bram Stoker. Starring Christopher Lee, Peter Cushing, Michael Gough, Carol Marsh, John Van Eyssen, Miles Malleson, Melissa Stribling, Valerie Gaunt.

The Horror of Dracula (aka *Dracula* in Britain, 1958) was the first and most successful of Hammer's vampire movies. Written by the great Jimmy Sangster, the film went back in principle to Bram Stoker's original novel, altering a number of relatively minor details to heighten suspense and hasten the pace. Dracula, though stripped of his powers to pass through walls or change himself into a bat or wolf, emerges as a chilling presence portrayed by Christopher Lee, while the eminent vampirologist Dr. Van Helsing, played by Peter Cushing, is his equal — undaunted, armed with crucifix, garlic flowers, and the other paraphernalia of his rather specialized trade. The screenplay also retains many of the original characters, including Jonathan Harker, Dr. Seward, Lucy, Mina, and Arthur Holmwood, as well as the period setting with its Victorian mores and gothic mystery. Faithful to the book, it is also an imaginative piece of filmmaking.

The film opens (much like the book) with Jonathan Harker's (John Van

Eyssen) diary entry of May 3, 1885. Because the coach driver has been reluctant to drive him to Castle Dracula, Harker is forced to walk the balance of his trip. When he arrives, he finds the genteel surroundings deserted and sits to eat a meal that has been left for him. But before Harker can complete the dinner, he is interrupted by a beautiful woman who claims that she is being held prisoner by Dracula. She is in fact one of Dracula's vampire wives and attempts to bite Harker before being frightened away by the Count. When he first appears in silhouette at the top of the stairs, Dracula (Lee), seems menacing to Harker, but after he descends the stairs, he is handsome and charming. He welcomes Harker to his castle and offers him all the hospitality of his home as well as quiet and seclusion. He even compliments his guest on the choice of a fiancée (upon viewing Lucy Holmwood's picture). However, when Harker later kills one of Dracula's brides in self-defense and inadvertently reveals his purpose to destroy the Transylvanian Count (in a major departure from the novel), Dracula turns into a yellow-eyed monster. He kills Harker, draining him completely dry, then sets out for London to take Lucy (Carol Marsh) as his own.

Several days later, Dr. Van Helsing (Cushing) arrives in Klausenburg looking for Harker. But the townspeople are afraid and refuse to cooperate with him. When he ventures to Castle Dracula, he discovers Harker's diary and quickly realizes that the evil menace has fled to England. Once he has destroyed Dracula's wives and his friend, the Dutch scientist returns to London, but is too late to prevent the death of Lucy. However, allied with Arthur (Michael Gough, who would later play Alfred in the 1989 *Batman*), he prevents Mina's (Melissa Stribling) demise and frees the soul of Lucy. He then chases the Count back to Europe, and in the climactic showdown between Dracula and Van Helsing at the former's castle, the two adversaries struggle hand to hand. Dracula's strength momentarily overcomes the doctor; however, in a desperate move, Van Helsing leaps across the room and pulls the drapes down, exposing Dracula to the purifying rays of the sun. The doctor has won (temporarily), having disposed of the vampire rather drastically by reducing him to dust, which is blown away in the final credits. But as we all know, it's difficult to keep a good vampire down, and Dracula would return in further sequels.

By sharp contrast with Universal's film, *The Horror of Dracula* was far more explicit. Terence Fisher, a pioneer in the field of British horror films, had been dissatisfied with Browning's version because much of the film's key action took place offscreen. He was determined not to make the same mistakes, even if it meant being visually explicit. Thus, when Harker stakes the vampire bride or Van Helsing destroys Dracula, the audience witnesses the event in brilliant Technicolor. Of course, the film raised a storm of outraged protest from newspaper critics who thought the film was too explicit about violence and implied sexuality. Fisher recently defended his film,

Christopher Lee took over the role of the Transylvanian Count in Hammer's series of Dracula films, and Lee was quickly recognized as Lugosi's successor. Photo courtesy of Hammer Films.

claiming, "The explicitness occurred in the [film's] most important moment, which is the destruction of the vampire. You can't do this by implication, or by shadows on the wall. You've got to show the beast's destruction.... It is a release!"

Fisher similarly restored the vampire's irresistible sexuality. "Dracula is a tremendously sensual creature," he added. "When he comes down those stairs, you see this totally attractive man, not a twisted grotesque!" He strongly objected to Lugosi's and Carradine's portrayal of Dracula and insisted that the gaunt, attractive Christopher Lee be cast in the title role. Lee, the veteran of several low-budget British productions, had impressed Fisher as the monster in *The Curse of Frankenstein* (1957). Slightly taller than Lugosi and less solid in his appearance, he resembled Stoker's original conception of Dracula. He also brought to the role a charisma and a quiet, chilling dignity that had been missing in previous portrayals. When Dracula approaches his victims, they actually enjoy, rather than resist, his neck biting. After all, the vampire's movements represent foreplay, and what woman can resist such attention? But beyond his tremendous sensuality, there was also an air of tragic melancholy. Christopher Lee explained that this made his Count more believeable: "I've always tried to put an element of sadness, which I've termed the loneliness of evil, into his character. Dracula doesn't want to live, but he's got to! He doesn't want to go on existing as the undead, but he has no choice." Lee's vampire was certainly memorable enough to be revived nine years later in *Dracula—Prince of Darkness* (1966), and he continued playing the character, or a relative vampire, in fourteen other productions.

Although the film is far from perfect, it is an ambitious, visually attractive production. Fisher's uncanny sense of atmosphere, use of pace and color, and ability to build suspense from divergent points had gone back to the roots and rituals of the traditional fairy tale in which good triumphed over evil. He had given the vampire story credibility again. With the added dimension of Technicolor, *The Horror of Dracula* is a real pleasure to watch, even today. And its commercial success (particularly in the United States) encouraged Hammer to produce a series of Dracula films.

1961 *The Bad Flower (Ahkea Kkots)*
South Korean, b/w, 75 min. Director-Writer: Youngmin Lee, based on *The Horror of Dracula*. Starring Chimi Kim, Yeehoon Lee.

Just as Universal Pictures and Junior Laemmle had arranged for the production of a foreign-language version of the 1931 *Dracula*, Hammer Films gave the nod to a Korean version of *The Horror of Dracula* (1958). Working from the Sangster screenplay (with a few scenes tailored for home

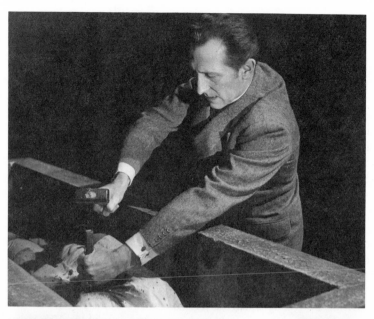

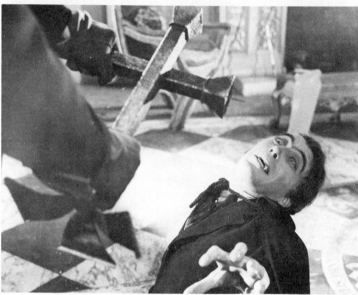

Top: Dr. Van Helsing (Peter Cushing) impales one of Dracula's victims in *The Horror of Dracula* (1958). Photo courtesy of Hammer Films. *Bottom: The Horror of Dracula* (1958). During their climactic struggle, Van Helsing fashions a cross from two candelabra and forces Dracula into the sunlight. Photo courtesy of Hammer Films.

audiences), principal photography was completed in South Korea by director Youngmin Lee. (Yechoon Lee took over the role of Dracula, and Chimi Kim played Mina.) Then footage from the Hammer version was added, and the result was an odd vampire entry entitled *Ahkea Kkots* (bad flower). The film works well in Korean and proves that the story of Dracula is universal.

1960 *The Brides of Dracula*

Hammer Films, 85 min. Director: Terence Fisher. Producer: Anthony Hinds. Writer: Jimmy Sangster. Starring Peter Cushing, David Peel, Martita Hunt, Freda Johnson, Yvonne Monlaur, Andrea Melly, Mona Washbone, Henry Oscar, Miles Malleson.

The Horror of Dracula was followed two years later by *The Brides of Dracula* (1960). Directed once again by Fisher, the film did not focus on Dracula but dealt with a Transylvanian nobleman who fancied himself a disciple of the Count. (This way, the producers didn't have to figure a clever solution to Dracula's demise in the previous film.) The inventive screenplay was written by Jimmy Sangster with the aid of Peter Bryan and Edward Percy, and featured Peter Cushing, reprising his role of Dr. Van Helsing as the critical link between the two films.

For several years (since the death of Dracula in the previous movie), vampire Baron Meinster (David Peel) has been held prisoner by his mother (Martita Hunt) at a deserted inn while she procures young maidens to satisfy his blood lust. However, the arrival of Marianne Danielle (Yvonne Monlaur), a young French teacher, upsets the delicate balance between mother and son. When the old baroness dies, the local villagers suspect Marianne and accuse her of being a vampire. She escapes and flees into the arms of Meinster, who desires her for his bride. Meanwhile, Van Helsing has destroyed all the other brides (vampires) and has followed the trail to Meinster's ancestral castle.

Cornered by the eminent vampirologist in a deserted windmill, the baron turns and inflicts his fatal bite. Van Helsing painfully struggles with the wound, then in desperation burns his neck with a white-hot branding iron before arranging the arms of a moonlit windmill to cast the shadow of the cross on the vampire. Though he has no religious fervor, Van Helsing believes in righteousness and the reasons why good can outthink evil. Cleverly, he calls upon the forces of darkness to destroy Meinster. The dark powers descend from the heavens in the form of a flurry of bats and like winged piranhas, viciously tear the baron to pieces. They then scatter his remains in the shadow of a cross. Van Helsing breathes a deep sigh of relief as the bats return to the black sky, and he heads for the village, exhausted, hoping for a peaceful night's rest.

Although *The Brides of Dracula* is not a direct sequel, it is a fine successor to *The Horror of Dracula*. The film has a good sense of pacing and period, and it features some wonderful performances, particularly from Cushing (who would play Van Helsing three more times in *Dracula A.D. 1972* [1972], *The Satanic Rites of Dracula* [1973], and *Legend of the Seven Golden Vampires* [1974]). However, when the motion picture was released in 1960, audiences were disappointed to learn that Hammer Films' key ingredient — Christopher Lee as Dracula — was missing. And the film's poor box-office showing caused executives at the studio to reconsider the direction their Dracula series was taking.

1966 *Dracula, Prince of Darkness* (aka *Disciple of Dracula, Revenge of Dracula, The Bloody*)

Hammer, 90 min. Director: Terence Fisher. Producer: Anthony Nelson Keyes. Writer: John Samson, based on an idea by John Elder and the characters created by Bram Stoker. Starring Christopher Lee, Barbara Shelley, Philip Latham, Andrew Keir, Francis Matthews, Suzan Farmer, Charles Tingwell, Thorley Walters.

Six years later, *Dracula, Prince of Darkness* (1966), under the able direction of Terence Fisher, brought Dracula back from the dead. The film opens by recalling the climactic struggle between Dracula and Dr. Van Helsing from *The Horror of Dracula* (1958). Once the vampire has been destroyed, Van Helsing leaves Castle Dracula (presumably to pick up the trail of Baron Meinster in *The Brides of Dracula*). Peace and tranquility have been restored to Klausenburg; the townspeople are happy once more, and groups of travelers regularly tour the late Count's estate. Klove (Philip Latham), a servant and faithful follower of Dracula, takes full advantage of one tour group and kidnaps one of its members (Charles Tingwell). Hanging him upside down over Dracula's tomb, he cuts the man's throat and pours the fresh blood (like a Catholic priest administering the Sacrament) over the ashes of his master. The Count subsequently returns to life, stronger and deadlier than before, and takes several women from the town (notably Barbara Shelley and Suzan Farmer) in revenge.

Meanwhile, Father Sandor (Andrew Keir), a local parish priest, believes that Dracula is not dead and hunts down his vampire brides between confession and Holy Communion. He represents the religious equivalent of Dr. Van Helsing, staking a vampire when he must and calling his fellow priests "superstitious, frightened idiots" when they refuse to help. He follows the trail of blood to Castle Dracula, and in the film's climax chases and traps the Count on a frozen lake. When the ice breaks, Dracula is seemingly drowned.

Ingeniously constructed around incidents of the previous movies, *Dracula, Prince of Darkness* quickly became the studio's most successful horror venture, rivaling even their original *Dracula* in both quality and box-office receipts. Part of that success was due to the imaginative scripting by John Samson and Anthony Hind (writing under the pseudonym John Elder). Even though Dracula had been destroyed at the end of the first film, their screenplay provided an ingenious resurrection for the Count. Another part of the success had to do with the creative use of sets, costumes, actors, and technical personnel from the Hammer stable. For budgetary reasons, the movie was filmed back-to-back with *Rasputin, the Mad Monk* (1965), yet it's quite impossible to tell that *Dracula, Prince of Darkness* had a modest budget, considering the lushness of the production. But the single most important factor in the success of the film was the triumphant reappearance of Christopher Lee as Dracula.

Christopher Lee had originally refused to play the part again for fear of being typecast, like Lugosi, as the Count and had taken a number of unusual roles with the hopes of shaking that image. In fact, he spoofed his characterization of Dracula in the low-budget *Tempi Duri Der I Vampire* (*My Uncle Was a Vampire*, 1959). Born in 1922, he started acting just after World War II in classical and Shakespearean drama. One of his big career breaks was in the 1948 film version of *Hamlet*, and the other was in Terence Fisher's *Curse of Frankenstein* (1957) as the monster. In the early sixties, Lee spent two years in Europe fine-tuning his acting talents in a number of undistinguished motion pictures, and his return to Hammer Films in 1964 was a propitious one. By relying on gestures and facial expressions (the very elements of mime), Lee demonstrated superior acting abilities in each part he undertook, from Rasputin to Sherlock Holmes to Fu Manchu. His performance as Dracula was critically acclaimed by the British film community: "Christopher Lee, eyes bloodshot and speechless, makes a powerful figure out of Dracula." He came to Hollywood in the middle seventies following Hammer Films demise, and distinguished himself in films like *The Man with the Golden Gun* (1973), *The Three Musketeers* (1974), *Airport '77* (1977), *House of Long Shadows* (1983), *Gremlins II* (1990), and others. However, in spite of his numerous other successes, this tall, gaunt British actor will always be remembered by many as the definitive Dracula.

1968 *Dracula Has Risen from the Grave*

Hammer, 92 min. Director: Freddie Francis. Producer: Aida Young. Writer: John Elder. Starring Christopher Lee, Rupert Davies, Veronica Carlson, Barbara Ewing, Barry Andrews, Ewan Hooper.

Christopher Lee's next film outing as the Count was *Dracula Has Risen from the Grave* (1968). Directed with a strikingly different style (than

Fisher's) by Academy Award winner Freddie Francis, this motion picture was a further departure in the Dracula series but once again featured some solid acting by Lee.

The movie opens as two priests, fighting their way through a raging snowstorm, attempt to place a golden cross on the gate to Castle Dracula. One of them accidentally falls through the ice, and blood from his wounds revives the vampire. Dracula is soon thawed from his frozen grave and again terrorizes the village in the shadow of his castle. He first enslaves, then kills Zena (Barbara Ewing). Then he abducts Maria (Veronica Carlson) and forces her to remove the cross from his gate (she unwittingly throws it into the chasm which surrounds Castle Dracula). When both Zena and Maria mysteriously die and return as vampires, a stranger arrives in the village to investigate. At first the villagers, incited by the leading citizen (Barry Andrews), suspect that the stranger is a vampire, but it is soon revealed that he is a monsignor in the Catholic church (Rupert Davies). The familiar pattern of bloodletting and staking occurs, eventually leading to the atheist hero (Andrews) and the Catholic priest joining forces to destroy the evil vampire. At Castle Dracula they corner the Count and force him off a parapet. Dracula falls into the chasm and is symbolically impaled on the golden cross.

The movie has moments of pure terror, but burdened with the traditional plot, it becomes tedious and repetitive. Freddie Francis, quite a different director from Terence Fisher, replaced atmosphere and tension with blood and gore. In fact, film critic Judith Crist called *Dracula Has Risen from the Grave* "a bloody bore." Also, the tension between the repressed Victorian sexual mores and Dracula's overt sexuality, clear in Fisher's adaptations, is missing here. Francis has gone to the opposite extreme of Browning and offers plenty of sexy women in various states of undress. Warner Brothers, Hammer's American distributor, felt that Fisher was much too subtle in his approach to the sexual issue and preferred Francis's more obvious style. Predictably, Warner's advertising campaign (featuring a nearly naked vampire) turned the film into one of the year's top moneymakers. And even though the Count had died, the ending (as expected) left room for another sequel.

1969 *Taste the Blood of Dracula*

Hammer, 95 min. Director: Peter Sasdy. Producers: Aida Young, Sir James Carreras. Writers: John Elder, Aida Young. Starring Christopher Lee, John Carson, Peter Sallis, Geoffrey Keen, Gwen Watford, Linda Hayden, Anthony Carlan, Ralph Bates.

Hammer Films brought Dracula back for a fourth time in *Taste the Blood of Dracula* (1969). Christopher Lee returned as the Count (but in a

Dracula Has Risen from the Grave (1968). Dracula (Christopher Lee) puts the bite on another female victim in the superior sequel to *The Horror of Dracula*. Photo courtesy of Hammer Films.

much diminished capacity). Newcomer Peter Sasdy, a Hungarian immigrant, directed the movie with style and panache, and elicited fine performances from John Carson, Peter Sallis, Geoffrey Keen, and Lee (who was incapable of giving a bad performance). However, the tension and suspense of the originals were missing from an otherwise innovative screen story, as the further adventures of Dracula became like installments in the James Bond series.

Working as a servant of Dracula, Lord Courtley (Ralph Bates), the depraved heir of an old, wealthy British family, searches for a ring, a black cloak, and a phial of red dust. He enlists the services of Samuel Paxton (Keen), William Hargood (Carson), and Jonathan Seeker (Sallis) to look for the valued artifacts but fails to tell them that the items are what he needs to bring the Count back to life. Convinced that the "treasure" will lead them to gold, they murder Courtley and accidentally spill his blood on the red dust. In a sequence strangely reminiscent of *Dracula, Prince of Darkness*, Count Dracula is brought back to life. Horrified, the three businessmen flee in terror, but not before Dracula identifies each one. He then arranges to avenge his servant by first seducing the three men's children (Anthony Corlan, Linda Hayden, and Isla Blair), then sending them to kill their fathers. The plan succeeds, but in the course of his revenge, Dracula plunges through a stained-glass window (which features a cross) and is cut to pieces.

Cleverly contrived, the story unfortunately reduced the character of Dracula to a static set piece of minor importance. He appears merely as a catalyst for the film's central action, but Warner Brothers seemed unconcerned, convinced that audiences really wanted to see women dressed in low-cut gowns or negligees writhing in ecstasy in sexually suggestive scenes and that Dracula's appearance was of secondary significance. Hammer Films had become financially dependent on its American distributor and was in no position to disagree. The real star of the film series, Christopher Lee, became disillusioned with this type of filmmaking and made numerous attempts to leave the role. But the studio kept offering him more money, and Lee continued unhappily in the role that made him famous. (Lee's struggle with typecasting and the Hollywood system is recounted in detail in his 1977 autobiography, *Tall, Dark and Gruesome*.)

1970 *Scars of Dracula*

Hammer, 96 min. Director: Roy Ward Baker. Producers: Harry Fine, Michael Styles. Writer: Tudor Gates, based on an original idea by John Elder. Starring Christopher Lee, Christopher Matthews, Anoushka Hemple, Jenny Hanley, Dennis Waterman, Patrick Troughton, Bob Todd, Michael Gwynn.

As the Dracula cycle began to wane in the late sixties and early seventies, studio executives began to see the writing on the wall and looked around for new ideas to spice up the old formulas. Aida Young, producing with director Roy Ward Baker and scripter John Elder (Anthony Hinds), reintroduced Klove (Dracula's servant) and made Dracula the central character again in *The Scars of Dracula* (1970). No attempt was made to link the resurrection of Dracula with his demise in the previous film. And by returning to Stoker's original novel (as well as his short story "Dracula's Guest"), the movie attempted to return to its earlier form. Warner Brothers also insisted that to increase the film's commercial appeal, more nudity and violence be added.

Paul (Christopher Matthews), a young man on the run, finds himself an unwitting guest of Dracula. After spending several sleepless nights in Castle Dracula, he is seduced by Tanya (Anoushka Hemple), one of the Count's vampire brides. (This parallels the original novel, with Jonathan Harker's arrival and subsequent discoveries.) Dracula learns of the seduction and brutally murders the young man. Meanwhile, Sarah (Jenny Hanley), Simon (Dennis Waterman) — respectively, Paul's girlfriend and his brother — and a local priest (Michael Gwynn) trace the young man to Dracula's clifftop castle. The priest is gruesomely killed by bats, and the remaining couple must enlist the aid of Klove (Patrick Troughton in a non–Dr. Who role), who has been beaten by the Count, to destroy Dracula. Climaxed on the battlements of the castle, the Count is struck by lightning and falls in flames into the chasm.

Executives at both Warner Brothers and Hammer were pleased with the box-office receipts of *The Scars of Dracula* and recognized for the first time the type of audience their films had attracted: a youthful one. They ordered future scripts appropriately tailored, and Warner suggested that Dracula's Victorian setting be contemporized. Financially troubled, Hammer speeded up production of the Dracula films, planning to release one every year.

1972 *Dracula, A.D. 1972*

Hammer, 95 min. Director: Alan Gibson. Producer: Josephine Douglas. Writer: Don Houghton. Starring Christopher Lee, Peter Cushing, Stephanie Beachum, Christopher Neame, Caroline Munro, Marsha Hunt, William Ellis, Michael Cross.

Both *Dracula A.D. 1972* (1972) and *The Satanic Rites of Dracula* (1973) moved the setting of the previous films into the twentieth century in a further attempt to vitalize the series. *Dracula A.D. 1972* begins in 1872 with Van Helsing's death and final (?) victory over the Count. The scene then shifts one hundred years later (with a jet flying overhead). Dracula (Lee) is revived by a group of 1970s swingers led by Johnny Alucard (Christopher Neame) and begins his familiar pattern of bloodletting to the beat of rock music. Lorimar Van Helsing (Cushing), a descendent of the eminent vampirologist, picks up the tools of his ancestor and stakes Dracula back to his grave. Directed by Alan Gibson and scripted by Don Houghton (who would team up to direct and write *The Satanic Rites of Dracula*), this film was unintentionally silly and appeared dated mere weeks after its release. (The American version of *Dracula A.D. 1972* added a three-minute commercial in which a Dracula impersonator swore members of the audience into the Dracula Society.)

1973 *The Satanic Rites of Dracula* (aka *Dracula Is Dead and Well and Living in London, Count Dracula and His Vampire Bride*)

Hammer, 87 min. Director: Freddie Francis. Producer: Roy Skeggs. Writer: Don Houghton. Starring Christopher Lee, Peter Cushing, Michael Coles, William Franklin, Freddie Jones, Richard Vernon.

The Satanic Rites of Dracula (1973) was released one year later and proved to be somewhat more interesting. The story is a curious cross between Dracula, Fu Manchu, and the James Bond films, with the Count plotting to annihilate mankind with a deadly bacterium. Dracula has given up his swinging ways (from the previous film) and become a wealthy Howard Hughes figure controlling a vast empire. (Parallels to the Bond villain Blofeld, particularly in *Her Majesty's Secret Service* [1969] and *Diamonds Are Forever* [1971], are rather obvious.) He has enslaved several pillars of the community (notably William Franklyn, Richard Vernon, and Patrick Barr) and a scientist (Freddie Jones) who has created a Black Death plague. Together with members of a satanic cult, he intends to destroy the world by reducing its inhabitants to mindless zombies. To insure that Lorimar Van Helsing (Cushing) does not interfere with his plans, he kidnaps the doctor's daughter (Joanna Lumley). Undaunted, Van Helsing sneaks into Dracula's country estate (complete with its Bond-like security system) and destroys the deadly bacillus. Imaginative, yet hardly in the same class as the original, *The Satanic Rites of Dracula* marked the final appearance of Lee as Dracula. (Coincidentally, Christopher Lee went on to play the Bond villain Francisco Scaramanga in *The Man with the Golden Gun*, 1973.)

Less artistically satisfying than the earlier films in the series, both movies have points of merit, the most important reintroducing Peter Cushing as Dr. Van Helsing to the Dracula cycle. Too many of the previous

motion pictures had produced weak counterparts to Dracula, and it was important to the formula that the Count have an equally strong nemesis. Both films also restored Dracula's vital, chilling presence, an essential ingredient that had been missing from the middle films of the series. Unfortunately, they failed to generate the box-office revenue necessary to sustain the series.

Production on a ninth film (*Dracula Walks the Night*) was begun in 1974, utilizing all that the producers had learned from past failures and successes. But when Hammer Films developed serious financial problems (and eventually folded in 1975), all new productions were halted. What a pity! The new project was to have combined the mythos of Sherlock Holmes with Dracula and was touted as the ultimate vampire film. Needless to say, *The Satanic Rites of Dracula* remains as the last film in the ambitious yet flawed Dracula series.

The Hammer Company, under the leadership of Michael Carreras, also produced another vampire series and five largely independent vampire movies. The Karnstein saga encompasses three films: *The Vampire Lovers* (1970), *Lust for a Vampire* (1971), and *Twins of Evil* (1972). (A fourth movie, *Vampire Virgins*, was in the preproduction stages when the studio folded.) Produced at a time when Hammer's Dracula cycle was winding down, this series was violent, sexually explicit, and full of box-office potential. Writer Tudor Gates explained that Carreras's (as well as Hammer's) new philosophy for success: "Nudity was very much an 'in' thing at the time I began thinking about the series. The doors of censorship were opening wide, and there was a liberty in what could be allowed on film. They [Hammer] had done some excellent work in the genre, and they were anxious to continue—provided we writers could come up with the twists that would make it profitable in the marketplace."

1970 *The Vampire Lovers*
Hammer, 91 min. Director: Roy Ward Baker. Producers: Harry Fine, Michael Style. Writers: Tudor Gates, Fine, and Style, based on *Carmilla*, by Joseph Sheridan Le Fanu. Starring Ingrid Pitt, George Cole, Dawn Adams, Douglas Wilmer, Peter Cushing, Pippa Steele, Madeline Smith.

Based on Joseph Sheridan Le Fanu's classic horror story *Carmilla*— which had already been made three times as *Vampyr* (1932), *Blood and*

Ingrid Pitt as Mircalla–Carmilla Karnstein, the lesbian vampire from Hammer's
The Vampire Lovers (1970). Photo courtesy of Hammer Films.

Roses (1961), and *La Cripta e l'Incubo* (1963) — *The Vampire Lovers* (1970)
introduced nudity and lesbianism to the vampire genre. Baron Hartog
(Douglas Wilmer), seeking revenge for the death of his loved ones, destroys
the Karnsteins, a family of vampires, in a beautifully rendered precredits sequence. But Mircalla (Ingrid Pitt), the eldest daughter, escapes. She later
reappears as Mircalla and Carmilla, and charms her way into wealthy
households where she befriends young women and makes them her "vampire lovers." She seduces, then vampirizes, young Laura (Pippa Steele),
daughter of General von Spielsdorf (Cushing); Emma (Madeline Smith); her
doctor (Ferdinand Mayne); her governess (Kate O'Mara); and her butler
(Harvey Hall). Outraged and sickened by his daughter's death, von Spielsdorf enlists the aid of Hartog and destroys the evil menace.
    Ingrid Pitt was voluptuous and sensual in her portrayal of the myste-

rious Carmilla, and Peter Cushing was fine as the dauntless vampire hunter. Capably directed by Roy Ward Baker, the film was a unique mixture of eroticism, soft-core pornography, and Grand Guignol horror. Hammer had learned from its Dracula series exactly what audiences wanted, and *The Vampire Lovers* was an immediate success critically and financially. A sequel followed one year later.

1971 *Lust for a Vampire*

Hammer, 95 min. Director: Jimmy Sangster. Producers: Harry Fine, Michael Style. Writer: Tudor Gates. Starring Yutte Stensgaard, Ralph Bates, Michael Johnson, Barbara Jefford, Suzanna Leigh, Mike Raven, Helen Christie.

Lust for a Vampire (1971) was the second film of the Karnstein saga, preferred by many critics over the first because of its imaginative plot. Mircalla (Yutte Stensgaard) is resurrected from the dead by her parents with the blood of a young girl, then enrolled as a pupil in an exclusive mid–European finishing school. Shortly after her arrival, several of the attendees die from the bite of the vampire. Local villagers are convinced that the evil Karnsteins have returned.

Late one night, Giles Barton (Ralph Bates), one of the school's professors, witnesses Mircalla kill another student. But even though he is an expert on the occult and should know better, he falls madly in love with her. She feigns interest and soon kills him in a loving embrace. Another professor, Richard Lestrange (Michael Johnson), is researching a horror story and accidentally stumbles upon Barton's notes. He too falls for the mysterious Mircalla, but when he insists that they consummate their love, she attempts to run away. Lestrange corners her in her family's castle and with the help of several villagers burns the Karnstein home to the ground. Mircalla dies in the blaze—and with her (hopefully), the Karnstein curse.

The film is leisurely paced yet never stately or static enough to become arty and never slow enough to become dull. Hammer horror screenwriter Jimmy Sangster directed (and cowrote) with a low-key style that allows the movie to develop crisply on its own. It is also a fascinating study of lesbianism and vampirism, with just the proper mixture of chills, thrills, and beautifully buxom girls. Trend-setting in its choice of subjects (once taboo), *Lust for a Vampire*, predictably, spawned another sequel.

1972 *Twins of Evil* (aka *Twins of Dracula, The Gemini Twins*)

Hammer, 87 min. Director: John Hough. Producers: Harry Fine, Michael Style. Writer: Tudor Gates. Starring Mary and Madeline

Lust for a Vampire (1971). Poster art from the sequel to *The Vampire Lovers*, featuring Yutte Stensgaard in the role Ingrid Pitt originated. Courtesy of Hammer Films.

Collison, Denis Price, Isobel Black, Kathleen Byron, Peter Cushing.

Twins of Evil (1972) is a somewhat weakened retelling of the first film. Mary and Frieda Gelhorn (played by real-life twins, *Playmate* centerfolds Mary and Madeline Collison) are the "twins of evil" (from the title), and their arrival in a small European village spells trouble for the local villagers. Under the guidance of Count Karnstein (Damien Thomas), they have come to avenge the death of the Karnstein family. They begin by draining several young men and women, turning the victims into vampires. When news of the twins leaks out, Gustav Weil (Cushing), a leader of a bloodthirsty, puritanical brotherhood, turns up to eradicate all evil from the town. He soon reveals that Mary and Frieda are descendants of the Karnstein family and incites the villagers to destroy them. In the carnage, he too is destroyed, along with Count Karnstein, while one of the twins is freed.

Peter Cushing is undoubtedly the best part of the film; in fact, his witch hunter, relentless and ruthless in his puritanism, is merely the other side of the vampiric coin. Both characters are perceived as evil, much in keeping with Vincent Price's role in *Witchfinder General* (1968) and other overly zealous characters. Working always in the shadow of Christopher Lee, Peter Cushing was the silent backbone of Hammer Films. Born in 1913, the British character actor of stage, television, and screen had performed in a number of undistinguished minor roles before going to Hammer. In 1957, Terence Fisher cast him as Baron Frankenstein (opposite Lee's monster) in *The Curse of Frankenstein,* and he was instantly acclaimed by the British film critics. Following that successful role, he played Van Helsing in *The Horror of Dracula* (1958), a part he was to become identified with and play on six more occasions. He also portrayed Sherlock Holmes twice, Dr. Who (the BBC time traveler) twice, and Baron Frankenstein in seven appearances. After Hammer's demise, his distinguished acting talents continued in films like *Star Wars* (1977), *Arabian Adventure* (1979), and *The House of Long Shadows* (1983).

From 1962 to 1972, during its most prolific period, Hammer Studios produced five other vampire movies. The films varied greatly in theme and approach, from a straight Dracula pastiche, as in *Kiss of Evil* (1962), to biting satire, as in *Captain Kronos, Vampire Hunter* (1972), or from historical romance, as in *Countess Dracula* (1972), to high camp, as in *Vampire Circus* (1973) or *The Legend of the Seven Golden Vampires* (1974). But they all shared the third great horror school's trademark for explicit violence and lurid sex. Unfortunately, toward the end of the sixties, the once highly regarded studio began to produce too many lower-budget B movies, and its later efforts were not seriously regarded by critics, reaching only limited distribution in the United Kingdom, Europe, and the United States. (*The Legend of the Seven Golden Vampires*, though completed in 1974, was not released until four years later.)

1962 *Kiss of the Vampire* (aka *Kiss of Evil*)

Hammer, 88 min. Director: Donald Sharp. Producer: Anthony Hinds. Writer: John Elder. Starring Noel Willman, Clifford Evans, Barry Warren, Elisabeth Valentine, Olga Dickie, Edward de Souza, Jennifer Daniel, Isobel Black.

Kiss of the Vampire (1962) was the first of Hammer's independent vampire films. Set in 1910, the story's focal point is Dr. Ravna (Noel Willman), a Bavarian disciple of Dracula. He lures a British honeymoon couple (Jennifer Daniel and Edward de Souza) to his château to seduce the wife and drain the husband. However, his opponent, Professor Zimmer (Clifford Evans), who was introduced in a precredit sequence staking his own daughter, discovers that Ravna is a vampire and leads a squadron of bats to destroy him. This unsubtle variation on the *Dracula* story, written by Anthony Hinds (as John Elder) and directed by Don Sharp, features a thrilling climax that seems lifted from *The Brides of Dracula* (1960) and evokes Alfred Hitchcock's *The Birds* (1963). But beyond that, the film is entirely too predictable.

1972 *Captain Kronos, Vampire Hunter*

Hammer, 91 min. Director-Writer: Brian Clemens. Producers: Albert Fennell, Brian Clemens. Starring Horst Janson, John Carson, Ian Hendry, Wanda Ventham, Caroline Munro.

Looking desperately for a fresh twist on their tired vampire series, Hammer introduced Horst Janson as *Captain Kronos, Vampire Hunter* (1972). This satirical, swashbuckling action film that had overtones of the 1930s serials and predicted *Raiders of the Lost Ark* (1981) relates the episodic tale of superhero Captain Kronos, late of the Imperial Guard, and his hunchback assistant Professor Grost (John Cater) in their search for vampires. Their hunt leads them to a nineteenth-century village that is being ravaged by a band of vampires. The two heros vanquish an evil doctor (John Carson) and rescue the raven-haired maiden Carla (Caroline Munro). Eventually their trail leads to a middle-aged lady of the manor (Wanda Ventham) and her resurrected husband (Shane Briant). Kronos wields his magic sword, then rides off into the sunset looking for more vampires. Although the film was intended to inaugurate a series, it failed commmercially at the box office, and no further adventures have been made about Captain Kronos.

1972 *Countess Dracula*

Hammer, 93 min. Director: Peter Sasdy. Producer: Alexander Paul. Writer: Jeremy Paul, based on an original story by Paul and Peter Sasdy. Starring Ingrid Pitt, Nigel Green, Sondor Eles, Maurice Denlam, Lesley-Anne Down.

Countess Dracula (1972) was considerably less pretentious and considerably more satisfying, with an excellent performance by Ingrid Pitt in the title role. Derived from parts of Stoker's *Dracula*, Le Fanu's *Carmilla*, and Valentine Penrose's *The Bloody Countess*, the film had some interesting moments. Countess Elizabeth Bathory (not really Countess Dracula) is obsessed with remaining young and uses virgin blood to rejuvenate herself in sixteenth-century Hungary. She also takes several boys and young girls as lovers, hoping to tap their youth and innocence. Aided by a servant (Nigel Green) and her old nanny (Patience Collier), she even kidnaps her daughter Ilona (Lesley-Anne Down) to seduce Ilona's young suitor. The masquerade eventually begins to unravel, and the truth about Elizabeth is revealed. Embarrassed, her royal family orders that she be imprisoned and sealed into her castle walls, forever. Director (and cowriter) Peter Sasdy, who had directed *Taste the Blood of Dracula* (1969), makes many of the familiar formulas look fresh in this better-than-average horror film. But in a much larger context, the motion picture thematically echoes the sentiments of the late sixties hippie movement, which had claimed that the older generation, frustrated with the waste of their lives, would feed upon the youth, and that sentiment carried through numerous films, including *The Graduate* (1967) and *Easy Rider* (1970). (Jose Grau remade *Countess Dracula* in 1973 as *Ceremonia Sangrienta*.)

1972 *Vampire Circus*

Hammer, 87 min. Director: John Hough. Producer: Michael Carreras. Starring Robert Tayman, Lynne Frederick, John Moulder Brown.

Burdened with a silly plot, *The Vampire Circus* (1972) also proved quite imaginative. In 1810, Count Rittenhouse holds the town of Stetl, Serbia, in his vampiric grasp. When the villagers trap and destroy him, he curses the town and its people for "all eternity." Fifteen years later, the plague-ridden village, quarantined from its European neighbors, is visited by the Circus

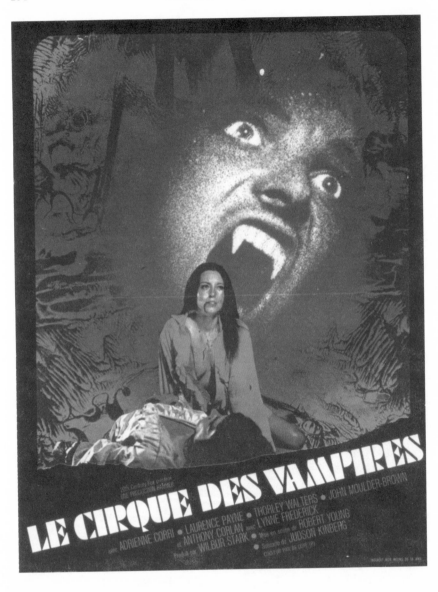

Foreign poster art for *Le Cirque des Vampires* (1972, *Vampire Circus*), the silly Hammer production which links high-wire circus acts with vampirism. Poster art courtesy of Hammer Films.

of Nights. This traveling troupe is really a circus of vampires (who can change into animals at will), and their gypsy owner (Robert Tayman) seeks revenge against those who murdered his cousin. They kill a number of villagers, kidnap (in an obligatory scene) the heroine (Lynne Frederick), then revive the Count for a bloodletting finale. Eventually the hero (John Moulder Brown) rescues the heroine and decapitates the head vampire. Though the film resembles a Fellini circus, with its odd assortment of strange characters, and represented an amalgam about Communist take-overs, it did not interest paying customers and was a box-office failure. (The script was written by George Baxt, whose *Circus of Horrors* [1959] had made such a splash in the late fifties.)

1974 *The Legend of the Seven Golden Vampires* (aka *The Seven Golden Vampires, The Seven Brothers Meet Dracula*)

Hammer, 110 min. Director: Roy Ward Baker. Producers: Don Houghton, Vee King Shaw. Writer: Don Houghton. Starring Peter Cushing, David Chiang, Julie Edge, Shina Szu, John Forbes-Robertson.

The last of Hammer's vampire films was *The Legend of the Seven Golden Vampires* (1974). Poorly dubbed, this far-out adventure story told of Van Helsing's (Cushing) trip to China in search of Dracula and his disciples. The eminent vampirologist becomes allied with his Chinese counterpart, Hsu Tien-an (David Chiang). Together with seven karate experts, they destroy the Chinese vampires, staking them village after village. Finally Van Helsing faces Dracula alone. Directed by Roy Ward Baker, the confused tale attempts to combine the vampire mythos with a Japanese kung-fu movie, but even the superb acting talents of Peter Cushing cannot help this horrible film. Hammer Films had tried to convince Lee to appear as Dracula, but after he refused, John Forbes-Robertson was hired for the part. His broadly camp approach to the role was the final nail in the coffin. Produced in 1974 when Hammer Films was facing bankruptcy, *The Legend of the Seven Golden Vampires* was one of the films they hoped would bail them out. Unfortunately, it was so bad that Warner Brothers refused to release it (along with several other embarrassingly poor efforts), and Hammer Films folded in 1975. (*The Legend of the Seven Golden Vampires* was finally released in 1978 by Dynamite Entertainment Group.)

Hammer Films, in its heyday from 1958 to 1969, created a number of fine quality films. Their production values were usually high quality, and they employed some of the finest talent of the British cinema. When the studio folded in 1975, it had produced nearly 150 motion pictures (7 to 8 major films a year). No wonder that many believe that they single-handedly represented the third great horror school. Some detractors will dispute the worth or impact of Hammer "horror," but it is quite clear that Hammer Films enriched and elevated the vampire movie above its B-film level and for a time made it a box-office bonanza. More important, the studio's high-quality prodigious output caused its American and European competitors to reconsider their efforts and begin producing quality horror films once again.

$$\boxed{5}$$

Western and
Atom Age Vampires
From *Curse of the Undead* (1959)
to *Horror of the Blood Creatures* (1971)

By the late fifties and early sixties, Britain's dominance of the horror industry was almost complete, which left American and European filmmakers struggling to compete. Since the final installment of Universal's horror cycle (eleven years before), Hollywood and its European counterpart had failed to make any successful vampire films. And they were reckless in their attempts to regain the audience they had once held. Archetypes of traditional horror fantasy were discarded in favor of conventional concepts of cinematic style like the Western and the science-fiction (sci-fi) film. Producers transposed elements like cowboys, shoot-outs, rocketships, alien invasions, and nuclear war to the vampire movie, making a desperate bid to reclaim that leadership, but instead producing for a few years an art form without a true identity of its own. Stripped of an atmosphere of terror and tension, the films became ludicrous caricatures, and it soon became apparent that as filmmakers unearthed old elements from the past or conceived new ones to play out the old formulas, the box-office potential of their hybrid was limited.

However, the period is far from undistinguished. Between 1959 and 1971, there were a number of notable exceptions, including *L'Ultimo Uomo*

della Terra (*The Last Man on Earth,* 1964), *Terrore nello Spazio* (*Planet of the Vampires,* 1965), and *Queen of Blood* (1966). In both plot and visual style, these films are really horror fantasies that coincidentally share a basic similarity in form to the science-fiction film. Their attempts at quasi-scientific explanations for vampires and vampirism provide a bond between science and gothic horror, a valuable link that can be historically traced back to Mary Shelley's *Frankenstein* (1818) and Robert Louis Stevenson's *Strange Case of Dr. Jekyll and Mr. Hyde* (1886) or *The Vampire Bat* (1933) and *The Return of Dr. X* (1939). The other films, like *Curse of the Undead* (1959), *Atom Age Vampire* (1961), and *Billy the Kid Versus Dracula* (1965), fail to make that connection with the past and become unwitting parodies of the form. Before the period was over, producers were again looking for new ideas, never realizing that the answers were right at hand.

1959 *Curse of the Undead* (aka *Mark of the West)*

Universal, b/w, 79 min. Director: Henry Cass. Producer: Joseph Gershenson. Writer: Edward Dein. Starring Michael Pate, Eric Fleming, John Hoyt, Bruce Gordon, Edward Binns, Kathleen Crowley.

The American Western had been a traditional favorite of the cinema for more than thirty years, and when Universal Pictures announced that it would make the first "Vampire-Western," audiences were dubious. *Curse of the Undead* (1959) is a dismal motion picture of the B variety. Relying heavily on the stock ingredients of both traditions, the film can never make up its mind whether it is a Western or a horror movie. Michael Pate plays a hired gunslinger (who also happens to be a vampire). He is brought into a range war between farmers and cattlemen to exact revenge for several murders. But instead of using his gun, he gets revenge by sinking his fangs into the necks of the bad guys (or were those the good guys?). Eventually, the story leads to a very predictable shoot-out between Pate and Preacher Dan (Eric Fleming), who has loaded his gun with a very special bullet. Directed by Edward Dein from a script by Henry Cass and his wife, Mildred, *Curse of the Undead* was better left buried.

1965 *Billy the Kid Versus Dracula*

Embassy, 89 min. Director: William Beaudine. Producer: Carroll Case. Writer: Carl K. Hittleman. Starring John Carradine, Chuck

Opposite: Curse of the Undead (1959). **In the cinema's first vampire Western, Michael Pate carries his victim (Kathleen Crowley) to his crypt for a late-night snack. Photo courtesy of Universal Pictures.**

Courtney, Olive Corey, Roy Barcroft, Harry Carey, Jr., Melinda
Plowman.

On a similar theme but a much larger budget was Embassy Pictures'
Billy the Kid Versus Dracula (1965). Directed by William Beaudine, a
veteran of numerous Westerns, the film was fast-paced and dimwitted. Billy
the Kid (Chuck Courtney), who has grown tired of being a gunslinger,
decides to settle down and marry his sweetheart (Melinda Plowman).
However, her uncle, who is really Count Dracula, has other plans. The
retired gunslinger must strap on his guns one last time and face the vampire
at twenty paces. Abysmal acting and a bad script contributed to the movie's
poor showing at the box office, and even the appearance of John Carradine
(as Dracula, in a film he considers his worst) couldn't resurrect the film for
even the late show. (John Carradine's son David would appear twenty-five
years later in a vampire–Western entitled *Sundown: The Vampire in
Retreat*, 1989.)

Producers were hesitant after the poor showing of *Curse of the Undead*
(1959) and *Billy the Kid Versus Dracula* (1965) to release more vampire–Westerns and turned instead to another form. (Predictably, the vampire–Western would resurface almost twenty-five years later in two very
different films.) The science-fiction film, its origins firmly rooted in European culture, had become a box-office bonanza in the fifties. In fact, it supplanted its blood relative (the horror film) for nearly a decade, by playing
on the anxieties and fears brought about by man's simultaneous discovery
of atomic power, the cold war, and the UFO threat from outer space.
"Creature-features" with men dressed in tacky monster suits dominated the
period and slowly, inevitably, took on the characteristics of the horror film.
Likewise, the vampire film began to deal with man's misuse of atomic power
and potential invasions from space.

1951 *The Thing (from Another World)*
RKO/Winchester Pictures, b/w, 86 min. Director: Christian Nyby
(and Howard Hawks). Producer: Howard Hawks. Writer: Charles
Lederer, based on the novella *Who Goes There?* by John W. Campbell. Starring Kenneth Tobey, Margaret Sheridan, Robert Cornthwaite, Dewey Martin, Bill Self, Douglas Spencer, James Arness.

Opposite: **Preacher Dan (Eric Fleming) destroys the vampire's coffin, then loads his
six-shooter with special bullets for a final showdown in** *Curse of the Undead* **(1959).
Photo courtesy of Universal Pictures.**

Before James Arness went on to play Marshall Dillon in TV's Gunsmoke, he played a "vegoid vampire" in Howard Hawks's superior *The Thing (from Another World)* (1951). Photo courtesy of RKO Pictures.

The thing (in *The Thing [from Another World]*, 1951) was not the metamorphosing creature of its source, John W. Campbell's 1938 novella *Who Goes There?* but a blood-drinking carrot man. If the one-line description sounds a trifle corny, don't be too premature in your judgment. Howard Hawks's superb science-fiction classic provides a wonderful departure from the traditional vampire legend. The roots of gothic terror, along with its staples of walking dead, dismemberment, and mutation, have been replaced by a "real" horror from beyond the solar system.

The movie opens with the discovery of a flying saucer embedded in the ice at the Arctic Circle. Members of an army research station (including Kenneth Tobey, Robert Cornthwaite, Dewey Martin, and Bill Self) have been alerted to UFO sightings but are confounded when they come upon the craft. They recover the only survivor of the crew, a "vegoid" (Gunsmoke's James Arness) and bring his frozen body to the safety of their encampment. When one of the soldiers accidentally thaws the creature, it begins to run amok, killing and draining men of blood. The station's resident mad doctor (Cornthwaite) urges the others to capture the thing alive, and leader Tobey believes that a "dead monster is a good monster." Ultimately, they trap the thing in the greenhouse and cook it to death. Journalist Spencer's final warning to "keep watching the skies" heightens our cold war paranoia and suggests that other things may be coming.

Rigorous pacing, thanks to the superior editing of Roland Gross, helped make *The Thing (from Another World)* one of the top moneymakers of 1951. Although some of the edge has been lost in time, the film is still a tight suspense thriller. It also has the distinction of having launched the invasion from space as the first science-fiction monster film. (John Carpenter remade *The Thing* in 1982, eliminating the vampire from space and returning to the original source material.)

1952 *Alraune* (aka *Unnatural, Vengeance, Mandragore*)

German, b/w, 92 min. Director: Arthur Maria Rabenalt. Producer: O. Lehmann. Writer: Fritz Rotter, based on the novel by H.H. Ewers. Starring Hildegard Knef, Erich von Stroheim, Karl Boehm, Julia Koschka.

The 1952 adaptation of *Alraune* was the fifth (and hopefully last) time that Hanns Heinz Ewers's 1913 best-seller was made for the silver screen. As with previous versions (two in 1918; 1928; and 1930), mad scientist Ten Brinken (overplayed by Erich von Stroheim) collects a hanged man's semen from under the gallows and artificially inseminates a prostitute. The resulting offspring of this unholy union is the cold, unfeeling Alraune. Needing blood and the souls of men to survive, Alraune (Hildegard Knef) begins killing those who try to love her. Ultimately, she and her creator are destroyed. This new version is the least satisfying (the 1928 version being the best).

Not of This Earth (1957) and Little Shop of Horrors (1960), the best of Roger Corman's low-budget films, dealt with these issues directly. (Corman would also make a gothic vampire film, Tomb of Ligeia [1964], as part of his homage to E. A. Poe.) Though somewhat limited by resources, both films are highly original and give the traditional vampire story a slightly different spin (taking their cues from Howard Hawks's The Thing [from Another World], 1951). They also share a number of striking similarities. The former concerns an extraterrestrial who, having survived a nuclear war on his home planet, must replenish his contaminated blood supply with that of healthy humans. The later deals with an intergalactic plant that has an insatiable thirst for blood. Both films were shot in a week or less with budgets that would barely pay for the special effects in many contemporary films of the day. And both films have the distinction of being remade into larger-budget camp productions of the eighties. (Little Shop of Horrors was resurrected first as a Broadway musical, then became a 1986 Frank Oz film.)

1957 Not of This Earth
Los Altos, b/w, 69 min. Director-Producer: Roger Corman. Writers: Charles B. Griffith, Mark Hanna. Starring Paul Birch, Beverly Garland, Morgan Jones, William Roderick, Jonathan Haze, Dick Miller.

Not of This Earth was one of the first of the science-fiction hybrid vampire movies. Produced and directed by Corman, this film also introduced his unique brand of suspense-horror-comedy that would find its way into future genre favorites. Mr. Johnson (Paul Birch), the alien in the gray flannel suit, has come to Earth looking for isotopically pure human blood and has sought out the services of Dr. Rocelle (Morgan Jones) and his pretty nurse, Nadine (Beverly Garland). The blood in his veins is drying up (just like the blood in the veins of his people) because of a devastating nuclear war that has turned his world, Davanna, into a radioactive hell. Johnson quickly discovers that a simple transfusion will not do and begins to send more derelicts (and even a vacuum-cleaner salesman, played by Dick Miller) through his matter transporter. He finally dies when the high pitch of a motorbike horn causes him so much pain that he crashes his car. Chillingly portrayed, particularly when Johnson removes his dark glasses to reveal eyes without pupils, this was one vampire that was beyond the ordinary.

1960 Little Shop of Horrors
Santa Clara Films, b/w, 70 min. Director-Producer: Roger Corman. Writer: Charles B. Griffith. Starring Jonathan Haze, Jackie Joseph, Mel Welles, Myrtle Vail, Dick Miller, Jack Nicholson.

Poster art for Roger Corman's *Not of This Earth* (1957), one of the first of the science-fiction hybrid vampire movies. Courtesy of Roger Corman Productions.

Little Shop of Horrors was derived from parts of Corman's earlier *A Bucket of Blood* (1959) and *The Spider Woman Strikes Back* (1946), in which Gale Sondergaard cultivates bloodthirsty plants. But what made this film unique was its approach. Nothing is sacred in this zany, crazy horror comedy, and certainly nothing is to be taken seriously. Seymour (Jonathan Haze), the underpaid, overworked Jewish nerd who tends Mushnik's Flower Shop, discovers a very unique plant, one that feeds not on fertilizer but on blood. Naming it Audrey II after the love his life (Myrtle Vail), he puts it on display. Suddenly business is blooming at Mushnik's as customers rush in to see the exotic potted plant. However, when it starts crying "Feed Me!" Seymour must find victims for its delicate digestive habits. Predictably, he takes to the street looking for buxom whores to feed Audrey. Suggested by John Collier's short story "Green Thoughts," this tale of a bloodthirsty vampire plant is irresistible. (Jack Nicholson appears in a minor role as a supermasochist.)

1958 *It! The Terror from Beyond Space* (aka *It! The Vampire from Beyond Space*)

United Artists, b/w, 69 min. Director: Edward L. Cahn. Producer: Robert E. Kent. Writer: Jerome Bixby. Starring Marshall Thompson, Shawn Smith, Kim Spalding, Ann Doran, Ray "Crash" Corrigan, Dabbs Greer.

Director Edward Cahn teamed up with noted science-fiction writer Jerome Bixby to create the first intergalactic vampire stowaway in *It! The Terror from Beyond Space* (1958). Although this low-budget shocker owes much to A. E. Van Vogt's 1950 novel *Voyage of the Space Beagle*, the plot is a direct descendant of the monster in the haunted-house story.

Returning from Mars, a space expedition discovers it has inadvertently taken a blood-drinking monster ("Crash" Corrigan) on board. Relentlessly, the vampire stalks members of the male and female crew and drains them of blood one-by-one. (As usual in films like this, the crew behaves rather stupidly and makes easy prey for the creature.) Captain Marshall Thompson and the remaining survivors attempt to contain the monster in the lower section of the ship, but it soon breaks free and pursues them section by section to the bridge. Backed up against the bulkhead, the crew is forced to decompress the ship and blast the monster into deep space. The special effects are laughable, and the rubber-suited monster is less than credible, but It! is a lively precursor to *Queen of Blood* (1966) and *Alien* (1979).

1963 *Atom Age Vampire (L'Erde di Satana)*

Italian, b/w, 87 min. Director: Robert McNamara. Producer: Mario Bava. Writers: Pierre Monviso, Gino de Santis, Alberto Bevilacqua. Starring Alberto Lupo, Suzanne Loret, Sergio Fantoni, Franca Parisi Strahl, Ivo Garrani, Andrea Scotti.

Intriguing though the concept may be in *Atom Age Vampire* (1963), the link between science and gothic horror is weak. Gothic science-fiction should emphasize danger and paranoia. Though the audience imagines itself in a well-lit comfortable world, it should be reminded that without technology everything is darkness. Unfortunately, this film does not live up to that promise. Mario Bava's photography is moody and atmospheric enough in this Italo-French film, but Anton Guilio Majano's (aka Robert McNamara) direction is never tense enough to draw us into the darkness. Although certain scenes are grimly horrific, the audience is always aware that it is only a movie.

The story focuses on Suzanne Loret, a once beautiful entertainer who has been scarred by a recent accident. She seeks the aid of a mad scientist (Albert Lupo) to restore her former beauty. During her first visit, he falls madly in love with her and decides to do anything, even commit murder, to help her. He strangles several women, then, using their fresh blood, he injects her with a formula that will rejuvenate her. Unfortunately, the formula turns her into an "atom age vampire," not totally unlike its gothic ancestors. She begins to lust for more blood, and the scientist is forced to destroy her.

Atom Age Vampire was neither a critical nor a box-office success, but it did encourage filmmakers to experiment further with the form, producing such motion pictures as *La Marca del Muerto* (*Creatures of the Walking Dead*, 1960), *World of the Vampires* (1961), *Frankenstein, the Vampire and Company* (1961), and others. However, none of these films were as chillingly effective as *L'Ultimo Uomo della Terra* (*The Last Man on Earth*, 1964).

1964 *The Last Man on Earth (L'Ultimo Uomo della Terra)*

Italian/Lippert Films, b/w, 88 min. Director: Sidney Salkow. Writers: Logan Swanson (Richard Matheson), William Leicester, based on the novel *I Am Legend*, by Richard Matheson. Starring Vincent Price, Franca Bettoia, Emma Danielli.

Direct, prophetic, *The Last Man on Earth* is a compelling horror fantasy that grabs the audience with the first frame and drags it into the darkness. It intends not merely to scare you with shock sequences and terror scenes but also to send you home thinking. The film is variable in style, its script sometimes overwritten and marred by a tendency at heavy-handedness, but as an exercise in sheer horror its worth is undoubted. There are few films that evoke its mood and feeling of loneliness and paranoia.

Robert Logan (Vincent Price) is the last man on earth, the lone sur-vivor of a plague that has killed most of the world's population and turned the remainder into vampire mutants. At first, he searches for a medical ex-planation of the ancestral stigmata of the vampire in symptoms of an illness and a cure. But quickly he realizes that there is no cure, only his survival. Then, armed with a mallet and stakes, the traditional tools of Dr. Van Hel-sing, he journeys through the deserted city by day, killing and burning as many of the vampires as he can. Terrified of the light, they hide in the shadows, awaiting darkness. And with the coming of dusk, he rushes to his fortress home to fight off the nocturnal mutations, using crosses, mirrors, garlic, and a stake-firing crossbow. There are glimmers of hope in his world, such as the appearance of a dog and female survivor, but they are fleeting. Lonely and weary enough to make mistakes, he eventually falls into the vampires' clutches. Robert Logan represents a threat to their new order as the last reminder of the world the vampires left behind, and they must destroy him. Unlike other vampire films, the roles of victim and menace are chillingly reversed. Man is pictured as the death master, and the vampires are representative of "society."

Though flawed by low production values, *Last Man* is still a master-piece of horror and science-fiction. This Italian-U.S. production was the first of two versions of Richard Matheson's classic vampire novel *I Am Legend* (the other being 1971's *The Omega Man*). Matheson wrote an original screenplay for *Last Man* in 1957 for Hammer Films, but when they optioned the rights to Lippert Films, the script was rewritten by William Leicester. Unhappy with the adaptation, even though it was a faithful retelling of his novel, Matheson withdrew his name and put his pen name, Logan Swanson, on the final film. When he learned that Charlton Heston intended to remake the movie, there was renewed hope for an adequate translation.

Richard Burton Matheson, an accomplished American writer of short stories, novels, and film scripts, didn't always have this difficulty with his writing. Born in 1926, he sold his first horror story in 1950, and his first novel *(I Am Legend)* in 1954. When he was called on to write the screenplay for his next novel *(The Shrinking Man)*, he so impressed the executives at Universal that he landed an assignment on Rod Serling's "Twilight Zone" (1959, CBS). He followed that successful collaboration with another by writing a series of Edgar Allan Poe adaptations for Vincent Price and Roger Corman.

Matheson has since written for "Star Trek" (1966, NBC), "Night Gallery"

(1971, NBC, including some distinctive vampire stories), and the highly successful *Night Stalker* (1972). His other films include *Duel* (1971, with Steven Spielberg), *Legend of Hell House* (1973, from his novel), *The Night Strangler* (1973), *Scream of the Wolf* (1974), *The Stranger Within* (1974), and *Somewhere in Time* (1979).

1968 *Night of the Living Dead*

Image Ten, b/w, 96 min. Director: George Romero. Producers: Russell Streiner, Karl Hardman. Writer: John A. Russo. Starring Judith O'Dea, Duane Jones, Karl Hardman, Keith Wayne, Julia Ridley, Marilyn Eastman.

Although not specifically a vampire film, George Romero's *Night of the Living Dead* (1968) was inspired thematically by Richard Matheson's *I Am Legend*. (Romero had attempted to purchase the rights to the novel, but they had just been sold to Warner.) The old conventions and legends which used to govern the behavior of monsters no longer exist; they have been replaced by the nightmare of science and technology out of control. Just as Robert Neville attempts to find a scientific explanation for vampirism, the protagonists struggle to understand what's gone wrong. Unfortunately, the ultimate irony reveals that answers are unnecessary in a world gone mad and that only survival matters.

Radioactive fallout from an aborted Venus probe revives the dead and turns them loose on an unsuspecting farmhouse (and reputedly the world). The mindless corpses stumble along at an unstoppable pace in search of humans for food. Society collapses, and a few people huddle together in a darkened house trying to stay alive until morning (when they hope the dead will return to their graves). Resourceful black hero Duane Jones and screaming heroine Judith O'Dea manage to survive wave after wave of the dead. Ironically, Jones emerges victoriously from the farmhouse only to be shot dead by members of a makeshift militia.

Filmed in Pittsburgh, Pennsylvania, with amateurs on weekends with borrowed money and equipment, Romero's low-budget effort went on to become the most successful independent of all time. The motion picture was a popular feature for midnight showings, and acquired cult status on college campuses. It has spawned two sequels—*Dawn of the Dead* (1979) and *Day of the Dead* (1985)—and a 1990 remake, as well as a host of imitators. When viewed as a document from the sixties, it tends to reflect the tone of rebellion, chaos, racial anxiety, confusion, paranoia, and mistrust of that time.

1971 *The Omega Man*

Warner Bros./Kinney, 104 min. Director: Boris Sagal. Producer: Walter Seltzer. Writers: John Williamson, Joyce Corrington, based on the novel *I Am Legend*, by Richard Matheson. Starring Charlton Heston, Anthony Zerbe, Rosalind Cash, Paul Koslo.

Predictably, *The Omega Man* (1971) was a further departure from Matheson's novel. Written by John Williamson and Joyce Corrington, the screen story radically transforms the thrust of paranoia and loneliness to action and melodrama. No longer is the last man on earth beseiged by vampires and haunted by the memory of plague and death. The vampires have been replaced with hooded zombies (thirsty for his blood), and loneliness is overcome by a normal woman and a band of youthful rebels. The chills and moody atmosphere are fine, but much of the bite of the original is missing.

In 1977, a plague resulting from a Sino-Russian war has decimated the world's population. Robert Neville (Heston), the last man on earth, wages a war against the loathsome survivors of the disease. Armed with an infrared sniper's rifle (instead of a mallet and stakes), he searches the deserted streets of Los Angeles for the plague-afflicted zombies. He has but one goal — survival. Then one day, as he is looking through a clothing store, Neville sees what appears to be a female mannequin move. The beautiful woman (Rosalind Cash) is the first normal person he has seen in two years, but unfortunately her appearance causes him to stumble into a trap.

On "trial," Neville is found guilty of "medicine, science, weapons, machine, electricity" by Matthias (Anthony Zerbe) and his hooded cult of zombie mutants, and sentenced to death. They view him as a relic of the destructive technology which destroyed their world; by killing him, they thus end the nightmare of his world. He is taken to a large stadium to be burned at the stake, but before the sentence can be carried out, the stadium lights come on, blinding the zombies, and he is rescued. Neville is taken by Dutch (Paul Koslo) and Lisa (Cash) to a fortress in the hills. The fortress protects the last eight survivors of the plague, each showing the first symptoms of the disease. Neville returns home to his laboratory, and using his own blood, he develops a serum that will save the last of mankind. However, Matthias and his Family have other ideas. They lure him into a trap with Lisa's unwitting help, destroy his home and laboratory, and mortally wound him. As the last rays of the sun chase the zombies into hiding, Dutch and the other survivors arrive too late to save Neville. But the serum, the key to their future, is safe. Robert Neville dies in a crucifixion pose in a nearby fountain.

The Omega Man was one of Warner's big hits for 1971, due in large part to Heston's bravura performance and a slick radio and television advertising

Two examples of poster art from *The Omega Man* (1971), a reworking of Richard Matheson's classic vampire novel *I Am Legend*. Courtesy of Warner Brothers.

campaign: "The last man alive . . . is not alone!" But it is pale in comparison to the film it could have been or even *The Last Man on Earth*. Both films are compelling in their own right, with some fine action sequences and marvelous photography. Both films also examine paranoia and the theme of science versus superstition. However, it is clear from both versions that the ultimate adaptation of *I Am Legend* has yet to be made. Ironically, George Romero's *Night of the Living Dead* (1968), the graphic and gruesome zombie movie which launched a whole subgenre of horror imitators and actually upstaged the vampire film for a number of years, comes the closest to the spirit of Matheson by advancing the theme of paranoia and survival in a world gone mad.

1965 *Planet of the Vampires (Terrore nello Spazio,* aka *Demon Planet)*

Italian, 85 min. Director: Mario Bava. Producer: Fulvio Luciana. Writers: I. B. Melchoir, Callisto Casulich, Antonio Roman, Bava. Starring Barry Sullivan, Norma Bengell, Evi Marandi, Angel Aranda, Fernando Villena, Franco Andrei.

One year after *The Last Man on Earth* (1964), Mario Bava directed *Terrore nello Spazio (Planet of the Vampires*, 1965). Bava had been Italy's leading cinematographer in the fifties and became a producer of a series of fine low-budget horror films in the sixties. His first foray into the science-fiction field has the visual pace and styling of a classic horror film, even though the alien sets are made from cardboard and the plot is derivative of *It! The Terror from Beyond Space* (1958) and a half dozen other films.

While surveying the planet Aura, the first of two rocketship expeditions mysteriously vanishes, and the second expedition, led by Barry Sullivan, sets out to investigate. But it too is forced off course and pulled down to a planet by a strange gravitational field. Once on the planet, the crew discovers the ruins of the first ship and the bodies of its crew. Sullivan orders that the dead astronauts be given a proper burial; however, after they are buried, the dead astronauts rise from the grave in a chilling sequence. Eventually Sullivan learns that the disembodied inhabitants of the planet have lured the rocketships there to take over his crew members' bodies and thus leave their world. Sullivan must quickly decide to destroy his ship or allow these "space vampires" to roam the galaxy.

Bava's film anticipates *Alien* (1979), *Aliens* (1986), and *Lifeforce: The Space Vampires* (1985) with his novel blending of gothic horror and science fiction. Though the script is innocuous, Bava's direction is compelling, his ever-moving camera creating an atmosphere of tension and menace. (Ridley Scott and James Cameron must have studied his technique before embarking on their classic efforts.) The elements in the film are somewhat banal, strangely familiar from a hundred or so other films from *Forbidden Planet* (1956) to *Creature* (1985). The same can be said of a number of other horror fantasies of the period, though on certain notable occasions filmmakers like Bava found it possible to create interesting approaches that make the material fresh. American International's *Queen of Blood* (aka *Planet of Blood*, 1966) was another exception.

1966 *Queen of Blood* (aka *Planet of Blood*)

George Edwards Productions/AIP, 88 min. Director: Curtis Harrington. Producer: George Edwards. Writer: Curtis Harrington, based on the novel by Charles Nuetzel. Starring John Saxon, Basil Rathbone, Judi Meredith, Dennis Hopper, Florence Marley, Forrest J Ackerman.

Dark, smoothly shot in shadowy interiors that recall the best work of Murnau and Browning, *Queen of Blood* is an anomaly. The plot is taken directly from *It! The Terror from Beyond Space* (and evokes Ridley Scott's *Alien*); the exterior stock footage is cannibalized from a superior Russian film, *Niebo Zowiet* (*The Heavens Call*, 1959); and the balance was shot in eight days with a budget of less than $50,000. Yet *Queen of Blood* manages to overcome those handicaps and become a compelling atmospheric piece of horror fantasy.

In 1990, an expedition is sent to Mars to investigate a mysterious phenomenon. Three astronauts — John Saxon, Judi Meredith, and Dennis Hopper — discover a spaceship that has crashed (at the center of the phenomenon) and its sole survivor, a green-tinted alien (Florence Marley). After they take her aboard the mother ship, crew members begin to die one by one, their bodies completely drained of blood. Marley is really a hemophiliac vampire, the sole survivor of her race, and she has come aboard their ship to breed a new race. Finally, during the climactic struggle with Meredith, the vampire is cut and bleeds to death. However, her nest of eggs is uncovered by the mission commander (Basil Rathbone, in his last role) and taken back to earth for study. (Forrest J Ackerman, the famous SF collector and editor of *Famous Monsters of Filmland*, appears in a cameo role.)

1967 *The Vampire-Beast Craves Blood* (*The Blood Beast Terror*)

88 min. Director: Vernon Sewell. Producers: Tony Tenser, Arnold Miller. Writer: Peter Bryan. Starring Peter Cushing, Robert

Fleming, David Griffen, Wanda Ventham, Vanessa Howard, Roy Hudd, Kevin Stoney.

Queen of Blood succeeds (in spite of its limitations), whereas *The Vampire-Beast Craves Blood* (1967), with a better budget and a more distinguished cast and crew, fails. Directed by Vernon Sewell, this British production (independent of Hammer Studios) employs Peter Cushing, Robert Fleming, Wanda Ventham, and scripter Peter Bryan, but it never manages to capture the imagination of the former film.

The story has the same familiar trappings of several older thrillers like *The Bat Whispers* (1930) and *The Devil Bat* (1940). A mad scientist (Fleming) creates a giant moth for his daughter (Ventham), who has the unfortunate ability to turn herself into a monster. He hopes the giant moth will stop her vampirelike assaults, but what he fails to realize is that the *moth* now needs blood. A Sherlock Holmes–like detective (Cushing) follows the trail of the gruesome murders to the scientist, and together they destroy the "blood beast."

1971 *Dracula Versus Frankenstein (El Hombre que Vina de Ummo,* aka *Assignment: Terror)*
Italian/Interantion Jaquar, 89 min. Director: Tulio Demichelli. Producer: Jami Prades. Writer: Jacinto Molina. Starring Michael Rennie, Karin Dor, Craig Hall, Paul Naschy, Patty Sheppard, Angelo del Rozo, Ella Gessler, Peter Damon, Gene Reyes.

Less amusing but rising to a special weirdness was *El Hombre que Vino de Ummo* (*Dracula Versus Frankenstein* 1971). This film attempted, in the form of an adult comic strip, to assign technological seriousness to the classic horror monsters. Unfortunately, the independent low-budget production fails to capture the true essence of horror fantasy and looks like a retread of *Plan Nine from Outer Space* (1959).

Michael Rennie (in a role similar to Klaatu in *The Day the Earth Stood Still,* 1951) is the leader of a vanguard of alien invaders. They have come to Earth (to claim it as theirs) from a dying world, and they must pave the way for the invading force. By reviving the famous monsters of popular culture — Dracula, the werewolf, the mummy, Reptile Man, and Frankenstein's monster — they hope to terrorize the world into submission. But eventually the aliens inhabiting the creatures' bodies succumb to their emotions and resort to interfighting. Rennie's assistant, Karin Dor, and the wolf man (Paul Naschy) take advantage of the situation and save the world from invasion. The advertised confrontation between Dracula and Frankenstein never occurs (leaving this critic to question the English-language title).

This film follows in the same path as *Planet of the Vampires* and *Queen of Blood*, but perhaps not as imaginatively. The script is weak, the direction poor, and the special effects far below the credibility level. Michael Rennie, who was never able to shake his Klaatu role, is embarrassingly stiff in a part that should have been familiar to him. The other actors are similarly amateurish, and the shadow of a comic strip looms over the entire project. It was becoming apparent that as filmmakers produced more and more cinematic nonsense, the linking of gothic horror and science-fiction had worn thin.

1971 *Horror of the Blood Creatures* (aka *Vampire Men of the Lost Planet*, *Creatures of the Red Planet*, and *The Flesh Creatures*)

Filippino, Independent International Films, 86 min. Director-Producer: Al Adamson. Writer: Sue Macnair. Starring John Carradine, Robert Dix, Vicki Volante, Joey Benson, Jennifer Bishop, Bruce Powers.

None of the films, however, were as memorably nonsensical as *Horror of the Blood Creatures.* This independent work was produced and directed by Al Adamson on a low-low budget and shot by Academy-Award–winning cinematographer Vilmos Zsigmond in the Philippines. Padded with stock footage from *One Million Years B.C.* (1940) and *Unknown Island* (1948), the movie is little more than a cartoon caricature of horror fantasy.

In the not too distant future, Earth is invaded by a colony of extraterrestrial vampires (much like *Lifeforce—The Space Vampires*), and Dr. Rynning (John Carradine), with his two colleagues (Robert Dix and Vicki Volante), must rocket to a faraway unknown planet (like *Flash Gordon's* Mongo) to destroy the bloodsucker's home base. Seeking Spectrum X, the secret power source, they battle bat creatures, cat men, claw demons, serpent people, and the like. Eventually they discover the base and emerge victorious. Their return to Earth signals not only the end of the blood creatures but the last of this type of vampire film.

As the cycle began to wane in the early seventies, producers once again looked around for new ideas to spice up the old plots. The form, created to compete with Hammer Films, had burned itself out quickly, its involved special effects making it less and less practical, its limited story potential appealing less and less to audiences. Their influence, however, can be appreciated only in retrospect as newer productions like *Alien* (1979), *Aliens* (1986), and *Lifeforce—The Space Vampires* (1985) venture into the same thematic territory. They may not have been classics or masterpieces, but films, like *Not of This Earth* (1957), *Little Shop of Horrors* (1960), *The Last Man on Earth* (1964), *Planet of the Vampires* (1965), *Queen of Blood* (1966), and *The Omega Man* (1970), are definitely an integral part of the vampire cinema.

6

Feasts of Blood
and Vampiric Orgies
From *I Vampiri* (1956)
to *Blood for Dracula* (1974)

While Hammer Studios was establishing itself as a leader in the field
of horror fantasy, a dozen independent filmmakers were attempting to
revive the European film industry. They were true *auteurs* who, discarding
the irrelevant patterns of the American vampire film, turned their idiosyn-
cratic talents to the genre. They wished to return the cinema of the fantastic
to its original illusionary form by stripping away its realistic approach and
replacing it with their own expressionistic avant-garde vision. Their work
led to the fourth great horror school in Europe, returning in part to the
place where horror began.

Mario Bava, Luis Bunuel, Roman Polanski, Roger Vadim, and other
leading filmmakers turned away from the traditional narrative approach
and adopted a surreal or imagistic design. Their films to a considerable extent moved away from plotting action and conventional methods of
storytelling to examine the psychological disorders of their characters. Just
as Fritz Lang, F. W. Murnau, and Carl Dreyer had learned to capture the
illusive nature of film, they strived to blend the "real" with the "unreal" and
to use the technology of film to present illusion and hallucination as reality.
Eventually their improvised images (of filmmaking) transcended the horror

genre to a higher form, one in which audiences found it increasingly difficult to distinguish between what was happening on screen and what was imagined by the characters' minds under stress. The vampire film, manipulated by these skillful craftsmen, became a reflection of the "dropout" counterculture and an expression of helplessness in a violent age of terrorism, campus unrest, and nuclear blackmail.

The tendency to dwell on violence, prolonged scenes of bloodletting, and sexual deviance also increased during the period (following the unprecedented success of *The Horror of Dracula*, 1958). As the restraints of censorship were withdrawn, the vampire film gained a new freedom, and the vampire, though still cloaked in ritual and superstition, took on an air of sadism and erotic sensationalism. Violent practices and sexual relationships of every kind in the human (and not so human) experience were explored, and those subjects that were considered too taboo "resurfaced" in underground films. The word (or a form of the word) *blood* appears in sixteen film titles, more than in any other cinematic period, in titles as lurid as *The Bloody Vampire* (1963), *Blood Bath* (1966), *Blood Drinkers* (1966), *Bloodsuckers* (1971), *Blood for Dracula* (1974), and many more.

However, during the fourteen-year feast of blood, the period produced only a handful of memorable vampire movies, including *Black Sunday* (1960), *Blood and Roses* (1961), *The Fearless Vampire Killers* (1967), and *Tristana* (1970). The others were either pale copies of Hammer films or cheap sexploitation movies. By 1970, the visionary avant-garde filmmakers of the fourth horror school had restored the vampire film to its previous dignity, while other schlockmeisters and pornographers had plunged it to new depths.

One of the directors largely responsible for reviving the vampire film in Europe was veteran Mario Bava. His four films—*Black Sunday* (1960), *Black Sabbath* (1963), *Blood and Black Lace* (1964), and *Planet of the Vampires* (1965)—are minor classics of the genre and allowed him to join a select group of artists, including Terence Fisher and Roger Corman, as a leader in the horror renaissance. (He also made the muscle-man farce *Ercole al Centro della Terra* [*Hercules Versus the Vampires*, 1961], which probably inspired the vampire-wrestling films of the sixties.) Born in San Remo, Italy, in 1914, Bava was the son of Eugenio Bava, one of the pioneering cameramen of the Italian silent cinema. After apprenticing with his father, he earned the chance to photograph *L'Avventura di Anabella* (*Anabelle's Adventure*, 1938). He followed that by shooting films for such legendary directors as Riccardo Freda, G. W. Pabst, Robert Rosselini, Jacques Tourneur, and Raoul Walsh. Bava won his first directing assignment when Freda walked out on *I Vampiri*, and he proved his worth by completing that fine horror film.

1956 *I Vampiri (The Devil's Commandment, Lust for a Vampire)*

Italian/Titanus/Athena Cinematografica, b/w, 90 min. Directors: Mario Bava, Riccardo Freda. Writers: Riccardo Freda, Piero Regnoli. Starring Gianna Maria Canale, Antoine Belpetre, Paul Muller, Carlo D'Angelo, Dario Michaelis, Wandissa Guida, Charles Fawcett.

I Vampiri was a modern retelling of the Elizabeth Bathory story set in contemporary Paris. A mad doctor (Antoine Belpetre) drains the blood of young women to maintain the youth of his aristocratic patient-lover (Gianna Maria Canale). Although the film was a flop, many critics contend that Bava's contribution actually marked the beginning of the horror renaissance by pointing the direction that landmark films like *The Horror of Dracula* (1958) and *The House of Usher* (1960) would take.

In the sixties, Mario Bava firmly established himself as one of Italy's finest filmmakers, and in the seventies, he brought his talents to the United States and produced a series of unforgettable spatter movies. Bava died in 1980 after a long, successful career.

His first important vampire film was *La Maschera del Demonio (The Devil's Mask*, American title *Black Sunday*, 1960), not *I Vampiri*, for which he shared directoral credit with Riccardo Freda. Bava confessed that *The Horror of Dracula* was largely responsible for his decision to make a vampire film: "I had seen Hammer's Dracula film, and I thought that I could make one better. Years earlier, I had read 'The Viy' by Gogol—a stupendous story! I used to read it to my children and, scared to death, they slept together in the middle of the bed. I wanted to bring that terror of witches, ghosts, and vampires to the modern screen!" He enlisted screenwriter Ennio De Concini and hired English actors Barbara Steele and John Richardson to play the key parts, hoping to attract an American or British distributor. Then, after only a few months of preproduction, he shot what was to become a horror classic—*Black Sunday.*

1960 *Black Sunday (La Maschera del Demonio,* aka *The Devil's Mask, Revenge of the Vampire)*

Italian/Galatea Films, b/w, 84 min. Director: Mario Bava. Producer: Massino de Rita. Screenwriters: Ennio De Concini, Marcello Coscia, Mario Serandrei, Mario Bava, based on "The Viy," by Nikolai Gogol. Starring Barbara Steele, John Richardson, Arturo Dominici, Andrea Cheechi, Ivo Garrani.

The film opens with an incredibly explicit scene of a group of torch-carrying villagers hammering a mask of spikes onto the face of a beautiful woman. She is really a witch, Princess Asa (Steele in half of a dual role), and she has been condemned by her brother, the local witch-finder general. One hundred years later, Princess Katia (Steele in the other half) is haunted by her ancestor. She attempts to break the spell but eventually succumbs to a power from beyond the grave. Asa is reincarnated in her virginal descendant's body with the single desire to destroy her brother's descendants in revenge for what he did to her. She prepares a ritual to resurrect her lover (Arturo Dominici) and her master Satan to aid her in unholy task. In the horrifying climax, Katia's lover (Richardson) fights with the devil for her soul and prevails.

Black Sunday is a masterpiece of gothic horror with an eerie atmosphere and chilling set pieces. It also made millions all around the world in its initial release and firmly established Bava as a master of the macabre. But it was not without controversy. American International Pictures (the U.S. distributor) edited major scenes because of the graphic violence, added a banal score by Les Baxter, and then released it with a notice: "Persons under 12 will not be admitted!" The British censors did not permit the film to be shown in England until 1968, and the motion picture encountered similar difficulties in Canada and Mexico — not to mention the ire it raised in the Catholic church!

Refusing to allow this adversity to affect him, Bava continued producing horror films. Three years later, he released *I Tre Volte della Paura* (*The Three Faces of Fear*, released in America as *Black Sabbath*, 1963), a horror anthology, and the year after that *Sei Donne per l'Assassino* (*Fashion House of Death*, released in America as *Blood and Black Lace*, 1964). Both movies feature vampires, and both movies have that uncompromising touch which would become characteristic of Bava.

1961 *Hercules Versus the Vampires (Ercole al Centro della Terra*, aka *Hercules at the Center of the Earth)*
Italian, 91 min. Director: Mario Bava. Producer: Achille Piazzi. Writers: Duccio Tessari, Alessandra Continenza, Franco Prosperi, Bava. Starring Reg Park, Christopher Lee, Leonora Ruffo, Giorgio Ardisson, Marisa Belli, Ida Galli, Ely Draco, Mino Dorro.

Mario Bava's sword-and-sandal epic *Ercole al Centro della Terra* (*Hercules Versus the Vampires*, 1961) has a wonderfully gothic sense of humor but does not compare with his other truly expressionistic visions. Legendary hero Hercules (played by muscleman Reg Park) must retrieve a golden apple from the fairy-tale island of Hesperides, then a magic crystal from

Black Sunday (1960). Mario Bava's innovative blood feast, which established a new approach to vampire films. Photo features horror queen Barbara Steele. Courtesy of American International Pictures.

Hades, to cure the madness of Princess Deianira (Leonora Ruffo). Along the way, he encounters the vampiric demons of Lico (Christopher Lee) and must defeat the monstrous Procrustes. The climatic finale provides Bava with a chance to experiment with horrific scenes (worthy of H. P. Lovecraft), but the outcome is all too predictable. However, for those who happen to enjoy watching scantily clad men flex their muscles, this exploitative spectacle provides plenty of titillation. (Fans of Christopher Lee will be disappointed to see his talents squandered in too few scenes.)

1963 *Black Sabbath* (*I Tre Volte della Paura*, aka *The Three Faces of Fear*)

Italian, 100 min. Director: Mario Bava. Producer: Paolo Mercuri. Writers: Marcello Fondata, Alberto Bevilacquen, Bava. Starring Boris Karloff, Susy Anderson, Mark Damon.

The final episode of the multipart *Black Sabbath* featured a Russian species of vampire known as the Wurdalak. Based on Tolstoy's short story, the tale tells of a Russian patriarch named Gorka (horror great Boris Karloff) who becomes infected by a vampire bite. Upon his return home, he unwittingly infects his little grandson, who infects his mother, who murders her husband, etc. The version is both humorous and terrifying, and by far the best segment of *Black Sabbath*'s anthology. (Karloff also appears as the "host" of the three-part film, which includes the insipid "Drop of Water" and the predictable "Telephone.")

1964 *Blood and Black Lace* (*Sei Donne per l'Assassino*, aka *Fashion House of Death*)

Italian, 87 min. Director: Mario Bava. Writers: Marcel Fondato, Guiseppe Barilia, Bava, based loosely on *Carmilla*, by Joseph Sheridan Le Fanu. Starring Cameron Mitchell, Eva Bartok, Thomas Reiner, Mary Arden.

Blood and Black Lace, on the other hand, lacks any humor or predictability and is deadly serious. Originally scripted as a murder mystery, Bava felt the motive of the homicidal maniac was weak and reconstructed it as a vampire story. But the audience is no longer asked to care who gets killed or why, just to relax and enjoy the carnage. What remains is a terrifying, sadistic journey into horror. (Mario Bava must have been influenced by Alfred Hitchcock's *Psycho* (1960); the central character and a number of murders greatly resemble that earlier thriller. *Blood and Black Lace* also evokes *The Texas Chainsaw Massacre* (1974), *Halloween* (1978), *Friday the 13th* (1980), and other sadistic terror films.)

Since the film is more a psychological study than a direct narrative, it is difficult to summarize the story in one or two paragraphs. Basically, models at Countess Christiana's beauty salon are being brutally murdered by a faceless killer who is determined to obtain the circulating diary of the first victim. The bodies are found half naked, their faces disfigured, their throats ripped out, their blood drained. Police describe the murderer as a sex maniac and attempt to find him. But the deaths continue, and the audience, like accomplices in the murders, are drawn into the bizarre, twisted world of a psychotic.

Starring Eva Bartok and Cameron Mitchell, *Blood and Black Lace* was surprisingly more successful than *Black Sunday* (or *Black Sabbath* for that matter) and was certainly far more violent. Vaguely necrophilic, the film languishes on graphic visuals of blood-red drapes, telephones, doors, dresses, fingernails, stoves, and bloodied bodies. It is definitely not for the squeamish, but a superior effort.

Though not as noteworthy as Mario Bava's expressionist visions, Italian filmmakers produced a number of other vampire films. Several, including *The Crypt of the Incubus* (1963) and *Dance Macabre* (1964), were inspired low-budget thrillers. Others, like *Goliath and the Vampires* (1961), *Playgirls and the Vampire* (1963), *The Island of Death* (1966), and *Malenka, the Vampire's Niece* (1968), were simply exploitative trash.

1960 *Uncle Was a Vampire* (*Tempi Duri per i Vampiri*, aka *Hard Time for Vampires*)

Italian, b/w, 85 min. Director: Stefano Vanzina. Producer: Mario Cecchi Gori. Writers: Edoardo Anton, Dino Verde, Alessandro Continenza. Starring Christopher Lee, Sylvia Koscina, Renalto Rascel, Antie Geerk, Lia Zoppelli, Kay Fisher.

Trading entirely upon the reputation of Christopher Lee (and his identification with the role of Dracula), comic director Stefano Vanzina hoped to tap into Hammer's successful formula with *Tempi Duri per i Vampiri* (*Uncle Was a Vampire*, 1960). Baron Rodrigo (Lee) passes on the vampiric heritage to his nephew, Count Osvaldo (Renalto Rascel), who in turn squanders the family fortune. Forced into bankruptcy by his creditors, Osvaldo sells his castle to a hotel chain and takes a job as the night porter. Predictably, he moves from room to room attacking female guests as they slumber in their beds. The love of a beautiful gardener (Sylvia Koscina) cures him of his vampire curse, and they live happily ever after. Played like a romantic comedy, the motion picture has little to offer fans of the *cinéfantastique*. Even Christopher Lee's talents are wasted in what amounts to a cameo appearance.

1961 *Goliath and the Vampires (Maciste Contro il Vampiro)*

Italian, 92 min. Directors: Sergio Corbucci, Giacomo Gentilhomo. Producers: Paola Moffa, Gentilhomo. Writer: Duccio Tessari. Starring Gordon Scott, Gianna Maria Canale, Jacques Sernas, Leonora Ruffo, Anabella Incontera.

Not to be confused with Bava's *Ercole al Centro della Terra* (1961), this Gentilhomo-Corbucci collaboration offered yet another variation of sword-and-sandal epic mixed with vampires. Muscleman Goliath (Gordon Scott) must journey to the lower regions to rescue his girlfriend (again played by Leonora Ruffo) from the evil clutches of vampire Kobrak (Guido Celano). More violent and less amusing than Bava's spectacle (and minus the acting talents of Christopher Lee), *Maciste Contro il Vampiro (Goliath and the Vampires)* is better left buried in the infernal depths of Hades.

1961 *The Vampire and the Ballerina (L'Amante del Vampiro,* aka *The Vampire's Lover)*

Italian, b/w, 86 min. Director: Renato Polselli. Producer: Bruno Bolognesi. Writers: Giuseppe Pellegrini, Ernesto Gastaldi. Starring Helene Remy, Maria Luisa Rolando, Walter Brandi, Tina Gloriani, Isarco Ravaioli.

1963 *Playgirls and the Vampire (L'Ultima Preda del Vampiro,* aka *The Last Victim of the Vampire* and *Desires of the Vampire)*

Italian, b/w, 85 min. Director-Writer: Piero Regnoli. Producer: Tiziano Longo. Starring Walter Brandi, Lyla Rocco, Mario Giovannini, Albert Rizzo, Tilde Damian, Erika di Centa, Marisa Quattrini.

L'Amante del Vampiro (The Vampire and the Ballerina, 1961) and its sequel *L'Ultima Preda del Vampiro (Playgirls and the Vampire,* 1963) were two avant-garde exercises inspired by the work of Mario Bava. Although on the surface they may appear to be sexploitation films, they are really explorations into the illusionary nature of sex and violence. The first film, by Piero Regnoli, who wrote Bava's *I Vampiri* (1956), is an Elizabeth Bathory tale set in an exclusive European dancing school and looks at a vampire's sexual blood lust. Two young ballet dancers, Luisa (Helene Remy) and Francesca (Tina Gloriani), entrust their instruction to a vampire countess (Maria Luisa Rolando) and her servant (Walter Brandi) but end up losing their talent and their lives. In the second motion picture, Brandi plays both a vampire and his brother, Count Gabor Kernassy, and the story line attempts to examine the sexual magnetism and power of the vampire. Five showgirls and two male companions take refuge at the Count's castle, and slowly, inexorably, the bloodsucker introduces each to his vampire charms. Both motion pictures came and went with very little fanfare and even less box-office appeal, but they were infinitely superior to the efforts then being lensed in the United States and demonstrated a definite commitment to the genre. They were also precursors (and in a sense paved the way for) of the sexy vampire films of Jean Rollin, starting with *Le Viol du Vampire* in 1967 and leading to *La Vampire Nue* (1969), *Frisson des Vampires* (1970) and *Requiem pour un Vampire* (1971).

1963 *The Crypt of the Incubus (La Cripta e l'Incubo, aka The Terror in the Crypt)*

Spanish/Italian, 84 min. Director: Thomas Miller. Producer: William Mulligan. Writers: Julian Berry, Robert Bohr, Maria del Carmen, Martinez Ramon, Miller, based on *Carmilla*, by Le Fanu. Starring Christopher Lee, Audrey Amber, Ursula Davis, Jose Campos, Mela Conjuri, Vera Valmont, Jose Villasonte, Angela Milland.

The Crypt of the Incubus (1963) was Thomas Miller's Spanish-Italian adaptation of Le Fanu's tale. Starring Christopher Lee as the aristocratic Count Ludwig von Karnstein, the story follows efforts to save his daughter, Laura (Audrey Amber), from the influence of vampire Lyuba (Ursula Davis), the incarnation of evil witch Sheena. Unlike Vadim's version, which appeared two years earlier as *Et Mourir de Plaisir (Blood and Roses)*, this film was faithful to the original, deemphasizing violence and focusing on the women's relationship. Rather crudely mounted from a technical standpoint, Miller's effort represented one of the sincerest attempts by Italian filmmakers to tap into the lucrative vampire market and produce a literate motion picture.

1963 *The Vampire of the Opera (Il Vampiro dell' Opera)*

Italian, b/w, 80 min. Director-Writer: Renato Polselli. Producer: Bruno Bolognesi. Starring John McDouglas, Vittoria Prada, Marc Marian, Barbra Howard, Catla Cavelli.

Loosely based on Gaston Leroux's famous *Phantom of the Opera*, Polselli's film chronicles the seduction, abduction, and conversion of a talented but unknown opera singer (Vittoria Prada) by a mysterious stranger (John McDouglas). The "phantom" of the opera house is not a disfigured monster but a hauntingly twisted vampire. When he takes her to his subterranean world, his need for blood overwhelms his interest in her musical abilities. She returns to the opera as a vampire and begins to suck her way through the chorus section. *Il Vampiro dell'Opera (The Vampire of the Opera,* 1963) is a silly mix of classic tales that never rises above the mediocre.

1964 *Dance Macabre (La Danza Macabra)*

Italian/French, b/w, 87 min. Director: Antonio Margheriti. Producer: Frank Belty. Writers: Sergio Corbucci, Gianni Grimaldi, based on an unpublished story by Edgar Allan Poe. Starring Barbara Steele, George Rivere, Margaret Robsahn, Henry Kruger.

Capitalizing on the worldwide success of Roger Corman's series of Edgar Allan Poe adaptations, a number of low-budget quickies were rushed into production. *La Danza Macabra (Dance Macabre),* one of those efforts, was a cut above the rest, thanks in large part to Antonio Margheriti's hauntingly atmospheric direction. Based on an unpublished story by Poe, the motion picture tells the familiar tale of a man named Alan (George Rivere) who must spend a night in a haunted house to win a healthy bet. Once there, he becomes involved in a series of ghostly goings-on, culminating in the appearance of Elizabeth (horror maven Barbara Steele). "Is she alive, or is she dead?"—that is the question Alan keeps asking as she disappears then reappears at will. Finally realizing the ghosts and ghouls need his blood to be reborn, he makes plans with Elizabeth to leave. But in their final embrace she turns into demon who scares him to death. The plotline may sound simple (and it is), but the way Margheriti skillfully handles the material makes this film a cut above the norm. The influence of Bava is evident as the audience is led from one set piece through another. (Antonio Margheriti later remade this film as *Nella Stretta Morsa del Ragno (Prisoner of Dracula)* in 1970 with funds from a West German financier who had enjoyed the first one.)

1970 *Prisoner of Dracula (Nella Stretta Morsa del Ragno)*

Italian/Spanish/West German, 102 min. Director: Anthony Dawson (Antonio Margheriti). Producer: Giovanni Addessi. Writers: Bruno Corbucci, Giovanni Grimaldi. Starring Anthony Franciosa, Michele Mercier, Peter Carsten, Klaus Kinski, Karin Field.

American actor Anthony Franciosa took over the role of Alan Foster, this time a journalist who is challenged by Edgar Allan Poe (Klaus Kinski) to spend a night in the haunted house. Margheriti's faithful remake of his *La Danza Macabra* (1964) is good but certainly not in the same league as the original.

1966 *The Island of Death (La Isla de la Muerte,* aka *The Island of the Doomed, Death Island, Bloodsuckers)*

Spanish/Italian, b/w, 78 min. Director: Mel Welles. Producer: George Ferrer. Writers: Ira Meltcher, Stephen Schmidt, Welles. Starring Cameron Mitchell, Elisa Montes, George Martin, Matilde Sampedro.

Tourists who visit *La Isla de la Muerte (The Island of Death,* 1966) off the Italian coast are terrorized by a vampire tree created by mad scientist Baron von Weser (Cameron Mitchell). Carnivorous plants and bloodthirsty flowers have been the subjects of previous films about vampires, notably *The Spider Woman Strikes Back* (1946) and *Little Shop of Horrors* (1960), but this time the novelty has worn a bit thin. (This film was released under several different titles to unsuspecting audiences in an effort to bolster box-office receipts.)

1968 *Malenka, the Vampire's Niece (Malenka—La Sobrina del Vampiro, Fangs of the Living Dead)*

Spanish/Italian, 94 min. Director-Writer: Amando De Ossorio. Starring Anita Ekberg, Audrey Amber, Maria Luisa de Benedictus, Paul Muller.

Malenka—La Sobrina del Vampiro (Malenka, the Vampire's Niece, 1968) was a low-low-budget vehicle for European star Anita Ekberg. Her stereotypic dumb-blonde character, Silvia, inherits a Transylvania castle from her departed uncle (Julian Ugarte). After she moves in, her uncle returns from the dead as a vampire and falls madly in love with her. (Apparently, she is the spitting image of his lost love, Malenka, a witch who was burned at the stake years earlier.) Several deaths occur in the village, and the local townspeople revolt by burning the castle. Both she and her uncle perish in the conflagration. Standard fare, with very lame acting, directing, and writing.

1961 *Blood and Roses (Et Mourir de Plaisir)*

French, 87 min. Director: Roger Vadim. Producer: Raymond Eger. Writers: Claude Brule, Claude Martin, Roger Vadim, based loosely on *Carmilla*, by Joseph Sheridan Le Fanu. Starring Mel Ferrer, Annete Vadim, Elsa Martinelli, Marc Allegret.

What Italy could do France could do better, and in 1961 Roger Vadim released *Et Mourir de Plaisir (Blood and Roses)*. This chilling but elegant horror film based on Joseph Sheridan Le Fanu's classic short told the familiar story of vampiress Carmilla. A young girl (Annette Vadim), jealous of the women around her, becomes possessed by the vampiric personality of her ancestress, Mircalla, whom she closely resembles. Then, taking revenge on those who made her life miserable, she commits a series of murders as a vampire. At one point she even takes Elsa Martinelli as her bride. When she accidentally harms the man (Mel Ferrer) that she once loved, she is forever damned to live as a vampire.

Clearly intended as an art-house horror film, *Blood and Roses* explores the eroticism and sexual deviance of lesbianism. That exploration is dark and sinister. Like Bava before him, Roger Vadim was interested in *outre* regions of man's soul and brought his avant-garde approach to that subject. Born in 1928 in Paris, the celebrated French writer and director, who sometimes appeared as an actor or worked as a journalist, had definite ideas about the nature of horror fantasy. He had skillfully crafted two psychological thrillers starring Brigitte Bardot, *And God Created Woman* (1956) and *Heaven Fell That Night* (1957), that demonstrate his fascination with bloody violence and plushy eroticism. He believed that juxtaposition revealed man's true nature stripped of all pretentions of good and evil. For *Blood and Roses*, he cast aside the traditional vampire formula and concentrated on a montage of images (blood, representing terror and violence, and roses, representing innocence and sexuality) against the backdrop of Le Fanu's story. All of this is beautifully photographed by Claude Renoir in brilliant color that shows off this wicked contrast. (In one scene, the color drains from the screen to highlight the vivid splash of blood on Carmilla's wedding dress.) *Blood and Roses* seems to take on a chilling reality of its own.

Unfortunately, censors and critics were not too kind to Vadim's French production. First, it was brutalized by Paramount Pictures (the U.S. distributor), which, fearing statewide censorship, cut more than thirteen minutes of lesbianism from the film. Then American critics called it "a boring half-hearted attempt to make a horror movie." Next, British censors refused to release it altogether. And finally, even in France, critics panned the film for its lack of imagination or wit. Roger Vadim remained undaunted and continued to make controversial films, including the science-fiction cult favorite *Barbarella* (1967, with Jane Fonda). *Blood and Roses* is occasionally shown on the late-night show in a much edited version, but even in this form, Vadim's expressionist vision and enormous talent are apparent.

Not as ambitious as Vadim's classic but still worth noting were Jean Rollin's sexy vampire films from *Le Viol du Vampire* (1967) to *Requiem pour un Vampire* (1971), which featured plenty of beautiful naked women succumbing to the advances of virile vampires.

1967 *Queen of the Vampires (Le Viol du Vampire* aka *The Rape of the Vampire)*

French, b/w, 100 min. Director: Jean Rollin. Producer: Sam Selsky. Writer: Jean Rollin. Starring Bernard Letrou, Solange Pradel, Ursule Pauly, Nicole Romnin, Catherine Devile, Barbara Girade.

Made on a shoestring budget with a group of his nonprofessional friends, Jean Rollin's *Le Viol du Vampire* (*Queen of the Vampires*, aka *The Rape of the Vampire*, 1967) created a whole subgenre (the nudie vampire film) and pushed the bounds of censorship to the limit. In the fall of 1966, Rollin, a photographer and producer of television commercials, was contracted by Sam Selsky to provide a half-hour sex film to accompany an hour-long American vampire film in theatrical release. He carefully studied the current works of Bava and Vadim and created a surreal sex fantasy that was far superior to the film it was meant to accompany. Producer Selsky was so pleased that he asked Rollin to add an hour more, and *La Reine des Vampires (The Queen of the Vampires)* was made and edited, together with the first thirty minutes. The result is an erotic (rather than pornographic) series of set pieces which convey (rather than tell, since the narrative structure is poor) the struggle of a psychiatrist to combat African vampires in modern France.

1969 *The Naked Vampire (La Vampire Nue)*

Les Films, French, 90 min. Director-Producer-Writer: Jean Rollin. Starring Oliver Martin, Maurice Lemaitre, Caroline Cartier, Ly Letrong, Bernard Musson, Jean Aron, Michael Delahaye, Ursule Pauly, Nicole Isimat.

Because of the overnight success of *Le Viol du Vampire* (1967), Jean Rollin decided to make a follow-up feature. *La Vampire Nue (The Naked Vampire,* 1969) was a sequel only thematically, again featuring a sense of surrealism that replaced the need for narrative coherence with poetic images of eroticism. While experimenting on a female vampire, mad doctor

Maurice Lemaitre is stopped by his son (Oliver Martin), who has fallen madly in love with her. The two flee the mad doctor's laboratory and become part of a strange vampire sect. Once the young man gets his fill of beautiful women, suicide rituals, and satanic masses, he returns home to Dad. In spite of the fact that the characterization and narrative are kept to a minimum, this strange mixture of science-fiction, horror and sex moves along relentlessly to a dramatic conclusion.

1970 *Vampire Thrills (Le Frisson des Vampires,* aka *Terror of the Vampires)*

Les Films, French, 96 min. Director-Producer-Writer: Jean Rollin. Starring Sandra Julien, Dominique, Nicole Nancel, Michael Delahaye, Jacques Robiolles, Michael Durand.

Frisson des Vampires (*Vampire Thrills,* 1970), the third entry into Jean Rollin's sexy vampire series, had a much stronger narrative than the other two but again moved along at a surreal, relentless pace. Two brothers, vampire hunters (Michael Delahaye and Jacques Robiolles), fall victim to the charms of Isolde (Nicole Nancel), the master agent of the world's vampire population. She wants to perpetuate the species and enlists their aid in this endeavour. When a honeymooning couple (Sandra Julien and Michael Durand) arrive at their medieval castle, the path to destruction is clear. Sadistic and erotic, Rollin's third production harkens back to Hammer's *Kiss of the Vampire* (1962) and may well represent the best of the series.

1971 *Requiem for a Vampire (Requiem pour un Vampire, Sex Vampires)*

Les Films, French, 95 min. Director-Producer-Writer: Jean Rollin. Starring Marie-Pierre Castel, Mireille Dargent, Phillippee Gaste, Dominique, Louis D'hour.

The weakest entry in Jean Rollin's vampire saga was *Requiem pour un Vampire* (*Requiem for a Vampire,* 1971). Borrowing a tired plot from Piero Regnoli's *L'Ultima Preda del Vampiro* (*Playgirls and the Vampire,* 1963), his last film in the series followed the sexploits of two female escapees from a reform school who take refuge in a castle of vampires. Predictably, the sadistic vampire count takes them for himself, then introduces the two girls to his lesbian brides. By the time this motion picture had debuted, the nudie vampire films had been replaced by soft- and hard-core pornographic ones. But even though his voyeuristic audience was no longer there, Rollin

Poster art from the third entry in Jean Rollin's sexy vampire series, *Le Frisson des Vampires* (*Vampire Thrills*, 1970). Courtesy of Les Films.

continued to make erotic movies, notably a horror adaptation of Romeo and Juliet in *Le Rose de Fer* (1973).

1967 *The Fearless Vampire Killers (Dance of the Vampires, Pardon Me But Your Teeth Are in My Neck)*

MGM/Cadre Films, 107 min. Director: Roman Polanski. Producer: Genne Gutowski. Writers: Gerald Back, Roman Polanski. Starring Jack McGowran, Roman Polanski, Ferdinand Mayne, Sharon Tate, Alfie Bass, Terry Downes, Iain Quarrier.

Roman Polanski was much too individual a filmmaker to be concerned exclusively with the cinema of the fantastic, but in *The Fearless Vampire Killers* (1967) he found the genre a convenient form to express his views on bloody violence and sexual voyeurism. Born in Paris in 1933, he had watched helplessly as his Polish father was brutalized and his mother killed by the Nazis in a World War II concentration camp. The international director (and occasional actor) brought that psychological terror and interest in the nature of evil into more than one of his films. In *Knife in Water* (1962), his first film, he examined the motives of rape and murder; in *Repulsion* (1965), the progression of madness; in *Rosemary's Baby* (1968), his most popular film, satanism and black magic; and in *The Fearless Vampire Killers,* the sexual and violent exploits of a coven of vampires.

Renowned professor of vampirology Ambrosius (Jack McGowran) and his bumbling, fearful assistant, Alfred (Polanski), follow the trail of vampires to a remote hideaway in Transylvania. Meanwhile, Count Von Krolock (Ferdinand Mayne) makes several attempts to put the bite on lovely maiden Sarah (Sharon Tate). In the film's funniest sequence, he falls through a skylight while watching her bathe in bubble bath, but because she has worn the wrong religious symbol, he prevails. She then becomes a vampire and joins his coven in their dance macabre. Eventually, the professor and his assistant learn that Von Krolock is the group leader, and they pursue him (stakes in hand) to the bloody climax. Ironically, even though they have rescued Sarah, she vampirizes Alfred in the back of their sleigh while Ambrosius unwittingly drives them to civilization.

A heavy, slow-moving parody of *Dracula*, the film is also visually attractive and subtly engaging. Douglas Slocombe, the famed British

Opposite: The Fearless Vampire Killers (1967). The Count (Ferdinand Mayne) puts the moves on lovely Sharon Tate (only months before her tragic death). Photo courtesy of MGM.

cinematographer who would later shoot *Raiders of the Lost Ark* (1981) and *Never Say Never Again* (1983), gives *The Fearless Vampire Killers* the look of a slick Hammer movie, long stretches of the film resembling *The Horror of Dracula* or *Dracula, Prince of Darkness*. But this is no pale copy—rather, a pastiche and a satiric parody of Hammer horror. And Polanski uses that effectively as a springboard to examine his views of sex and violence. It is unfortunate that two years after the film was released his wife, Sharon Tate, and several others were brutally killed in a ritual massacre by Charles Manson and his Family, and the underlying themes in his films (of sex and violence) became glaringly real. Manson testified under oath that he and his accomplices had murdered the others to drink their blood in some satanic ritual.

1970 *Tristana*

French, ? min. Director-Writer: Luis Buñuel. Starring Catherine Deneuve, Fernando Rey.

Like *The Fearless Vampire Killers*, Luis Buñuel's *Tristana* (1970), photographed like a surrealistic dream, using the vampire motif to explore the bounds of illusion and reality, though with infinitely more cinematic skill than Polanski. While the story tells of an innocent girl (Catherine Deneuve) who becomes the mistress and victim of her elderly guardian (Fernando Rey), a vampire, it really focuses on the psychological implications of incest and domination. Deneuve, who would play a dominant vampiress in Tony Scott's *The Hunger* (1983), is trapped by someone she trusts and forced into a nightmare world of vampirism and sexual perversion. Although this vision, as well as the others like it, was chilling and harsh, it helped raise the consciousness of the film industry and revive the European vampire film.

Evolving parallel to the works of Bava, Vadim, Polanski, Buñuel, and the fourth great horror school, though hardly in the same class, were a number of low-budget exploitation vampire movies from Mexico, the Philippines, and the United States. Some were X-rated pornographic versions of the traditional formulas. Others were halfhearted, dimwitted attempts to restore a struggling film economy, and still others were little more than trash.

Whether the success of the 1931 foreign-language version of *Dracula* prompted Spanish-speaking filmmakers to make their own horror movies or not, Mexico became one of the busiest vampire-movie industries during the late fifties and early sixties, producing four separate series of films and many individual efforts. This output was more than any other country or motion-picture studio. Of course, the quality of these films wasn't very high, with uneven production values, repetitive storylines, and downright poor acting. Most of them were derivative of their American and European rivals and relied more on familiar formulas than experimentation. But the worldwide box-office receipts certainly proved that Mexican filmmakers were a force to be reckoned with. Films like *El Vampiro* (1958), *El Ataúd del Vampiro* (1959), and *La Maldición de Nostradamus* (1960) established German Robles as a worthy successor to Bela Lugosi and a competitor of Christopher Lee; others, like *Santo Contra las Mujeres Vampiras* (1963) and *Santo y Tesoro de Dracula* (1968), created a whole subgenre known as the wrestling horror movie.

1958 *The Vampire* (*El Vampiro,* aka *The Lurking Vampire*)

Mexican, b/w, 84 min. Director: Fernando Mendez. Producer: Abel Salazar. Writer: Ramon Obson. Starring Abel Salazar, German Robles, Ariadna Welter, Carmen Montego, José Luis Jimenez, Mercedes Soler, Alicia Montoya, José Chavez.

Even though *El Vampiro* (*The Vampire,* 1958) had a limited budget, director Fernando Mendez made great use of his limited resources to create a solid effort that has a certain lyricism. This disguised adaptation of Stoker's *Dracula* has Hungarian Count Karol de Lavud (German Robles) relocating to Mexico's Sierra Negra and purchasing an estate known as Sicomoros. Upon arrival, he begins to terrorize several locals, including Eloisa (Carmen Montego) and María Teresa (Alicia Montoya). He also enslaves a servant named Emilio (José Luis Jimenez). María Teresa's niece, Marta (Ariadna Welter), enlists the services of a man of science, Dr. Enrique (producer Abel Salazar), to combat the evil menace. Like his thematic predecessor Dr. Van Helsing, Enrique pursues Lavud to his subterranean lair and stakes him to the wall. But like all famous vampires, Count Luvad was only temporarily destroyed. He would return in the sequel *El Ataud del Vampire* (1959).

Clearly one of the best Mexican vampire films, *El Vampiro* shows the influence of Hammer Films' *Horror of Dracula* (released earlier in the year) even though Robles's performance is presented as a tribute to the late Bela Lugosi. He deftly handles the cape and aristocratic manner as if he were born to play the part and would continue to play vampires in a host of horror films. This adaptation of the familiar story is not to be missed. (An America version directed by Paul Nagle and produced by K. Gordon Murray replaced twenty minutes with additional scenes featuring Dick Barker, Edward Tucker, and Lydia Melon.)

1959 *The Vampire's Coffin (El Ataúd del Vampiro, aka The Return of the Vampire)*

Mexican, b/w, 86 min. Director: Fernando Mendez. Producer: Abel Salazar. Writers: Raul Zenteno, Ramon Obon. Starring Abel Salazar, German Robles, Ariadna Welter, Yerge Beirute, Alicia Montoya.

Hurried into production to take advantage of the continuing box-office fanfare of *El Vampiro* (1958), this sequel was equally engaging. A mad scientist steals the body of Count Lavud (again Robles) and revives him. The aristocratic vampire quickly dispatches him and takes up residence at a wax museum, terrorizing patrons from the Gallery of Horrors. Partly out of vengeance and partly to lure his nemesis to his doom, Lavud encases María Teresa (Alicia Montoya) in wax. Dr. Enrique (Abel Salazar) follows his bloody trail, saves the female hostage, and spears him just as Lavud changes into a bat. Derivative of *The Mystery of the Wax Museum* (1933) and Vincent Price's *House of Wax* (1953), *El Ataúd del Vampiro* proved to be a well-mounted sequel. (An American version by Nagle and Murray was also produced.)

1959 *Castle of the Monsters (El Castillo de los Monstruos)*

Mexican, b/w, 90 min. Director: Julian Soler. Producer: Jesus Soto-mayor. Writers: Fernando Galiana, Carlos Orellana. Starring Antonio Espino, German Robles, Evangelina Elizondo, Carlos Orellana.

German Robles parodied his role of Hungarian Count Karol de Lavud in the comic monster team-up *El Castillo de los Monstruos* (1959). Little more than a rehash of *Abbott and Costello Meet Frankenstein* (1948), itself an abominable mess, this film represented a low point in the Mexican cinema.

1960 *Curse of Nostradamus (La Maldición de Nostradamus)*

Mexican, b/w, 77 min. Director: Federico Curiel. Producer: Victor Parran. Writers: Carlos Enrique, Federico Curiel. Starring German Robles, Julio Aleman, Domingo Soler, Aurora Alvarado, Manuel Vegara.

During a break in the productions of *El Vampiro* (1958) and its sequel, *El Ataúd del Vampiro* (1959), German Robles headlined a serial of twelve

25-minute installments, later reedited and released as four motion pictures between 1960 and 1963. Not since Louis Fevillade's silent classic *Les Vampires* (1915–16) had the vampire been the subject of a multipart series. Frederico Curiel had seen Fevillade's work and despite the restrictions of a low-low budget was able to blend the right mixture of horrific thrills and gallows humor into an episodic framework. The series focuses on the son of Nostradamus (not the famous sixteenth-century prophet and occultist), who has become a vampire, and the twelve installments chronicle his demonic adventures.

The prelude sets the whole series in motion: Duran (Domingo Soler), a man of science, denounces the existence of vampires as superstitious nonsense at the same time that the famous vampire returns from a visit to his father's tomb. He confronts the aged professor and challenges him to a contest of wills. Episodes 1–3 concern Nostradamus's attempts to promote a vampire cult by murdering thirteen villagers. He then buries one of the professor's colleagues and finally kidnaps Duran's daughter (Aurora Alvarado). Duran pursues him to his mountain lair and in the climatic struggle between good and evil buries Nostradamus under a rock slide.

Typical of the action-packed serials of the thirties and forties (and anticipatory of Steven Speilberg's *Raiders of the Lost Ark,* 1981), *Curse of Nostradamus* was a popular success. It spawned three sequels, utilizing material from episodes 4–12. (These four motion pictures should not be confused with Juan Bastillo Oro's 1936 historical epic *Nostradamus.*)

1961 *The Blood of Nostradamus (La Sangre de Nostradamus)*

Mexican, b/w, 77 min. Director: Federico Curiel. Producer: Victor Parran. Writers: Carlos Enrique, Federico Curiel. Starring German Robles, Julio Aleman, Domingo Soler, Aurora Alvarado, and Manuel Vegara.

Federico Curiel makes effective use of the element of science-fiction in the second installment, *La Sangre de Nostradamus (The Blood of Nostradamus,* 1961). The son of Nostradamus (German Robles) is rescued from the rock slide and uses an electromagnetic device to manipulate an eclipse of the sun. Dispatched again by the good doctor Duran (Domingo Soler), his body is burned and the ashes scattered.

1962 *Nostradamus and the Genie of Tinebra (Nostradamus y el Genio de las Tiniebras)*

Mexican, b/w, 75 min. Director: Frederico Curiel. Producer: Victor Parran. Writer: Carlos Enrique. Starring German Robles.

In episodes 7–9, the son of Nostradamus is resurrected by the genie of Tinebra and falls madly in love with her while Professor Duran attempts to steal the body of the vampire's father.

1963 *Nostradamus and the Monster Demolisher (Nostradamus y el Destructor de Monstruos)*

Mexican, b/w, 75 min. Director: Frederico Curiel. Producer: Victor Parran. Writer: Carlos Enrique. Starring German Robles, Julio Alemán.

The fourth (and final) film in the series features a return to science-fiction. Professor Duran has created a device that destroys bats through sound waves. Making use of his invention, he forces the son of Nostradamus off a cliff, then stakes him to the ground. Immensely popular, these four films continue to be shown today.

1960 *Creatures of the Walking Dead (La Marca del Muerto)*

Mexican/Alameda Films, b/w, 84 min. Director: Fernando Cortés. Producers: Cesar Santos Cralino, Alfredo Ripstein, Jr. Writers: Cortes, José María Ferandes, Alfredo Varez, Jr. Starring Fernando Casanova, Sonia Furio, Pedro de Aguillon, Aurora Alvarado.

Besides the popular film series about Count Lavud and Nostradamus, Mexican filmmakers produced a number of individual vampire features. One of the most interesting was *La Marca del Muerto* (*Creatures of the Walking Dead*, 1960).

In 1890, Dr. Malthus (Fernando Casanova) kills several young women for their blood. He mixes the blood with a formula and injects it into his heart for eternal youth. Local officials discover his insane plot and hang the mad doctor. Years later, the Malthus's great-grandson Gonzalo (Casanova again) and his fiancée (Sonia Furio) move into the ancestral home. While looking through the doctor's notes, he discovers the formula and revives him. Dr. Malthus must have additional treatments of blood to stay alive and he terrorizes the local town. Ultimately, his great-grandson recognizes the menace and destroys him. Similar to *The Man in Half Moon Street* (1944), this popular effort was reshot by Jerry Warren (with additional scenes featuring Rock Madison and George Todd) and released in the United States.

1960 *World of the Vampires (El Mundo de los Vampiros)*

Mexican, b/w, 85 min. Director: Alfonso Corona Blakke. Producer: Abel Salazar. Writer: Paul Zenteno. Starring Mauricio Gareces, Silva Fournier, Guillermo Murray, Erna Martha Bauman, José Baviera, Marí Carmen Vela, Wally Barron, Alicia Moreno.

El Mundo de los Vampiros (1960) was a typical potboiler about resurrected vampire, Sergio Sotubai (Guillermo Murray), and his attempt to drink a small town dry of blood. Professor Kolman (José Baviera), who just so happens to have two beautiful nieces (Silvia Fournier and Erna Martha Bauman), constructs a sound-wave device and drives the vampire back to his grave. Ludicrous and hardly worth the effort, this low-budget quickie spawned several like features.

1961 *Invasion of the Vampires (La Invasión de los Vampiros)*

Mexican, b/w, 100 min. Director-Writer: Miguel Morayta. Producer: Rafael Perez Grova. Starring Carlos Agnosti, Martha Bauman, Tito Junco, Rafael Del Rio, Berta Moss.

1963 *The Bloody Vampire (El Vampiro Sangriento)*

Mexican, b/w, ? min. Director-Writer: Miguel Morayta. Producer: Rafael Perez Grova. Starring Carlos Agnosti, Andrias Roel.

La Invasión de los Vampiros (1961) and its sequel, *El Vampiro Sangriento* (1963), feature Carlos Agnosti as vampire Count Frankenhausen. In the first film, Frankenhausen and his daughter, Brunilda (Martha Bauman), retire to a small village, and suddenly several unexplained deaths occur. Local physician Dr. Albaran (Rafael del Rio) suspects the work of a vampire and follows the bloody trail to Frankenhausen. In the climatic struggle, the count raises his victims from the dead and sets them on the village. By the second film, the "bloody vampire" has moved on to another village and is experimenting, like most mad doctors, with reanimating the dead.

Because of their popularity in Mexico, Paul Nagle and K. Gordon Murray were encouraged to prepare versions for release in the United States. They both failed miserably at the box office.

1961 *Bring Me the Vampire (Enchenme al Vampiro)*

Mexican, 100 min. Director: Alfredo Crevenna. Producer: Mario Garcia Camberos. Writers: Camberos, Alfredo Ruanova. Starring Fernando Soto, Joaquin Garcia Vargas, José Jasso, Roberto Cobo, María Eugenia San Martin.

Composed of three separate episodes, this rare horror comedy featured the familiar haunted-house tale as the framing device. Episode three dealt with a mad murderer who pretends to be a vampire to scare off his rival inheritors. Standard stuff.

1961 *Frankenstein, the Vampire, and Company (Frankenstein, el Vampiro, y C^{ia})*

Mexican, b/w, 79 min. Director: Benito Alaraki. Producer: Guillermo Calderon. Writer: Alfredo Salazar. Starring Manuel Loco Valdes, José Jasso, Martha Elena Cervantes, Nora Veryan, Quintin Bulnes, Jorge Mondragon, Roberto Rivera.

Similar to *El Castillo de los Monstruos* (1959) and derivative of *Abbott and Costello Meet Frankenstein* (1948), this effort was yet another monster rally disguised as a horror farce. Wax replicas of the famous monsters of filmland come to life for predictable results. Quintin Bulnes appears as the vampire.

1967 *Empire of Dracula (El Imperio de Dracula)*

Mexican, 90 min. Director: Federico Curiel. Producer: Enrique Veragara. Writer: Ramon Obon. Starring Cesar del Campo, Eric del Castillo, Lucha Villa, Ethel Carrillo, Rebeco Inturbide, Athia Michel, Gigi Monet, Raoul Ferrer.

Debuting as the first Mexican film in color, *El Imperio de Dracula* (*Empire of Dracula*, 1967) was an uncredited remake of Hammer's *Horror of Dracula* (1958). A dying mother sends her son Luis (Cesar del Campo) to Castle Draculstein to avenge his father, who was killed by the vampire (Eric del Castillo). Endowed with an atmosphere of eroticism, the familiar story of *Dracula* seems fresh in the hands of Federico Curiel. Obviously his years of training (producing serials) allowed Curiel special insight into the effective use of horror.

1967 *Mark of the Wolf Man (La Marca del Hombre Lobo,* aka *The Vampire of Dr. Dracula)*

Mexican, 133 min. Director-Producer: Enrique Eguiluz. Writer: Jacinto Molina. Starring Paul Naschy, Diane Konopka, Julian Ugarte, Rosanna Yanni, Michael Manz.

A semisequel remake of *Frankenstein, el Vampiro, y Cia* (1961), this low-budget film featured the debut of Paul Naschy as werewolf Count Waldemar Daninsky (a role he would play a dozen times or more). Vampire legends are mixed with werewolf ones, adding to the confusion that would haunt moviegoers for years to come.

1967 *The Vampires (Las Vampiras)*

Mexican, b/w, ? min. Director-Writer: Federico Curiel. Producer: K. Gordon Murray. Starring John Carradine.

Very little information is available regarding this John Carradine vehicle. By all accounts, American producer K. Gordon Murray purchased an unfinished Curiel tale about a female bloodsucker who preys on peasant farmers and added Carradine as a Dracula-like count. Typical low-budget nonsense.

1972 *Angels and Cherubs (Angelas y Querubines)*

Mexican, ? min. Director: Rafael Corkidi.

No further information is available on this film.

1972 *Capulina Versus the Vampires (Capulina Contra los Vampiros)*

Mexican, 73 min. Director: Rene Cordona. Writers: Gaspar Henaine, Cordona. Starring Gasper Henaine.

Popular comic Gaspar Henaine plays Capulina, a vampire hunter, in this Mexican farce.

1963 *Santo Versus the Vampire Women (Santo Contra las Mujeres Vampiras)*

Mexican, b/w, 90 min. Director: Alphonso Corona Black. Producer:

Alberto Lopez. Writer: Ferrando Galiana. Starring Santo, Claudio Brook.

Released at about the same time, the Mexican series of wrestling horror movies were somewhat incompetent and mindless but were aimed at a slightly different audience. When the first of these wrestling fantasy films appeared, the Mexican film industry, which had produced a number of inferior vampire movies, including *World of the Vampires* (1960), *Curse of Nostradamus* (1960), and *The Bloody Vampire* (1963), was on the edge of bankruptcy. The overnight success of *Santo vs El Estrangulador* (*Santo vs the Strangler*, 1963), *El Azul Demonio* (*The Blue Demon*, 1963), and *Santo Contra las Mujeres Vampiras* (*Santo vs The Vampire Women*, 1963) revived the failing industry, and by the following year, most of Mexico's filmmakers were producing monster-wrestling movies. Since then, there have been literally hundreds of wrestling films, rich in fantasy and horror elements. But the most popular were the team-ups of a young energetic grappler, Santo (Huerta, the Silver Masked wrestler), and a mysterious blue-masked loner, the Blue Demon. Together they fought werewolves, mad scientists, zombies, aliens, killer robots, and vampires in a lurid, exploitative series of bloody adventures, including *Santo y el Tesoro de Dracula* (*Santo and the Treasure of Dracula*, 1968), *La Venganza de las Mujeres Vampiras* (*Revenge of the Vampire Women*, 1969), and *Santo y Blue Demon Contra Dracula y el Hombre Lobo* (*Santo and the Blue Demon vs Dracula and the Wolf Man*, 1970). Despite the enormous popularity of these films, the audience eventually grew bored with the repetitious violence, and the entire genre came to an end in the midseventies after a long run.

For Santo's third adventure, *Santo Contra las Mujeres Vampiras* (*Santo vs the Vampire Women*, 1963), the famous grappler is enlisted by Dr. Orloff, a distinguished Egyptologist, to save his daughter from the clutches of vampire women. Inadvertently, the absentminded professor has brought several Egyptian priestesses, who need the blood of a young girl (his daughter) to resurrect their queen, back from the dead. Santo battles with the vamipre women and their "batmen," saves the girl, and returns to live happily ever after. The strange mix of comic-strip violence, naked women, and a wrestling grand finale was an unbeatable combination, and the masked muscleman would return to battle other vampiric demons.

1968 *Santo and the Treasure of Dracula (Santo y Tesoro de Dracula)*

Mexican, 81 min. Director: Rene Cordona. Producer: Guillermo Calderon. Writer: Alfredo Salazar. Starring Eric Del Castillo, Santo,

Noelia Noel, Aldo Monti, Carlos Agosti, Albert Rojas, and Roberto Rivera.

Five years later, Santo returned in *Santo y Tesoro de Dracula* (*Santo and the Treasure of Dracula*, 1968) to battle the king of vampires in a hybrid science-fiction–horror tale. When a scientist's daughter, Luisa (Noelia Noel), uses his time machine to travel back to nineteenth-century Transylvania, she is captured and terrorized by Count Dracula. Utilizing high-tech computer equipment in his scientific batcave, Santo watches the abduction, then travels back in time himself to effect a rescue. He battles with the Count's henchmen, rescues the girl, and steals Dracula's treasure. The open-ended conclusion left plenty of room for the sequel which followed a few months later.

1968 *Santo and the Blue Demon Versus the Monsters (Santo y el Blue Demon Contra los Monstruos)*

Mexican, 81 min. Director: Rene Cordona. Producer: Guillermo Calderon. Writer: Alfredo Salazar. Starring Eric Del Castillo, Santo, Noelia Noel, Aldo Monti, Carlos Agosti, Albert Rojas, Robeerto Rivera.

In this semisequel to *Santo y Tesoro de Dracula* (1968), Santo enlists the aid of his grappler buddy, the Blue Demon, to battle Dracula and the famous monsters of filmland. Predictably, the Count escapes at the end, to return a few years later.

1969 *Vengeance of the Vampire Women (La Venganza de las Mujeres Vampiros)*

Mexican, 90 min. Director: Federico Curiel. Producer: Garcia Besne. Writers: Garcia Besne, Fernando Oses. Starring Santo, Aldo Monti, Norma Lazareno, Gina Romand, Victor Junco, Patricia Ferrer.

The vampire women (from the third Santo movie) returned in *La Venganza de las Mujeres Vampiros* (*Vengeance of the Vampire Women*, 1969). Led by Countess Mayra (Gina Romand), who has been revived with the blood of a nightclub dancer, they enlist the aid of a mad scientist. Apparently Dr. Brancor (Victor Junco) has created an indestructable monster, Razos (Nathaniel Leon), who can defeat Santo. The famous grappler prevails, rescues an attractive journalist (Norma Lazareno) held captive by the mad doctor, and sends the vampire women to the morgue.

1970 *Santo and the Blue Demon Versus Dracula and the Wolf Man (Santo y Blue Demon Contra Dracula y Hombre Lobo)*

Mexican, Cinematográfica Calderón, 87 min. Director: Miquel Delgado. Producer: Guillermo Calderon. Writer: Fernando Oses. Starring Eric Del Castillo, Gina Romand.

In his final outing, Santo again teamed with the Blue Demon to battle the Count (Eric Del Castillo) and the wolf man. What results is a free-for-all tag-team match worthy of Hulk Hogan and the World Wrestling Federation.

1971 *Chantoc Versus the Tiger and the Vampire (Chantoc Contra el Tigre y el Vampiro)*

Mexican (no further information available).

Low-low-budget rip-off of the Santo wrestling movies featuring a battle with vampires.

1963 *Blood Feast*

H. G. Lewis Productions, 61 mi. Director-Writer: Herschell Gordon Lewis. Producers: David F. Friedman, Stanford Kohlberg, Lewis. Starring Thomas Wood, Mel Arnold, Connie Mason, Scott Hall, Lyn Bolton, Toni Calvert, Gene Courtier.

Far worse than the exploitative wrestling adventures of Santo, a series of cheap American films better suited for the trash heap than the movie screen throve (like cinematic vampires) upon the bloodthirsty tastes of its audiences. They were made for sick, twisted minds that derived pleasure from explicit mutilations and bloody carnage, and they lacked any cinematic style or intellect. Herschell Gordon Lewis, the man who created the "splatter movie," made a number of highly successful motion pictures, including *Blood Feast* (1963), *2000 Maniacs* (1964), and *Color Me Blood Red* (1965), which featured psychotics who thought they were vampires, but any chances at psychological study were traded for exercises in the Grand Guignol school of gore.

Blood Feast has the notorious distinction of being the first splatter movie. Shot in Miami over a period of nine days for less than $75,000, the film concerns the efforts of an Egyptian caterer to plan a "blood feast" to bring an Egyptian love goddess back from the dead. Unfortunately, the limited narrative (which had its possibilities) took a backseat to the bloody carnage. Ranking high on the gross-out scale, *Blood Feast* was one of the most gruesome films ever made.

1964 *2000 Maniacs*

H. G. Lewis Productions, 73 min. Director-Writer: H.G. Lewis. Producer: David F. Friedman. Starring Connie Masion, Thomas Wood, Jeffrey Allen, Ben Moore, Shelby Livingston, Vincent Santo, Gary Bakeman.

2000 Maniacs (1964), Herschell Gordon Lewis's follow-up to *Blood Feast*, told the story of a small southern town that magically reappears one hundred years after Union soldiers in the Civil War have burned it to the ground. Seeking revenge, the townspeople terrorize visiting tourists with mutilation, cannibalism, and blood drinking. Visually graphic, the film's gory sequences are enough to turn a coroner's stomach.

1964 *Tomb of Ligeia*

AIP, 81 min. Director: Roger Corman. Producer: Pat Green. Writer: Robert Towne, based on a short story by Edgar Allan Poe. Starring Vincent Price, Elizabeth Shepherd, John Westbrook, Oliver Johnson, Derek Francis, Richard Vernon.

One singular exception to all the bloody carnage taking place in American films was *Tomb of Ligeia* (1964). The final entry in Roger Corman's definitive Edgar Allan Poe series, the motion picture is an unusual blend of necrophilia, witchcraft, and vampirism. Drug-addicted Verden Fell (beautifully played by Vincent Price) is so haunted by the memory of his dead wife that his grief conjures up her spirit. Raven-haired Ligeia (Elizabeth Shepherd) needs the blood and soul of Fell's new wife, Rowena (also Shepherd), to live again and sends her familiar (a black cat) to the grief-stricken husband to aid in her request. Slowly, inexorably, blond-haired Rowena begins to take on the characteristics and personality of Ligeia. Finally, as Rowena is lured to her death atop the bell tower, Fell repents, perishing along with his beloved Ligeia, and his second wife is rescued by her young lover. Expertly mounted with a British crew (and looking like a classic Hammer film), this was Corman's finest motion picture.

1966 *Blood Bath* (aka *Track of the Vampire*)

AIP/Italian, 80 min. Directors-Writers: Jack Hill, Stephanie Rothman. Producer: Roger Corman. Starring William Campbell, Linda Summers, Marissa Mathes, Sandra Knight, Jonathan Haze.

Blood Bath (1966), Roger Corman's composite of *The Mystery of the Wax Museum* and *A Bucket of Blood,* featured William Campbell as a schizophrenic beatnik vampire who gets high on blood. In fact, the film itself is somewhat schizophrenic, representing a composite of a horror film and an art-house sex film. (In an interview years later Campbell explained that Corman had spliced together two films [which he starred in] to create *Blood Bath.*)

1966 *Dr. Terror's House of Horrors*

Amicus, 98 min. Director: Freddie Francis. Producer-Writer: Milton Subotsky. Starring Peter Cushing, Mitch Evans, Neil McCallum, Ursula Howells, Peter Madden, Bernard Lee, Jeremy Kemp, Roy Castle, Donald Sutherland.

Dr. Terror's House of Horrors (1966) had a gallery of vampires, werewolves, zombies, anxious to drink blood, dismember body parts, and generally gross you out. The film is not particularly good.

1966 *Orgy of the Dead*

b/w, 78 min. Director: A. C. Stephen. Producer-Writer: Edward D. Wood, Jr. Starring Criswell, Fawn Silver, Pat Barringer, Tor Johnson, Lon Chaney, Jr., Vampira.

Probably the worst of all was Edward D. Wood, Jr.'s *Orgy of the Dead* (1966), wherein Tor Johnson, Vampira, and Lon Chaney, Jr., lend their talents to this inept horror film. A horror writer and his girlfriend drive to a cemetery to acquire a new story idea but stumble into a living nightmare. The undead Criswell and a female vampire capture the young couple, tie them to poles, and force them to watch the "orgy of the dead." But the orgy isn't really an orgy. It's just a chance for topless female werewolves, vampires, and zombies to dance (bumping, jiggling, and grinding) through the night. This film is a mindless, incompetent exercise in horror fantasy and ranks, along with Wood's *Plan Nine from Outer Space* (1959), as one of the worst movies ever made.

1969 *Blood of Dracula's Castle* (aka *Dracula's Castle*)

A & E Film Corporation, 84 min. Director: Al Adamson. Producer-Writer: Rex Carlton. Starring John Carradine, Paula Raymond, Alex D'Arcy, Robert Dix, Ray Young, Vicki Volante, John Cardos, Kent Osborne, Lon Chaney, Jr.

Blood of Dracula's Castle (1969, aka *Dracula's Castle*), another piece of low-low-budget trash from the undisputed king of Z movies, Al Adamson, totally wasted the talents of John Carradine and Lon Chaney, Jr. (in his last film). Here Carradine plays butler to Count and Countess Townsend (Alex D'Arcy and Paula Raymond), who are really Count and Countess Dracula. Luring a young couple to their estate in the Mojave Desert, the traditional bloodletting begins but is soon interrupted by the appearance of Chaney as the wolf man. A considered sequel, *Dracula's Coffin*, was thankfully never filmed.

1971 *Bloodsuckers* (aka *Incense for the Damned*)

Lucinda Films, 87 min. Director: Robert Hartford-Davis. Producer: Graham Harris. Writer: Julian More, based on the novel *Doctors Wear Scarlet*, by Simon Raven. Starring Peter Cushing, Patrick MacNee, Imagen Hassell, Alex Davian, Johnny Sekka, Madeline Hinde, Edward Woodward, David Lodge, Patrick Mowler.

1971 *I Drink Your Blood*

Jerry Gross Productions, 83 min. Director-Writer: David Durston. Producer: Jerry Gross. Starring Bhaskar, Janine Wong, Ronda Fultz, George Patterson, John Dammon, Riley Mills, Iris Brooks.

Bloodsuckers (1971, aka *Incense for the Damned*) and *I Drink Your Blood* (1971) were two other entries into the lucrative "blood freak" market. The former, based on the novel *Doctors Wear Scarlet*, dealt with a physician who kills his patients for their blood. The latter, a low-grade Z movie, found satanic hippies drinking tainted blood to get high. Both films, poorly received by the American board of censors, were forced to make extensive cuts to avoid an X-rating.

By the middle to late sixties and early seventies, before the time-honored classics were remade by the fifth school of horror, the familiar vampiric patterns found their ways into motion pictures produced by Spanish, German, Japanese, and Filipino filmmakers. The folkloric popularity of Dracula and his descendants, as realized in films by Universal and Hammer, had translated into big box-office receipts worldwide, and local auteurs were anxious to introduce their own cinematic nightmares into the competitive market. Unfortunately, the chilling expressionist visions of their contemporaries were far superior. Films like *Der Fluch der Gruenenaugen* (1963), *Un Vampiro para Dos* (1965), *Blood Drinkers* (1966), and *Bloodthirst* (1971) were generally uninspired retreads of traditional stories that had been told much more effectively before. The introduction of the samurai motif and other Oriental concepts in *Onna Kyuketsuki* (1963), *Kuroneko*

(1968), and the Michio Yamamoto trilogy were the only interesting additions to the vampire mythos. As a whole, the films contributed very little to the world cinema and have since faded into the dark shadows of obscurity.

1963 *The Woman Vampire (Onna Kyuketsuki)*
Toho/Japanese, b/w, 98 min. Director: Nabuo Nakagawa. Producer: Mitsuga Okura. Writer: Shin Nakazawa. Starring Shigeru Amachi, Yoko Mihara, Keinosuke Wada.

Onna Kyuketsuki (*The Woman Vampire*, 1963) was the first vampire film produced in Japan. Having distinguished itself with *Godzilla* (1954), *Rodan* (1956), *Mothra* (1961), and a host of other monster movies, Toho Films turned its attention to the lucrative horror-film market. The most popular form of literary horror in Japan was the Kaidan Eiga (the ghost story). Although the Islands had their legends about the "undead," most were far removed from their European counterparts. In fact, many of the traditions generally associated with vampirism (such as the symbolism of the cross and methods of destruction) were foreign to them. But determined to make a film for worldwide release, director Nabuo Nakagawa (making his fifth motion picture that year) and writer Shin Nakazawa collaborated on what can only be termed a strange hybrid of cultures.

Set in Japan during the fifties, the story follows the efforts of a samurai-sword-wielding vampire (Shigeru Amachi) to win the hand of a beautiful woman in matrimony. Niwako (Yoko Mihara), the wife of an atomic scientist and daughter of an old Christian family (that dates back hundreds of years), is the object of the vampire's affections. He tries numerous maneuvers to romance her, but because she is married to someone else, she rejects his advances. Finally, unable to contain his lust, he kidnaps her to his castle fortress with the help of a dwarf, a witch, and a bald wrestler. Somewhat predictably, her husband comes to the rescue and duels with the vampire for her life.

A silly, uneven concoction of vampire myths, this film is still noteworthy as the first of its kind in Japan. Some reports suggest that Nabuo Nakagawa actually introduced the vampire film to his country several years earlier with *Kyuketsuki Ga* (1956), but this fact could not be confirmed. Prints of the film are no longer available, and records from the period are sketchy. Contradictory reports suggest that *Onna Kyuketsuki* and this earlier film are one and the same and that it was released in the late fifties (possibly 1958 or 1959). Whatever the case may be, the film did not make a huge impact on the market, and it would be several years before the Japanese would attempt another vampire movie. (Five years later, Kaneto Shindo would offer *Yabu No Naka Kurenoko*.)

1963 *Cave of the Living Dead (Der Fluch der Grünenaugen,* aka *Night of the Vampires, Curse of the Green Eyes)*

German, b/w, 89 min. Director: Akos Von Rathony. Producer: Richard Gordon. Writer: Carl Von Rock. Starring Erika Remberg, Carl Mohner, Adrian Hoven, Emmerich Schrenck, Wolfgang Preiss, John Kitzmiller, Vida Juvan, Stane Sever.

One of the worst films of the period, *Der Fluch der Grüenenaugen* (*Cave of the Living Dead,* 1963) was an exploitative sadistic fantasy. Dreadfully produced, the story told the familiar tale of female vampires luring men to their death. Several bodies are found at the entrance to a cave, and Detective Doren (Adrian Hoven) follows the trail into the caverns of Professor Adelsberg (Wolfgang Preiss), a local mad doctor who is also a vampire. He has been experimenting with several of the villagers' wives and daughters to produce an army of bloodsuckers. Surprise! Featuring plenty of women in black lace and panties, the motion picture is predictable trash.

1965 *A Vampire for Two (Un Vampiro para Dos)*

Spanish, b/w, 85 min. Director: Pedro La Zanga Sabater. Writers: José Marice Palacio, Sabater. Starring Gracita Morales, José Luis Lopez Vazquez, Fernando Fernan Gomez.

Un Vampiro para Dos (*A Vampire for Two,* 1965) was another predictable mess. In this horror comedy, a young Spanish couple (Gracita Morales and José Luis Lopez Vazquez) go to work as servants of vampire Baron von Rosenthal (Fernando Fernan Gomez) and his bloodsucking family. The usual shenanigans unfold, leading to the couple's early dismissal. Director Pedro La Zanga Sabater tried to make this low-budget farce look like classic Hammer horror, but the material is worse than outtakes from "The Munsters" (1964, CBS).

1966 *Blood Drinkers* (aka *Vampire People*)

Filipino, 87 min. Director: Gerardo de Leon. Producer: Danilo Santiago. Writer: Cesare Amigo. Starring Amelia Fuentes, Ronald Remy, Eddie Fernandez, Eva Montez, Celia Rodriguez, Jess Roman, Felisa Salcedo, Renato Robles, Vicky Valasquez.

The first of two vampire films by Gerardo de Leon, *Blood Drinkers* (1966, aka *Vampire People*) is a bizarre retelling of the Elizabeth Bathory tale. Hoping to bring his love Christine (Amelia Fuentes) back from the dead, wealthy aristocrat Marco (played by Filipino great Ronald Remy) travels to a small town to steal the heart and blood of his lover's twin sister, Charita (also Fuentes). He and his three compatriots—a bat, a sexy seductress (Eva Montez), and a hunchback dwarf—make several unsuccessful attempts before a traveler (Eddie Fernandez) recognizes the danger they represent. He rallies the villagers against them, and the "vampire people" are hunted down and killed (all except Marco, who escapes for the unrealized sequel). The straightforward plot is rather dull, and the poor dubbing and inept editing make the feature impossible to watch. De Leon would later team with Roger Corman to make a number of low-budget cheapies like *Women in Cages* (1971).

1968 *Kuroneko (Yabu No Naka Kuroneko)*
Japanese, 87 min. Director-Writer: Kaneto Shindo. Producer: Nobuyo Horiba. Starring Kichiemon Nakamura, Kiwako Taichi, Nobuko Otawa.

Released as a companion piece to the famous *Onibaba* (1964), *Yabu No Naka Kuroneko (Kuroneko,* 1968) was a strange tapestry of ghostly images, vampiric legends, and samurai justice. In medieval Japan (the eleventh or twelfth century), an old woman (Nobuko Otawa) and her daughter-in-law (Kiwako Taichi) are raped and killed by a band of renegade samurai, but they return as vampires to destroy all samurai. When their bloodsucking vengeance threatens to engulf the entire country, a noble warrior (Kichiemon Nakamura) is sent to hunt down the two women and destroy them. He soon discovers that they are his mother and wife, and he is unable to fulfill his promise to his lord. The samurai must therefore commit suicide or be dishonored. Wanting to preserve her husband's dignity, Taichi voluntarily returns to the grave after one last night with him. The old woman resists, and destroys them both. Despite the lack of narrative coherence, the film is quite powerful and led to further explorations into the vampire mythos.

1969 *A Vampire's Dream (Um Sonho de Vampiros)*
Brazilian, 80 min. Director-Writer-Producer: Ibere Cavalranti. Starring Ankito, Irma Alvarez, Janet Chermoni, Sonelia Costa, Robson Bob, Zuza Curi, Tuna Espinheira.

Um Sonho de Vampiros (A Vampire's Dream, 1969) was a satiric comedy that seemed influenced by Woody Allen's short play *Death Knocks.* Death gives Dr. Pan (Ankito) a choice between dying or becoming a vampire. The mad doctor opts for the latter and begins a hedonistic lifestyle that includes traditional bloodletting and sex orgies. When a young couple (Janet Chermoni and Sonelia Costa) wander into his trap, the motion picture becomes most predictable, with one too many sight gags.

1970 *Night of the Vampire (Chi O Suu Ningyo,* aka *The Vampire Doll)*

Toho/Japanese, 71 min. Director: Michio Yamamoto. Producer: Tomoyuki Tanaka. Writers: Eli Ogawa, Hiroshi Nagano. Starring Kayo Matsuo, Akira Nakao, Atsuo Nakamura, Yukiko Kobayashi.

1971 *Dracula's Lust for Blood (Chi O Suu Me,* aka *Lake of Dracula)*

Toho/Japanese, 82 min. Director: Michio Yamamoto. Producer: Fumio Tanaka. Writers: Eli Ogawa, Katsu Takeura. Starring Mori Kishida, Midori Fujita, Oashide Takahashi, Sanae Emi.

1974 *The Evil of Dracula (Chi O Suu Bara)*

Toho/Japanese, 87 min. Director: Michio Yamamoto. Producer: Fumio Tanaka. Writers: Eli Ogawa, Masaru Takasue. Starring Toshio Kurosawa, Mariko Mochizuki, Shin Kishida, Hunie Tanaka.

Chi O Suu Ningyo (Night of the Vampire, 1970), *Chi O Suu Me (Dracula's Lust for Blood,* 1971), and *Chi O Suu Bara (The Evil of Dracula,* 1974) formed Michio Yamamoto's famous trilogy about vampires. Though dramatically different in style and content, they were thematically linked. Each dealt with loss, contracts with the devil, and the price of vengeance. In *Night of the Vampire,* Keiko (Kayo Matsuo), a woman raped by a physician at the end of World War II, offers her daughter, Yuko (Yukiko Kobayaski), to the devil in exchange for revenge. Both mother and daughter suffer from the unholy bargain, and Yuko loses her lover, Kuzuhiko (Atsuo Nakamura), to her vampire mother. In *Dracula's Lust for Blood,* a young woman painter, Akiko (Midori Fujita), and her sister, Natsuko (Sanae Emi), fall victim to a vampire (Mori Kishida). When Natsuko dies, Akiko must travel into the depths of hell to destroy the evil bloodsucker (in a sequence copied from Hammer's *Horror of Dracula,* 1958). In *The Evil of Dracula,* a young psychology teacher (Toshio Kurosawa) must enter into a demonic pact to destroy the vampire couple (Hunie Tanaka and Mio Ota), descendants of Dracula, who run a girl's school.

All three films are unusually atmospheric and recall the best of Hammer's *Dracula* series. Apparently, Yamamoto was impressed with the work being produced in England during the third great horror school and lifted many of his best set pieces from those efforts. The single drawback to Yamamoto's trilogy is the synthesis of traditional European vampire rituals into the predominantly Oriental story and setting.

1970 *Curse of the Vampires (Dugong Vampira,* aka *Creatures of Evil)*

Filipino, 90 min. Director: Gerardo de Leon. Producer: Amalia Muhlack. Writers: Ben Fello, Pierre Salas. Starring Amelia Fuentes, Eddie Garcia, Mary Walter, Romeo Vasques.

De Leon's second vampire film, *Dugong Vampira (Curse of the Vampires,* 1970), concerned the trials and tribulations of a family of vampires in the modern day. Leonora (Amelia Fuentes) and her brother (Eddie Garcia) return home to find that Mama (Mary Walter) has become a vampire. They release her from the basement crypt to which Dad (Romeo Vasques) has chained her, and soon all members of the family become "creatures of evil." The family descends upon a small village and begins to suck the locals dry. Lurid and Oedipal in nature, Gerardo de Leon's film revels in images of blood and incest with its garish colors and attempts at pretentiousness.

1971 *Bloodthirst*

Filipino, b/w, ? min. Director: Newt Arnold. Starring Robert Winston.

Bloodthirst (1971) was an American coproduction that went awry. Made in the Philippines in 1965, finished with funds from a U.S. banker in 1970, and finally released in 1971, the picture already looked twenty years out of touch with current offerings when it debuted. The ludicrous tale follows an American Sherlock Holmes (Robert Winston) in search of a strange vampire sun cult.

1971 *The Vampire Happening (Gebissen wird nur nachts)*

West German/Aquilla Films, 102 min. Director: Freddie Francis. Producer: Piere A. Caminnecci. Writers: August Rieger, Karl Heinz Hummel. Starring Ferdinand Mayne, Pia Degermark, Thomas

Hunter, Lyvia Bauer, Joachim Kemmer, Daria Damier, Yvor Murillo.

Freddie Francis's *Gebissen wird nur nachts* (1971, *The Vampire Happening*) was an unfunny parody of Polanski's *Fearless Vampire Hunters* (1967). A Hollywood beauty (Pia Degermark) who resembles her vampiric ancestor travels to the Balkans to initiate "a vampire happening." Ferdy Mayne lampoons his earlier vampire role, but otherwise there's very little to offer besides the ubiquitous naked women.

During the same period, the vampire became the focus of soft- and hard-core pornographic films. Though daring, these motion pictures utilized vampirism simply as a gimmick to link coupling (and tripling) scenes together. The traditional formulas of the vampire movie were used over and over again to provide a rudimentary narrative. For the most part, they deemphasized blood and violence and concentrated more on sexual relations of every conceivable type. The majority of these films were cheaply sensational, often sexploitative. Others, like *Dracula, the Dirty Old Man* (1969), *The Mad Lust of a Hot Vampire* (1971), *A Vampire's Love* (1973), and *Vampire Playmates* (1974), were outright obscene, while two in particular, *Spermula* (1974) and *Andy Warhol's Dracula* (1974), represented the high and low points of the X-rated vampire film.

Because the anonymity of those involved was often protected by fake or nonexistent screen credits, the ability to provide accurate filmographic entries was greatly undermined. Similarly, since the plot lines of many films were interchangeable, summaries and synopsis may appear repetitious. The problem of multiple versions with sex scenes grafted onto them from other films also makes a complete listing impossible.

1962 *House on Bare Mountain*

b/w, ? min. Director-Writer: R. L. Frost. Starring Jeffrey Smithers, Bob Cresse.

House on Bare Mountain (1962) was the first soft-core vampire picture. Filmed at a cost of $70,000, the plot takes the audience to Granny Good's School for Good Girls (run by Bob Cresse in drag). Dracula (Jeffrey Smithers) pays a visit on the training school for girls and gives them private instruction.

1963 *Kiss Me Quickly* (aka *Dr. Breedlove*)

80 min. Director-Producer-Writer: Russ Meyer. Starring Jackie DeWitt, Fred Coe, Althea Currier, Claudia Banks, Sexton Friendly.

Soft-core filmmaker Russ Meyer's first entry into the lucrative market was *Kiss Me Quickly* (aka *Dr. Breedlove*). Alien Fred Coe arrives on Earth from planet Sterilox in search of female partners and meets Dr. Breedlove (a parody of Peter Sellers' *Dr. Strangelove*). The mad doctor has been experimenting with the famous monsters of filmland and offers to create an artificial woman for Coe. Predictable and forgettable.

1965 *La Bonne Damme*
French, b/w. Director: Pierre Phillipe. Starring Valeska Gert.

Pierre Phillipe's *La Bonne Damme* provided a vehicle for European star Valeska Gert and revitalized her career. She plays a bloody fairy who enjoys bathing in the blood of her victims.

1968 *Sexyrella*
French, b/w (no further information available).

An uneven retelling of the Cinderella story mixing vampires and sado-masochism.

1968 *La Fée Sanguinaire*
Belgian, b/w. Starring T. Katinaki (no further information available).

La Fée Sanguinaire is a sexploitative version of the Elizabeth Bathory tale with T. Katinaki playing the bloody countess.

1969 *Dracula, the Dirty Old Man*
William Toiano Limited. Director-Writer: William Edwards. Producer: William Toiano. Starring Vince Keeley, Bill Whitton.

Dracula, the Dirty Old Man (1969) anticipated the direction that Hammer's series of Karnstein films would take. Count Dracula (Vince Keeley) turns a local villager (William Whitton) into a werewolf to kidnap his girlfriend for (not himself!) his vampire bride. The traditional lesbian sex scenes are meant to satisfy male fantasies and are very unrealistic. Dracula has a vibrating coffin for better effect, and the wolf man's unbelievably long staying power makes him a hit with local housewives.

1970 *Dracula's Vampire Lust* (aka *Do You Know What Happened to Count Dracula? Guess What Happened to Count Dracula?*)

Switzerland. Director: Laurence Merrick. Starring Des Roberts.

This film covers the same ground as *Dracula, the Dirty Old Man* (1969).

1970 *The Body Beneath*

Director-Writer: Andy Milligan.

The Body Beneath (1970) was a 16-mm horror quickie by Andy Milligan which combined vampires, sex, and violence for the S & M crowd.

1970 *Bite Me, Darling (Beis mich Liebling)*

German. Director: Helmut Fornbacher. Starring Eva Renzi, Patrick Jordon, Dieter Augustin.

Beis mich Liebling (1970) was released in America as *Love-Making, Vampire Style*, with major reediting and additional scenes by Anthony Baker. Eva Renzi plays a descendant of Count Dracula who wants to suck her share of men, including postman Patrick Jordon and psychiatrist Dieter Augustin.

1970 *Lesbian Vampires (Vampyros Lesbos, aka The Heritage of Dracula)*

Spanish/German, 92 min. Director: Franco Manera (aka Jesús Franco). Producer: Arturo Marcos. Writers: Jesús Franco, Jamie Chavarri. Starring Dennis Price, Soledad Miranda, Eva Stromberg, Paul Mueller, Victor Feldman, Jésus Franco, Michael Berling.

Vampyros Lesbos (*Lesbian Vampires*, 1970) explored the same territory as *Blood and Roses* (1961) and *The Vampire Lovers* (1970) but with a great deal more explicitness. Jesús Franco (Jess Frank) produced a number of impressive vampire films from *La Fille de Dracula* (1971) to *El Conde Dracula* (1972) during the early seventies, but his reworking of Joseph Sheridan Le Fanu's classic tale of forbidden vampire love caused much controversy. Combining material from *Carmilla*, Stoker's "Dracula's Guest," and historical records about the blood countess (Elizabeth Bathory), his film chronicles the exploits of a descendant of Count Dracula named Nadina (Soledad

Miranda). Isolated to a small Mediterranean island, Nadina entices young women to her estate to bathe in their fresh blood. She falls in love with one of her victims and tragically perishes at her hands.

Franco's mix of sex and sadism proved very daring for the time and was banned in several countries. An edited version appeared in his native country, Spain, in 1974, but the German version, minus his screen credit as director, contains scenes of explicit lesbianism and sadomasochism.

1971 *Incredible Sexy Vampire*
Annati Films/Italian. Director-Producer: L. Annati.

No further information available.

1971 *Mad Lust of a Hot Vampire*
Starring: Jim Parker.

No further information available.

1971 *Vampire of the Highway* (*El Vampiro de la Autopista*, aka *The Horribly Sexy Vampire*)
Cinefilms/Spanish, 94 min. Director-Writer: José Luis Madrid. Producer: Al Peppard. Starring Patricia Loran, Waldemar Wohlfahrt, Luis Iduni, Adela Tauler, Victor Davis, Mary Trovar.

El Vampiro de la Autopista (1971) was another haunted-house challenge. Count Oblensky (Wohlfahrt) and his lover (Loran) must spend the night among vampires to claim his inheritance, but Baron Von Winninger has other erotic plans for them. Typical nudie vampire film.

1972 *Casual Relations* (aka *A Vampire's Love*)
78 min. Director-Producer-Writer: Mark Rappaport. Starring Mel Austin, Margaret Smith.

Casual Relations (aka *A Vampire's Love*, 1973) examined the victim-love act, Mel Austin and Margaret Smith gracefully attempting numerous sexual positions. (The film opens and closes with stills and footage from *Nosferatu* [1922]).

1972 *Count Erotica, Vampire*
Lobo Productions. Director: Tony Teresi. Producer: Kelly Estelli. Starring John Peters, Mary Simon, Paul Robinson.

One of the most widely circulated of the pornographic vampire films, *Count Erotica, Vampire* retells the story of *Dracula* with wildly erotic sex scenes Bram Stoker never wrote about.

1972 *Dracula Vampire Sexuel*
Switzerland. Director: Laurence Merrick. Starring Des Roberts.

Dracula Vampire Sexuel (1972) is the same motion picture as *Dracula's Vampire Lust* (1970), simply rereleased under a new title with a few additional sex scenes.

1973 *Jacula* (*Les Avaleuses*, aka *Yacula, the Midnight Party, The Last Thrill*)
General Films/French/Belgian. Director: Jesús Franco. Producers: Marius Mesoseur, Pierre Querut. Writers: Jesús Franco, Gerard Brissaud. Starring Linda Romany, Alica Arno, Jack Taylor.

Although considerably more artistic than *Deep Throat* (1972), Jesús Franco's *Jacula* (1973) did not enjoy the same popular success. Countess Irina Karlstein (Linda Romay), a deaf-mute vampire, fellates her male lovers to death and enlists the aid of her bosom buddies in a sucking orgy. Director Franco appears as Dr. Roberts, the vampire hunter who must stop her before she can work her way through the entire country. Nicely done, *Jacula* anticipates *Spermula* (1974).

1974 *Immoral Tales*
Italian/New Line Cinema, 75 min. Director-Writer: Wallerian Borowazyk. Producer: Anatole Dauman. Starring Lise Danvers, Fabrice Luchini, Pascale Christopher, Charlotte Alexandra, Florence Bellamy, Palama Picasso.

Immoral Tales (1974) retells Elizabeth Bathory's story in a much nastier and more sexual way.

1974 *Spermula*

French/Parlafrance. Director-Producer-Writer: Charles Matton. Starring Dayle Haddon, Udo Kier, Georges Geret, Ginette Le Clere, Joyclyne Boisseau, Francious Dunoyer, Isabelle Mercanton.

Spermula (1974, released in the United States in 1976) was the perfect example of what is best about bad vampire movies. Bad vampire movies can be good nonsensical fun. The film does not trouble the intellect, but it scares you when it should, titillates you with erotic sensationalism, startles laughs out of you, and holds your attention to the last frame. It is also expertly expressionistic, melding the real and the surreal through a contrast of contemporary and Art Deco designs. Simply because it was an X-rated film, *Spermula* should not be discounted.

The story is a true parody of the science-fiction vampire movie. Dayle Haddon, in the tradition of other femme fatales, leads a race of virgin vampire women, in 1930s dress, from a distant planet to Earth. Their objective: sperm (which they consume through fellatio). Once on Earth, they make slaves of mankind and bosom buddies of fellow females. However, the local mad scientist (Udo Kier) has other ideas. With his bumbling assistants, he momentarily turns the tide of the invasion, but eventually, he too falls for the lovely Haddon.

Spermula is a beautifully done French production much in the style of Bava or Vadim, and when it is over, the audience exits from their seats in good humor. Is *Spermula* a good, or classic, vampire film? No, but it is full of inane pleasure.

1974 *Blood for Dracula (Dracula Cerca Sangue di Vergine e ... Mori di Sette, aka Andy Warhol's Dracula)*

Italian, 103 min. Director: Anthony Dawson. Writer (and codirector, uncredited): Paul Morrissey. Producer: Andrew Braimberg. Starring Udo Kier, Arno Juerging, Vittoria de Sica, Joe Dallesandra, Roman Polanski, Dominique Darel, Stefania Casini, Silvia Dioniso.

Blood for Dracula (released in America as *Andy Warhol's Dracula*, 1974) is not very good and could easily have earned a XXX rating if the code measured the pornography of violence in addition to sex. Its cast suffers every sadistic act that the twisted minds of Anthony Dawson and Paul Morrissey could imagine. If female characters are not being forcibly raped or beaten, then male characters are being dismembered. In the course of the film's two-hour running time, there are several decapitations, numerous mutilations, a few rapes, and as much blood and gore as can be imagined. Coupled with the explicit sexual acts, this film is *very* sick.

Count Dracula (played again by Udo Kier) is rapidly aging in a Transylvania depleted (by him) of noncontaminated virgin blood. He and his dim-witted servant (Arno Juerging) move his coffin to Italy, a country in which (he believes) women save their virginity for the marriage bed. Once there, the wealthy Count is embraced by an impoverished yet noble clan who have three charming virgin daughters. Dracula begins his bloodsucking but soon comes to odds with the local handyman (Joe Dallesandra), who saves the vampire's potential victims by deflowering them.

This sadistic, cold-blooded production represents the worst of the X-rated vampire movies. "Supervised" by Paul Morrissey (not the avant-garde imagist Andy Warhol), *Blood for Dracula* exploits the sadomasochistic freak market with its visual images of blood, sex, and gore. Although the film was intended as a stylistic art piece, it fails even as cinema. It ranks with trash like *Blood Feast* (1964) and *Orgy of the Dead* (1966), and is unworthy of further comment. (This film was released in 3-D as a companion piece to *Il Mostro e in Tavola* [*Andy Warhol's Frankenstein*, 1963].)

Please note: This film was released unfairly under several titles (with little or no reediting) to unsuspecting audiences in an effort to recoup its original investment.

By the end of the period, most cinematic approaches to the vampire film had run their course. The expressionistic avant-garde visions of Bava, Bunuel, Polanski, and Vadim, characteristic of the fourth great horror school, had restored the dignity of the horror genre in Europe and given the vampire film a new lease on life. And the other more violent and sexually explicit form had tested the bounds of censorship and good taste, and had emerged with a new understanding of cinematic freedom and responsibility. There may have been better films from other periods, but it was the influence of these efforts that would shape future cinematic nightmares.

The following films were also released during the period but no further information beyond the production credits is available:

1962 *Vampire Woman (Xi Xuefu)*

Hong Kong, b/w, 97 min. Director: Li Tie. Producer: Zhu Ziqui. Writer: Cheng Gang. Starring Bai Yang, Zhang Houyou, Haiang Manli, and Rong Xiaoy.

1964 *Batman Versus Dracula*

Independent. Starring Jack Smith.

1964 *Bloodless Vampire*

Director: Michael Du Pont. Starring Charles Macauley.

1964 *Devils of Darkness*

90 min. Director: Lance Comfort. Producer: Tom Blakeley. Writer: Lyn Fairhurst. Starring William Sylvester, Hubert Noel, Tracy Reed, Diane Decker, Rona Anderson, Peter Illing, Gerald Heinz.

1966 *Carry on Vampire*

97 min. Director: Gerald Thomas. Producer: Peter Rogers. Writer: Talbot Rothwell. Starring Kenneth Williams, Fenella Fielding, Harry H. Corbett, Joan Sims, Jim S. Dale, Charles Hawtrey, Dennis Blake.

1971 *Curse of the Vampyr (La Llamada del Vampiro)*

Arco Films/French, 102 min. Director: Joseph de Lacy. Producer: Riccardo Vasquez. Writers: de Lacy, Enrico Gonzalez Macho. Starring Beatrix Lacy, Nicholas Ney, Ines Skorpio, Diana Sorel.

1971 *The Macabre Dr. Scivano*

Brazilian. Director: Raul Calhado. Producer: Rosalvo Cacador. Starring Raul Calhado.

1971 *The Velvet Vampire* (aka *The Waking Hour*)

Independent Productions, 80 min. Director: Stephanie Rothman. Producer: Charles Swartz. Writers: Rothman, Maurice Jules. Starring: Celeste Yarnell, Michael Blodgett, Sherry Miles, Sandy Ward, Jerry Daniels, Bob Tessler, Chris Woodley.

1972 *Les Chemins de la Violence*

French. Director: Ken Ruder. Starring Michael Flynn.

1972 *The New Blood (La Novia Ensangrentada)*

Spanish. Director: Vincente Aranda. Starring Alexandra Bastedo.

1972 *Vampire 2000 (Vampiro 2000)*
Italian. Director: Riccardo Ghione. Starring Nino Castelnovo and Dominique Boscheo.

1973 *Vaarwhel*
Dutch. Director: Guido Peters.

1974 *The Bat People*
AIP, 81 min. Director: Jerry Jameson. Producer-Writer: Lou Shaw. Starring Stewart Moss, Mariane McAndrew, Michael Pataki, Paul Carr.

1974 *Blood*
Bryanston/Kent Productions, 74 min. Director-Writer: Andy Milligan. Producer: Walter Kent. Starring Allen Berendt, Hope Stansbury, Eve Crosby, Patti Gaul, Pamela Adams.

7

New Bottles, Old Wine

From *Count Yorga, Vampire* (1970)
to *Dracula* (1979)

The vampire film entered the seventies in a much healthier state than it had been in forty years. The critical successes of Bava, Buñuel, Polanski, and Vadim had elevated the vampire film from the B level, and the box-office appeal of the Hammer Films had made the genre attractive once again to producers. The vampire film also achieved various and divergent levels of sophistication with treatment of certain subjects (particularly violence and sex), technical excellence, the use of color, and special effects. Although the impact of television meant viewership was down for other genres, theater attendance increased for horror fantasy (and it wasn't until television horror caught up with the cinema that the shift came in audience).

With the dissolution of the studio system on which Hollywood had thriven for many years, there were fewer vampire films produced by Universal, Columbia, Warner Brothers, MGM, and others, and independent producers, who were largely responsible for the product, made films aimed at specific markets and target groups. Youth had become an influential force (both good and bad) at the box office, and filmmakers were quick to initiate and follow trends. Coupled with the fast-changing social, moral, and political values of the seventies, horror movies tended to reflect pop culture. Thus the fifth (not so) great horror school arose, combining traditional concepts and formulas of the past (old wine) with trends borrowed from other fields (new bottles). Dracula became a hip, swinging socialite of the new era in *Count Yorga, Vampire* (1970), *Old Dracula* (1973), and *Dracula* (1979) or a racially equal vampire in *Blacula* (1972), *Scream, Blacula, Scream* (1973), and *Blood Couple* (1974). Dracula's sons, wives, and dog (?) appeared in *Son of Dracula* (1974), *Dracula and Son* (1976), *Dracula's Dog* (1976), and *Lady Dracula* (1976).

By the close of the period, there could be no doubt that a new form of great potential had developed (from the various trends) and that at the same time a new formula of equal pretention was evolving. The success of *Star Wars* in 1977 began a new upward trend in big-budget films, and film companies rushed large fantasy pictures like *Alien* (1979) for $12 million, *Dracula* (1979) for $14 million, and others into the works. They believed that the more money they spent on their projects, the higher the box-office take would be. Conversely, the success of Tobe Hooper's *Texas Chainsaw Massacre* (1974) and John Carpenter's *Halloween* (1978) signaled a new trend in quickie splatter movies. With the formula of a psychotic murdering innocent teenagers, horror films proliferated. They weren't generally very good, but they racked up big box-office returns and made the careers of many independent filmmakers. The tension between these two traditions would converge to form the last great horror school, with some rather strange results.

1970 *Count Yorga, Vampire*

AIP, 90 min. Director-Writer: Bob Kelljan. Producer: Michael Macready. Starring Robert Quarry, Roger Perry, Michael Murphy, Michael Macready, Donna Anders, Judith Lang.

Count Yorga, Vampire (1970) was one of the first vampire films of the seventies. Originally begun as a college film project by Bob Kelljan and Michael Macready, this low-budget horror film gained national release through American International Pictures. (AIP was an independent production company founded in 1955 by Samuel Z. Arkoff and James Nicholson. They produced a number of low-low-budget horror movies in the late fifties on money grosses that would not have covered the advertising budget on A pictures. After a profitable splurge of Z movies like *Blood of Dracula* [1957], *I Was a Teenage Vampire* [1959], *Dragstrip Dracula* [1962], and the Roger Corman films, the company set its sights on the big time. However, it invested in a number of poor projects, and in 1980 the ailing company was taken over by Filmways [taken over by Orion in 1982].) *Count Yorga, Vampire* was to have been one of AIP's big horror films, but its weak scripting and minimal production values produced a big failure.

The story is very similar to Stoker's *Dracula*, but the locale has been shifted from Transylvania to the United States. Count Yorga (Robert Quarry), a Transylvanian vampire, is perturbed at being hauled back to life and kills his likely savior. He then moves his residence to an eerie castle just outside Los Angeles and begins to terrorize the local population. This suave foreign visitor becomes a member of the wealthy socialite community. He holds seances in his mansion as a means of attracting victims and soon holds two beautiful women (Donna Anders and Judith Lang) under his control. Ander's boyfriend (Michael Macready, the producer's son) and a sympathetic doctor (Roger Perry) eventually discover Count Yorga's secret and travel to his hideaway to put a stake through his heart.

Critics who suggested that this plot could be taken seriously were lamentably mistaken, but as in many films of the period, *Count Yorga, Vampire* did contain many of the traditions of the vampire film. Count Yorga is much like Dracula; he thirsts for blood yet regrets his immortal situation. He also hungers for the love and affection of another individual. His nemesis is a hip young professional (Perry) in much the same tradition as Dr. Van Helsing. He strives to destroy the vampire before any more of his fellow yuppies are killed. The eerie castle and setting remind one of Browning's *Mark of the Vampire* (1935), yet the soul and essence of the vampire film seem strangely absent.

1971 *Return of Count Yorga*
AIP, 97 min. Director: Bob Kelljan. Producer: Michael Macready. Writers: Kelljan, Yvonne Wilder. Starring Robert Quarry, Roger Perry, Mariette Hartley.

The sequel, *Return of Count Yorga*, followed one year later. AIP had been disappointed by the original's poor showing, but they were convinced that a larger budget and better production values would improve the sequel. However, *Return of Count Yorga* was only minimally better than the original.

Return of Count Yorga opens with a comic detective duo accidentally stumbling over the vampire's lair. They remove the stake that had killed the vampire in the first film and are quickly dispatched by the awakened count. Yorga moves his residence to San Francisco and infiltrates local society. Like Dracula, he attends fancy-dress parties, the theater, and other cultural events. He also watches television and dines on the best San Francisco meals. Eventually, a deaf-mute girl (Yvonne Wilder) and the fiancée of the doctor in the first film (Mariette Hartley) fall under his control, and that connection in turn leads to several deaths at a nearby orphanage. News of the vampire attacks reaches the doctor (Perry) in Los Angeles, and he tracks

Yorga to his new home and again destroys him. In a surprise twist ending, as the lovers are united, he reveals that he has been turned into one of the undead.

Director Bob Kelljan demonstrates a better understanding of the vampire mythos in the sequel, and William Butler's superior cinematography adds a fine texture to the film, but it is just not able to rise above its low-budget fare. Perhaps there is not enough inventive attention to detail. Perhaps the story line is too predictable. *Return of Count Yorga* (and its predecessor) appear like pale copies of *Dracula* that have been updated to appeal to contemporary tastes. Their sole purpose seems to have been to compete in the lucrative vampire film market. In fact, AIP was so satisfied with the box-office receipts of the sequel that they continued to produce other new-wave vampire films, including *Blacula* (1972), its sequel, and *Disciple of Death* (1973), for that market. Quarry also returned in a semi-sequel, *The Deathmaster* (1972), in which his long-haired vampire, washed up in his coffin on the beach in southern California, becomes guru to a band of hippies. Predictable, it was technically inadequate in all areas of production.

1970 *House of Dark Shadows*

MGM, 97 min. Director-Producer: Dan Curtis. Writers: Sam Hall, Russell Gordon, based on the television series. Starring Jonathan Frid, Kathryn Leigh Scott, Joan Bennett, Grayson Hall, Thayer David, Roger Davis, David Hensley.

On the other hand, *House of Dark Shadows* (1970) was the theatrical version of the long-running daytime adult drama (refer to Chapter 8 for details on the series "Dark Shadows"). The popular success of the daytime serial and the freedom of the cinema to explore sex and violence prompted producer Dan Curtis to make two full-length features. (*Night of Dark Shadows* [1971] dealt with witchcraft and did not feature vampires.) On television the network censors prevented Curtis from exploring the sensual-sexual nature of the vampire (except in veiled suggestion) and prohibited him from detailing the violence inherent in the vampire formula. But Curtis was determined to make up for the serial's shortcomings and hired some of the finest technicians in the business to make *House of Dark Shadows*.

The film opens on the New England estate Collinwood (actually the Jay Gould estate in Tarrytown, New York). The gardener, anxious to find a lost treasure, unlocks a chained coffin in the family crypt and accidentally unleashes a 375-year-old vampire. Apparently, 200 years before, Barnabas Collins (Jonathan Frid) had tried to marry a local girl, Josette (Kathryn

Leigh Scott), but when she discovered that he was a vampire, she refused the engagement and threw herself off the cliff at Widow's Hill. Believing that Barnabas was the reason for the girl's death, his father chained him in the coffin for all eternity.

Barnabas Collins goes to the main house and explains that he is a long lost relative who has been in England for many years. Elizabeth Collins (Joan Bennett), the handsome matriarch of Collinwood, welcomes him into her home and invites him to stay as their guest. Barnabas does and soon falls for Elizabeth's daughter Carolyn (who resembles Josette). He makes her a vampire and takes her for his bride, but Eliot Stokes (Thayer David), the local doctor, discovers her undead body and destroys it. Meanwhile, Dr. Julia Hoffman (Grayson Hall) falls for Barnabas and undertakes to cure him of his vampirism. She eventually discovers an extra cell in his blood and gives him a series of injections that will cure him. Barnabas Collins's thirst for blood disappears, and he's able to enjoy the sunshine and a normal life.

He begins his new "life" by courting Victoria Winters (Laura Parker), the governess and the image incarnate of Josette. But Julia, who really loves him, fouls the injection, and Barnabas rapidly ages 165 years before her eyes (thanks to makeup wizard Dick Smith). He then kills Julia and reverses the aging process by drinking her fresh blood. Angered and realizing that the others must know his secret, he carries Victoria off to make her his vampire bride. But Jeff (Roger Davis), her fiancé, chases after the vampire and using a crossbow with wooden stakes, kills Barnabas. Or does he? As Barnabas is struck by the wooden bolt, he turns instantly into a vampire bat and flies off into the night!

House of Dark Shadows was one of MGM's big summer successes in 1970. This version of the long-running soap opera was largely episodic, with segments that seem lifted from its original source. Despite Robert Colbert's eerie music and Dan Curtis's atmospheric direction, the film unfortunately doesn't have an identity of its own. The graphic violence and sexually explicit scenes, which appear to evoke the later Hammer films, add little to the overall effect. The characters certainly appear comfortable in their roles, particularly Jonathan Frid, Grayson Hall, and Thayer David, and the set pieces are well developed, but there is a disjointed quality and the suspicion that you (and the rest of the audience) have come in in the middle of the action.

Opposite: **Modern vampire Count Yorga (Robert Quarry) rises from his coffin in the 1971 sequel *The Return of Count Yorga* (1973). Courtesy of American International Pictures.**

1971 *Dracula Versus Dr. Frankenstein (Dracula Contra el Dr. Frankenstein,* aka *Daughters of Dracula)*

French/Spanish, 87 min. Director-Writer: Jésus Franco. Producers: Robert de Nesle, Arturo Marcos. Starring Britt Nichols, Dennis Price, Howard Vernon, Alberto Dalbes, Anne Libert, Brandy, Luis Barboo, Genevieve Delori.

Less interesting but rising to their own special weirdness were two films that followed the year later. *Dracula Contra el Dr. Frankenstein (Dracula Versus Dr. Frankenstein,* 1971), not to be confused with *El Hombre que Vino de Ummo,* was a throwback to the forties and resembled *House of Dracula* (1945) and *Abbott and Costello Meet Frankenstein* (1948). This strange concoction of werewolves, vampires, and other monsters told the preposterous tale of Dracula (Howard Vernon) and his efforts to prevent a mad Dr. Frankenstein (Dennis Price) from destroying the world. However, this film was little more than a color-and-effects-laden rehash of the Universal monster team-ups.

1971 *In Search of Dracula*

(Documentary), Independent International. Director: Calvin Floyd, based on the book by Raymond McNally and Radu Florescu. Starring Christopher Lee.

In Search of Dracula (1971) was also an oddity. Produced in Sweden and narrated by Christopher Lee, the film was billed as the first horror documentary. It not only discussed the common history of the vampire through paintings, drawings, written passages, and film footage of early Murnau, Dreyer, and Browning but also examined the "history" of Vlad Tepes, or Vlad the Impaler. Lee actually appears as Vlad in several semidocumentary scenes. Based on the book by Raymond McNally and Radu Florescu, the film avoids all the trappings of the vampire film, but in doing so also misses several opportunities to bring the message home. A very strange effort. (Recently, a made-for-television special about the real Dracula, starring George Hamilton, covered the same thematic group and featured an appearance by Radu Florescu.)

1972 *Count Dracula (El Conde Dracula,* aka *Nights of Dracula, Dracula)*

Tower of London Productions, 98 min. Director: Jesús Franco. Producer: Harry Alan Towers. Writer: Peter Welbeck, based on the novel *Dracula* by Bram Stoker. Starring Christopher Lee, Herbert Lom, Klaus Kinski, Frederick Williams, Maria Rohm, Solidad Miranda.

Infinitely more sophisticated than Franco's *Dracula Contra el Dr. Frankenstein* (1971) was his *Count Dracula* (finished in 1970 but not released until 1972). Produced in Spain with both Italian and German backing, this film was the most faithful of the adaptations of Bram Stoker's classic. Christopher Lee is exactly right in the role; Herbert Lom is ideally cast as his nemesis; Klaus Kinski (who would play the role of Dracula in *Nosferatu,* 1979) is perfect as the mad Renfield, and the balance of the cast performs handsomely. Although the production values are low, Franco makes good use of his limited budget.

As in the novel, Dracula is portrayed with a mustache and white hair, and actually grows younger as the story progresses. Following Jonathan Harker's (Frederick Williams) visit to Dracula's castle, the scene quickly shifts to London. Once there, a younger-looking Count Dracula takes up residence at Carfax Abbey and proceeds to terrorize Mina Harker (Solidad Miranda) and Lucy Westenra (Maria Rohm). His servant Renfield aids the Count in his London conquests from Dr. Seward's sanitarium, and soon he becomes raving mad. When Lucy dies and Mina becomes ill, Dr. Van Helsing is called in to investigate. The Dutch scientist, confined to a wheelchair because of a recent stroke, is revitalized with the knowledge of a vampire. Together with Dr. Seward and Quincy Morris (the only cinematic appearance to date of Stoker's American character), he drives Dracula from London. On the road to his gothic castle, the evil Count is eventually destroyed by the brave young men, who set his coffin ablaze.

El Conde Dracula represents the best of the period. This smooth, tight thriller achieves some truly memorable sequences in the course of ninety-eight minutes, and it never condescends to the material or attempts to make it contemporary for viewers. The sex and violence are internalized and help provide an atmosphere of terror rather than blood and gore. Franco would return to the vampire motif in *La Fille de Dracula* (*The Daughter of Dracula,* 1972).

1972 *Grave of the Vampire*
Pyramid Entertainment. Director: John Hayes. Producer: Daniel Cady. Writer: David Chase. Starring William Smith, Michael Pataki, Lyn Peters.

Grave of the Vampire (1972) shares this approach but on a much smaller budget and scale. Written by David Chase (who would later be the

El Conde Dracula (*Count Dracula*, 1972). Christopher Lee appears as a silver-haired, mustached Dracula in Jesús Franco's very faithful adaptation of Bram Stoker's novel. Courtesy of Tower of London Productions.

story editor on *Kolchak: The Night Stalker*, 1974, ABC), the film is a handsome tale of horror fantasy. Though it pulls from traditional formulas of past vampire films, its mixture of savagery and terror makes it a unique, interesting nightmare.

Caleb Croft (played by Michael Pataki) is a European vampire who has been transplanted to the United States. Rising from his tomb one night, he discovers a young couple making love in his graveyard. Angered, Croft breaks the spine of the boy, drains him of blood, and rapes the girl in his open coffin. Several months later, the girl gives birth to a small gray infant who craves mother's blood instead of milk. When the baby grows up, he turns out to be a very attractive college student (William Smith). He has learned over the years to control his blood need, but a chance meeting with his father, who teaches occult studies at the university, revives his vampiric longings. Eventually he kills Croft and is sentenced to the electric chair for murder. However, as in *The Return of Dr. X* (1939), he survives the chair and continues his studies.

Grave of the Vampire was popular among college students when it finally received general release in 1973, but the film was never a box-office success for the general audience. The story was simple enough; however, only youth could understand the confused and sinister nature of the movie's central character. Like *The Rocky Horror Picture Show* (1975), which combined depravity and rock music to satirize horror movies, *Grave of the Vampire* functions best as an examination of how the adult culture attempts to drain life from its youth. And it succeeds quite well on that level as well as a straight horror fantasy.

1972 *Blacula*
AIP, 93 min. Director: William Crain. Producer: Joseph T. Narr. Writers: Joan Torres, Raymond Koenig. Starring William Marshall, Vonetta McGee, Emily Yancy, Thalmus Rosalula, Gordon Pinsent, Charles Macauley.

Lacking the sophistication of Franco's *El Conde Dracula*, *Blacula* (1972) nevertheless succeeded in putting forward some intriguing speculations about voodoo and vampirism. Produced by American International Pictures and directed by William Crain, the film also added a racial twist to the old vampire theme.

A black African prince (William Marshall), who was turned into a vampire by the original Dracula (Charles Macauley) in an impressive precredits sequence, is resurrected inadvertently by art collectors in Transylvania and brought to Los Angeles. There Prince Mamuwalde takes up residence and begins to feed upon the local population. "Man or woman, black or white,"

Blacula (1972). William Marshall, the very talented Shakespearean actor, plays Blacula in the first of a highly successful series of blaxploitation films. Photo courtesy of American International Pictures.

he doesn't discriminate in his victims. At first he rampages freely among the unsuspecting people, but then he falls for a woman (Vonetta McGee) who appears to be the reincarnation of his lost wife. This discovery leads to his downfall, as a professor of archeology learns the truth and burns him to death.

Blacula was so successful for AIP among black filmgoers that they quickly realized there was a large untapped audience out there. They decided to capitalize on that audience and hurried other efforts (known as blaxploitation films) into production. Like Hammer's revival of the Universal monsters in the fifties, the gimmick of featuring blacks in the roles of classic monsters in the seventies was well inspired. *Blacula* was followed by its sequels *Scream, Blacula, Scream* (1973), *Blackenstein* (1973), *Blood Couple* (1973), *Dr. Black, Mr. Hyde* (1976), and many, many others. William Crain was soon replaced by Bob Kelljan (of *Count Yorga, Vampire* fame), and greater emphasis was placed on sex and violence.

Poster art for *Le Vampire Noir* (*Blacula,* 1972). Poster art courtesy of American International Pictures.

1973 *Scream, Blacula, Scream*

AIP, 96 min. Director: Bob Kelljan. Producer: Joseph T. Marr. Writers: Joan Torres, Raymond Koenig. Starring William Marshall, Pam Grier, Michael Conrad, Don Mitchell, Richard Lawson, Lynne Moody, Barbara Rhoades, Beverly Gill, Don Blackman.

Scream, Blacula, Scream (1973) was much better than it had a right to be, considering AIP's decision to increase the blood and gore. Prince Mamuwalde (once again portrayed by William Marshall) is brought back to life by an adherent of the black arts (Richard Lawson) when his bones are used in a voodoo ritual. After some random bloodletting, he falls in love with a voodoo girl (Pam Grier) who he believes will bring peace to his soul. However, she cares nothing for him and dispatches Blacula by the novel means of driving a stake into a voodoo doll replica of the prince. She has freed him from his troubled vampiric role and given him peace.

1973 *Blood Couple* (aka *Ganja and Hess, Double Possession*)

Kelly Jordon Production, 110 min. Director-Writer: William Gunn. Producer: Chris Schultz. Starring Duane Jones, Marlene Clark, Bill Gunn, Sam Waymon, Mabel King.

Remakes of well-known "white" horror films brought a whole range of roles for black performers, and the trend continued for several years until 1977. Most were simple remakes of the originals with very little identity of their own; however, one example that stands out above the rest is *Blood Couple*. This unique vampire story chose an entirely different path for its central character. Black anthropologist Hess (Duane Jones), studying the ancient black culture of Mythia, is infected with a strange blood disease by an ancient germ-laden knife wielded by his assistant Mena (William Gunn). Killing Mena, he finds the blood nourishing and makes him invulnerable to pain. He sets himself up as a black god and takes his assistant's wife, Ganja (Marlene Clark), as his queen. Predictably, his passion for her leads to his undoing. Produced by Chris Schultz and directed by William Gunn, the two men responsible for a number of blaxploitation films, *Blood Couple's* offbeat approach and humor are its best qualities and make this film definitely a cut above the rest.

1973 *Werewolf Versus the Vampire Woman* (*La Noche de Walpurgis*, aka *The Black Harvest of Countess Dracula*)

Spanish, Ellman, 86 min. Director: Leon Klimovsky. Producer: Salvadore Romero. Writers: Jacinto Molina, Hans Mankell. Starring Paul Naschy, Baby Fuchs, Barbara Capell, Patty Sheppard, Andrew Reese.

Spain's *Werewolf Versus the Vampire Woman* (1973) lacked *Blood Couple*'s style, but the film was in its own way a masterpiece of the Z movie. Set predictably in Transylvania, the story details the efforts of a werewolf to find a vampire bride. (The title lies: There is no conflict between a werewolf and vampire woman.) When two pathologists arrive at a hospital morgue to perform an autopsy on a recently killed werewolf, they remove a silver bullet. Count Waldemar Daninsky (Paul Naschy), the reluctant werewolf, returns to life and dispatches the two men. He then escapes to terrorize the countryside and search for a bride. Eventually he teams with two Parisian coeds to search for the tomb of a long dead vampire witch, Waldesa (Patty Sheppard). Waldesa is resurrected by fresh blood (provided by the coeds), and she and the werewolf unite to create a vampire baby. Abysmal acting and low production values helped to contribute to the film's poor quality, but like the other films of the period, it played to an audience who would watch anything that had to do with vampires. (Naschy, who had played a werewolf in *Los Noches del Hombre Lobo* [*Nights of the Werewolf*, 1968] and *El Hombre que Vino de Ummo* [*Dracula Versus Frankenstein*, 1971], would continue in *La Furia del Hombre Lobo* [*The Fury of the Werewolf*, 1971], *El Retorno de Walpurgis* [*The Curse of the Devil*, 1973], and *La Maldición de la Bestia* [*Night of the Howling Beast*, 1975].)

1973 *Curse of the Devil (El Retorno de Walpurgis, aka The Return of the Walpurgis)*

Loyus Films, Spanish, 87 min. Director: Carlos Aured. Producer: Luis Mendez. Writer: Jack Moll. Starring Paul Naschy, Faye Falcon, Vinc Molina, May Oliver, Maria Silva, Anna Farra, Patty Sheppard.

Count Waldemar Danisky (Paul Naschy), the reluctant werewolf, returned a few months later to meet Princess Bathory (Faye Falcon) and became involved in her lust for virgin blood. The material was pretty stale in the previous film and is worse here.

Too many motion pictures from the early seventies shared the same outlook as *Werewolf Versus the Vampire Woman*. Filmmakers were convinced that the vampire film did not need a big budget to scare or titillate its audiences. In an era of sexual freedom, they believed (wrongly) that all the films had to feature were plenty of beautiful naked women and buckets

of blood. Historically, this period of the fifth (not so) great horror school
would witness a proliferation of vampire films. Many of them were very
cheap, featured poor writing and acting, and were made on a limited
shooting schedule. If *El Conde Dracula* (1972) was representative of the
best, films like *La Orgía de los Muertos* (1972), *Ceremonia Sangrienta* (1973),
Il Plenilunio delle Vergine (1973), and *El Gran Amor del Conde Dracula*
(1973) represented the worst. But as in other periods, there were a number
of gems (hidden in the rough) waiting to be discovered.

1972 *The Blood-Spattered Bride (La Novia Ensangrentada,* aka *The Bloody Fiancée, 'Til Death Us Do Part)*

83 min. Director-Writer: Vincent Aranda. Producer: José Lopez
Merino. Starring Maribel Martin, Alexandra Bastedo, Simon Andreu.

La Novia Ensangrentada (1973) was yet another retelling of Joseph
Sheridan Le Fanu's *Carmilla* and a copy of Hammer's *The Vampire Lovers*
(1970). A young frigid newlywed (Maribel Martin), unable to consummate
her marriage to husband Simon Andreu (who is also a virgin), flees into the
arms of a vampire seductress (Alexandra Bastedo). The two women begin
a lesbian love affair, and Martin willingly offers her blood to Bastedo. When
the husband arrives to confront the "vampire lovers," they choose to die in
each other's arms rather than be separated. The unusual twist ending
(which rejects the traditional macho fantasy) was not enough to save this
effort and was buried along with the undead.

1972 *Dracula, the Terror of the Living Dead (La Orgía de los Muertos)*

Spanish/Italian, 97 min. Director: José Luis Merino. Producer: Ramon Plana. Writers: Enrico Colombo, Merino. Starring Stan Cooper,
Gerard Tichy, Dianik Zurakowska, Paul Nashy, Pasquale Basile.

Often confused with Edward D. Wood, Jr.'s *Orgy of the Dead* (1966),
La Orgía de los Muertos (1972) was actually a zombie movie masquerading
as an entry in the lucrative vampire market (with the English title *Dracula,
the Terror of the Living Dead*). Set in nineteenth-century Transylvania, the
story follows the familiar efforts of a mad doctor (Gerard Tichy) to resurrect
the dead. Using a device that harnesses "nebula electricity," he creates an
army of zombies and unleashes them on a nearby village. Local hero Stan

Cooper arrives to do battle and turns the zombies on the mad scientist. Somewhat common, the film's title lies: There is no "orgy" of the dead, and Dracula does not make an appearance.

1972 *Night of the Devils* (*La Notte dei Diavoli*, aka *Night of the Vampires*)

Italian. Director: Giorgio Ferroni. Producer: Luigi Mariana. Writers: Romano Migliorini, Giem Battista Musseto, Eduardo M. Bochero, based on Tolstoy's *The Wurdalak*. Starring Gianni Garko, Agostina Belli, Mark Roberts, Cinzia de Carlos, Teresa Gimpera, Luis Saurez.

Although the credits list Tolstoy's *The Wurdalak* as the inspiration, *Night of the Devils* was really a thinly disguised reworking of George Romero's *Night of the Living Dead* (1968). A young, heroic aristocrat, Nicola (Gianni Garko), finds himself stranded in the Russian countryside battling peasant vampires. Director Giorgio Ferroni attempts to draw parallels to the Russian Revolution in this extended version of Tolstoy's story (previously filmed by Bava as a segment of *I Tre Volti della Paura*, 1963), but they are lost in the muddled mess of bloodletting.

1972 *The House That Dripped Blood*

Amicus, 102 min. Director: Peter John Duffell. Producers: Milton Subotsky, Max Rosenberg. Writer: Robert Block. Starring Jon Pertwee, Ingrid Pitt, Denholm Elliott, Joanna Lumley, Tony Adams, Robert Lang.

1973 *Vault of Horror* (aka *Further Tales from the Crypt*)

Amicus, 99 min. Director: Roy Ward Baker. Producers: Milton Subotsky, Max Rosenberg. Writer: Subotsky. Starring Anna and Daniel Massey, Michael Pratt.

The House That Dripped Blood (1972) and *Vault of Horror* (1973) were two anthology films which featured segments about vampires. Amicus had scored big with its first anthology, *Torture Garden* (1967), and followed that with five other films in the same omnibus format. Utilizing actors and production staff from Hammer, these motion pictures probably represented the best of an otherwise poor field of choices.

"The Cloak," the fourth tale from *The House That Dripped Blood*, was adapted by Robert Bloch from a story which had originally appeared in *From Unknown Worlds*. A veteran horror star (Jon Pertwee of *Dr. Who* fame) purchases a cloak that once belonged to a famous vampire actor (possibly Lugosi). When he dons the garment, he suddenly changes into a real vampire and must satisfy an unquenchable thirst for blood. This dark comedy follows predictable lines until his leading lady (Ingrid Pitt) decides to give the cloak a try. He then becomes her first victim.

"Midnight Mess," from *Vault of Horror*, was based on a fifties tale from the E.C. horror comics of Al Fedstein and William Gaines. A desperate man (Daniel Massey) murders his sister (Anna Massey) to get the family fortune. Later that night, when he goes to dinner, he discovers that he has entered a restaurant for vampires. The man tries to play along with them, but when a curtain opens to a huge mirror, his reflection reveals the truth. The final scene, which finds him hanged upside down with a faucet at his neck and the vampires gathered for a drink, is memorable and worth the price of admission.

Both anthologies proved financially rewarding for Amicus and inspired a host of imitators. (HBO's award-winning *Tales from the Crypt*, 1990, is a direct descendant.)

1973 *Dracula's Great Love (El Gran Amor del Conde Dracula)*

Spanish, 83 min. Director-Writer: Javier Aguirre. Producer: Paul Naschy. Starring Paul Naschy, Rosanna Yannie, Ingrid Garbo, Mista Miller.

Dracula's Great Love (1973) was one of the worst films of the period. It attempted to imitate the Hammer gothic style, but the high-camp explicit violence and poor dubbing lowered the film beyond the Z-movie level. The story was just as bad. Count Dracula (Paul Naschy) is residing at an abandoned sanitarium and desperately needs a virgin to restore his dead daughter. When a broken carriage strands four ladies, he has plenty of blood to choose from. Unfortunately he falls for one of them (Haydee Politoff), who in rejecting his love breaks his heart.

There is almost nothing good that can be said about this awful film, but it did make money. It also touched a nerve in audiences that made them overlook its desperate lack of merit. The film had all the right ingredients: a vampire, swelling bosoms, plenty of bloodletting, and the bare bones of a gothic horror fantasy. And it opened the door for dozens more like it from shoestring producers and get-rich-quick investors (the real cinematic vampires). This trend would continue for over half a decade until John

Carpenter's *Halloween* (1978) pioneered a new path of low-budget horror films.

1973 *Full Moon of the Virgins (Il Plenilunio delle Vergine,* aka *The Devil's Wedding Night)*

Virginia Cinematografica, Italian, 85 min. Director: Paolo Solvay. Producer: Ralph Zucker. Writers: Ralph Zucker, Alan Harris. Starring Sara Bay, Mark Damon, Frances Davis, Miriam Barrios, Stan Pappas, A. Getty, Sergio Pislar.

Full Moon of the Virgins, 1973, was yet another excuse for nudity and sexploitation. Twin archeologists (played by Mark Damon) seek the ring of the Nibelungs, rumored to have magical powers. The less intelligent brother learns that the ring is in the possession of Countess Dracula (Sara Bay) but falls victim to her vampiric charms. Following his sibling's trail, the other brother arrives too late to save him or to prevent the ring from being used to evoke a witches sabbath. According to the legend, every twenty-five years the ring has the power to lure every local virgin into the service of the vampire countess. Predictably, the intelligent brother stakes them both and takes the ring for his own erotic pleasures.

1973 *Legend of Blood Castle (Ceremonia Sangrienta)*

Luis Films, Italian, 88 min. Director: Jorge Grau. Producers: José Maria, Gonzalez Sinde. Writers: Juan Tebor, Sandro Continenza. Starring Lucia Bose, Erva Aulin, Espartoco Santoni, Ana Farra, Franca Grey, Silvano Tranquila, Loal Goas, Enrico Vico.

1979 *Thirst*

Australian, F. G. Films, New South Wales Film Corporation, 98 min. Director: Ron Hardy. Producer: Anthony I. Gannane. Writer: John Pinkney. Starring Chantal Contouri, David Hemmings, Henry Silva, Max Phipps, Shirley Cameron.

Legend of Blood Castle (1973) and *Thirst* (1979) followed Peter Sasdy's *Countess Dracula* (1972) to the screen as additional variations of the Elizabeth Bathory myth. Unfortunately, neither was as effective.

Set in seventeenth-century Hungary, *Legend* follows the tragic tale of Count Karl (Espartoco Santoni), the resident vampire, and his efforts to find a reliable blood supply for his wife, Elisabeth (Lucia Bose). She remains young by bathing in the blood of her female victims. Similarly, in the

Australian production *Thirst*, young women are taken to a modern psychiatric clinic where they are "milked" of blood for a descendant of the evil countess (Chantal Contouri).

1973 *The Vampires' Night Orgy (La Orgía Nocturna de los Vampiros, aka Night of the Vampires)*

Spanish, 91 min. Director: Leon Klimovsky. Writers: Juan José Daza, Carlos Pumares, Juan José Porto. Starring Emma Choen, Carlos Ballesteros, Vicky Lusson.

Leon Klimovsky's low-low-budget feature *La Orgía, The Vampires' Night Orgy* (1973) crossed cannibalism with bloodsucking. A tour bus breaks down in the Transylvanian village of Tonia (located somewhere in the Carpathian mountains), and the bewildered occupants become the dinner guests of the local vampire population. Typical of Klimovsky (who made many of the werewolf movies for Naschy), the film features a bevy of beautiful naked bodies and plenty of violent scenes of bloodsucking.

La Orgía Nocturna de los Vampiros should not be confused with *La Notte dei Diavoli* (1972) or *La Orgía de los Muertos* (1972).

1973 *Young Hannah, Queen of the Vampires (La Tumba de las Isla Maldita, aka The Crypt of the Living Dead)*

Coast Industries, U.S./Spanish, 93 min. Director: Ray Danton. Producer-Writer: Lou Shaw. Starring Andrew Prine, Mark Damon, Patty Sheppard, Teresa Gimpera, Edward Walsh, John Alderman.

Young Hannah, Queen of the Vampires (1973) was a slow-moving but fascinating variation of the vampire mythos. In 1260, young Hannah (Teresa Gimpera), the beautiful bride of King Louis VII, is suspected of being a vampire and buried alive on Vampire Island after the king returns from the Crusades. Seven hundred years later, Professor Bolton accidentally releases the bloodsucker while on an archeological dig and becomes Hannah's first victim. She then uses her vampiric powers to drain all the male inhabitants of a Greek island. When Bolton's son (Andrew Prine) arrives looking for his father, he becomes so entranced with Hannah that his friend (Mark Damon) must stake her to save his life. Directed by former actor Ray Danton, the film wearily plods along. If not for the unique story line, *Young Hannah* would be better left buried.

1974 *Leonor*

Spanish/French/Italian, 100 min. Director: Louis Buñuel. Writers: Buñuel, Phillippe Buridzany, Pierre Maintigneaux, Jean Claude Carriere, Clement Biddle Wood. Starring Michel Piccoli, Liv Ullmann, Ornella Mutti, Antonio Ferrandis.

Leonor (1974) was Louis Buñuel's artistic remake of Roger Corman's *Tomb of Ligeia* (1964) with Liv Ullmann essaying the role of Leonor and Michel Piccoli playing a fourteenth-century knight who's obsessed with his dead wife. This film is often credited to Buñuel's son Juan, but the expressionistic vision (similar to *Tristana*) is clearly that of the great director.

1974 *Tender Dracula* (*Tendre Dracula,* aka *The Big Funk, Confessions of a Blood Sucker*)

French. Starring Peter Cushing, Christopher Lee.

Tendre Dracula (1974) wasted the talents of Peter Cushing and Christopher Lee in this poor story of a movie actor who plays the role of a vampire one too many times. No further information is available.

1974 *Old Dracula* (aka *Vampira*)

MGM/EMI, 88 min. Director: Clive Donner. Producer: Jack Weiner. Writer: Jeremy Lloyd. Starring David Niven, Freddie Jones, Peter Bayliss, Veronica Carlsen, Linda Hayden, Teresa Graves, Jennie Linden, Nicky Henson, Bernard Bresslaw.

By sharp contrast, *Old Dracula* (1974) satirizes youth and attempts to glamorize its ageless vampire, Dracula, much in the same tradition as Hammer's *Dracula A.D. 1972* (1972). The film is typical of the vampire films of the seventies in that it embraces many of the familiar traditions of the vampire motif and treats those attitudes as contemporary farce. Producer Jack Weiner defended his project, saying: "We've tried not to disappoint those people who have been going to see horror films for years; but at the same time, we're trying to get away from those films that publicize lots of nudity and gore." The motion picture was completed in 1973 as *Vampira*, but when MGM officials screened it, they were very disappointed. In fact, the film was withdrawn from general release and stayed in the vaults for several months. However, the success of Mel Brooks's *Young Frankenstein* (1974) encouraged the studio to rerelease the film under the new title *Old Dracula* in 1974.

The late David Niven plays a charming and debonair modern Dracula.

He conducts tours through his horror castle, and even judges finalists in a *Playboy* magazine Most Biteable Playmate of the Month contest by using samples of each girl's blood in a cocktail. His wife, Vampira (Teresa Graves), has been dead for fifty years because of an overdose of anemic blood and awaits revival in a nearby crypt. Once he names the perfect playmate, he uses a transfusion of her blood to revive Vampira. But her revival causes all manner of confusion as this camp comedy develops into a slapstick farce of mistaken identity and bedroom antics.

The popularity of this farce would encourage other filmmakers to look at the Dracula myth in an irreverent manner.

1975 *Dracula in the Provinces (Dracula en Brianza)*

Coralta Cinematografica, Italian, 100 min. Director: Lucio Fulci. Producer: R. Marini. Writers: Pupi Avati, Bruno Corbucci, Mario Amendola, Lucio Fulci. Starring Lando Buzzanca, Sylva Koscina, Christa Linder, Rossano Brazzi.

Dracula en Brianza (1975) was a knockoff of *Old Dracula* (1974) featuring Italian comic Lando Buzzanca as a homosexual victim of the great Count.

The phenomenal box-office bonanza of *Young Frankenstein* (1974) and to a lesser extent *Old Dracula* (1974) inspired filmmakers to introduce other members of the horror family to the silver screen. Dracula's son appears in *Count Down — Son of Dracula* (1974), *Deafula* (1975), *El Jovencito Dracula* (*Young Jonathan Dracula*, 1975), and *Dracula and Son* (1976); his daughter in *La Fille de Dracula* (*Dracula's Daughter*, 1971); his granddaughter in *Nocturna* (1978); his wife in *Lemora, Lady Dracula* (1973), *Lady Dracula* (1977) and *Mama Dracula* (1980); and his dog shows up in *Dracula's Dog* (*Zoltan — Hound from Hell*, 1976). The seeds of this trend actually date back years earlier to the horror classic *Dracula's Daughter* (1935), but many of the current crop of filmmakers thought their efforts were unique. Most of the motion pictures lack any style or originality and have largely vanished except on late-night horror movies. But one or two were a cut above.

1971 *Daughter of Dracula (La Fille de Dracula)*

French, 90 min. Director-Writer: Jesús Franco. Producer: Victor de

Opposite: Old Dracula (1974). David Niven, as a modern Count Dracula, awaits the rebirth of his bride in a coffin built for two. Onlooking butler (Peter Bayliss) is done up in a parody of Lugosi. Photo courtesy of American International Pictures.

Costa. Starring Britt Nichols, Anne Libert, Howard Vernon, Jesús Franco, Alberto Dalbes, Daniel White.

Although the concept dates back to Universal's *Dracula's Daughter* (1936) and *Son of Dracula* (1942), Jesús Franco (Jess Frank) is generally identified as the creative force responsible for initiating the current trend with his 1971 *La Fille de Dracula (Daughter of Dracula)*. Influenced by the style of Hammer's Karnstein films, Franco turned to Joseph Sheridan Le Fanu's classic *Carmilla* for source material and further inspiration. The result was a competent though sadistically violent thriller.

Several months after the Transylvanian Count's demise, a dying woman tells her daughter Maria Karnstein (Britt Nichols) that she is a descendant of Dracula. Frightened and confused, Maria flees her home and takes refuge at a large estate where she befriends a lonely young girl. The two become fast friends and lesbian lovers. Eventually Maria's blood legacy overwhelms her, and she turns her lover into a fellow creature of the night.

Because the motion picture uses violence and sex to cover a lack of narrative coherence, many critics contend that *La Fille de Dracula* is among Franco's weaker offerings. There may be some truth to that contention. Numerous scenes seem to collide with one another, with little setup and poor editing. Jesús Franco made three films, including *Dracula Contra Frankenstein* (1971) and *Les Experiences Erotiques de Frankenstein* (1972), in the relatively short time of twelve months, utilizing the same actors, production staff, and sets, and he may not have had as much time to devote to postproduction. The film appears like an afterthought and is certainly not in the same league with his far superior *El Conde Dracula* (1970).

Note: This film should not be confused with *Daughters of Dracula* (1974).

1973 *Lemora, Lady Dracula* (aka *Legendary Curse of Lemora*)

90 min. Director: Richard Blackburn. Producer: Robert Fern. Writers: Fern, Blackburn. Starring Lesley Gibb, Cheryl Smith, William Whitton, Steve Johnson, Hy Pike, Maxine Ballantine, Parker West, John Drury.

Lemora, Lady Dracula (1973) was an artistic offbeat vampire movie which recalled the best of Bava and Bunuel. Set in rural America in the 1920s, the story follows the efforts of Lemora (Lesley Gibb), a wife of the Transylvanian Count, to seduce a young girl into the pleasures of lesbian sex and vampirism. When Lila (Cheryl Smith), the thirteen-year-old daughter of fugitive gangster Alvin Lee (William Whitton), receives word from Lemora that her father is dying, she escapes the puritanical home of the Reverend Mueller (played by director Richard Blackburn) and begins a perilous journey to see him.

On her bizarre odyssey through the nightmarish forest and hills of the rural South, she encounters all manner of monsters and zombies (actually "undead" members of Lemora's coven), but she finally arrives at the vampire's home. Lady Dracula becomes a surrogate mother and tries repeatedly to make her one of the undead. Predictably, the Reverend Mueller arrives and puts an end to the "legendary curse of Lemora."

Hastily written and directed, *Lemora, Lady Dracula* does have a certain innocent charm (as expressed by Smith) and an erotic sensationalism. Regrettably, the Catholic Board of Review in the United States didn't think so (perhaps because of the stereotypic portrayal of religious figures) and condemned it with one of their stiffest ratings. Competition from the far superior *The Exorcist* (1973) further buried the film, which is rarely seen today, even on late-night television.

Note: The film should not be confused with Buñuel's *Leonor* (1974).

1973 *The Saga of the Draculas (La Saga de Los Dracula)*

Profilmes, Spanish, 100 min. Director: Leon Klimovsky. Producer: José Antonio Perez Giner. Writer: Lazarus Kaplan. Starring Tina Saenz, Tony Isbert, Helga Line, Narciso Ibáñez-Menta.

La Saga de Los Dracula (1973), Leon Klimovsky's companion piece to *La Orgía Nocturna de Los Vampiros* (1973), was really a thinly disguised remake of Polanski's *Rosemary's Baby* (1968). Desperate to have an offspring to carry on the family name, Count Dracula invites his pregnant niece Berta (Tina Saenz) and her husband (Tony Isbert) to his castle. (We are told that Dracula's offspring has become a stupid monster because of too much inbreeding.) The husband makes himself right at home but is dubious of the vampire's motives. Once she gives birth, Berta is repulsed to learn that her baby is a bloodsucker. She kills the newborn infant, then stakes both her husband and Count Dracula before dying at the hands of the loyal hunchback servant (Narciso Ibáñez-Menta). In a bizarrely twisted ending, one drop of blood falls on the baby's lips and brings Dracula's descendant to life. Extremely violent, Klimovsky's entry makes an interesting addition to the trend.

1974 *Vampyres, Daughters of Dracula* (aka *Vampyres, Daughters of Darkness*)

Cambist Films, 87 min. Director: Joseph Lorraz. Producer: Brian Smedley-Aston. Writer: Diana Daubeney. Starring Marianne Morris, Anulka, Murray Brown, Brian Deacon, Sally Faulkner, Bessie Love, Michael Byrne, Carl Lanchberry, Elliot Sullivan.

The other *Daughters of Dracula* (1974) were Fran and Miriam (Marianne Morris and Anulka), two young lesbian vampires who live in the late Transylvanian Count's decaying castle. As black-leather-jacketed bikers, they lead unsuspecting motorcycle enthusiasts to a dead end. As hitchhikers, they lure motorists to their doom. As fellow campers, they feed upon picnicking tourists who vacation on the grounds of the castle. Life as a gay female vampire is exciting until a young male victim (Murray Brown) introduces Fran to the pleasures of heterosexual love. Cheap, predictable, sexploitative, *Daughters of Dracula* is every male's fantasy film. Pity director Joseph Lorraz didn't lift some of the style of Hammer's *Vampire Lovers* (1970) when he stole the story line. (An X-rated version with explicit scenes of lesbian sex was released under the title *Vampyres*.)

1974 *Count Down—Son of Dracula* (aka *Son of Dracula*)

Cinema Industries. Director: Freddie Francis. Producer: Ringo Starr. Writer: Jay Fairbanks. Starring Harry Nilsson, Ringo Starr, Freddie Jones, Dennis Price, Peter Frampton, Keith Moon.

Count Down (1974) is not a remake of the Lon Chaney, Jr., film but a rock fantasy with all the standard vampire clichés. Produced by former Beatle Ringo Starr and directed by Academy Award winner Freddie Francis, the story concerns the efforts of Dracula's son to avenge his father. Several years earlier, Dr. Frankenstein (Freddie Jones) killed Count Dracula, and Count Down (Harry Nilsson), the vampire's son, was secreted away and raised by Dr. Van Helsing. With the aid of Merlin (Starr), Count Down challenges Frankenstein to a duel as they vie for the supremacy of the "netherworld." The film makes little sense, and its production design looks like something out of a Jack Kirby comic. But once again the bizarre mixture of rock, sex, and vampire images proved a winner on college campuses. *Count Down—Son of Dracula* also evokes *The Rocky Horror Picture Show* and *The Lost Boys*, both of which would use a horror theme to the rock beat.

1975 *Deafula*

Signscope, b/w, 90 min. Director-Writer: Peter Wechsberg. Producer: Gary Holmstrom. Starring Wechsberg, Holmstrom, James Randall, Dudley Hemstreet, Lee Darrel.

Deafula (1975), on the other hand, has an interesting concept but suffers from poor production values. The film was shot in black-and-white and featured "Signscope," the first closed-caption signing for deaf viewers. Written, directed, and starring Peter Wechsberg, who is deaf, the motion picture examines the sensitive issues of deaf people. A vampire is loose in Portland, Oregon, and the authorities are baffled. But one man, Steve Adams, begins to suspect the truth — that he is really a vampire. Periodically he grows fangs and a distinctive nose, and dons a black cape to become Deafula. He has an unquenchable taste for warm blood and stalks pretty maidens in the center city. Eventually he learns that the real Count Dracula (Gary Holmstrom) was his father, who cursed him from birth. He becomes saddened and allows himself to be trapped in a church where he dies exposed to all the religious symbols. There is great pathos in his portrayal of the character and unintentional humor from the very odd circumstances.

1975 *Young Jonathan Dracula (El Jovencito Dracula)*
Los Films del Mediterraneo, Spanish, 95 min. Director-Writer-Producer: Carlos Benpar. Starring Carlos Benpar, Susanna Estrada, Victor Israel, Marina Ferri, Veronica Miriel, Norma Kerr.

1975 *Jonathan, Vampire of the Night (Jonathan Vampiren sterben nicht)*
West German, Beta Films, 103 min. Director-Writer: Han Geissendorfer. Producer: Ullrich Steffen, based on the first chapter of *Dracula*, by Bram Stoker. Starring Jergen Jung, Paul Albert Krumm, Herta Von Walter, Oscar Von Schab, Hans-Dieter Jenreyko, Elconarc Schminke, Ilona Grubel, Arthur Brauss.

Both *Young Jonathan Dracula* and *Jonathan, Vampire of the Night* (1975) deal with the male offspring of the infamous Transylvanian Count. In the first film, young Jonathan Dracula (Carlos Benpar), a student of the occult at the University of Venice, inherits his father's estate and moves in with Mina Harker (Susanna Estrada) and her friend Lucy (Marina Ferri). Things move along smoothly until a descendant of Dr. Van Helsing (Victor Israel) arrives, determined to wipe out the last survivor of the vampire clan and turn the castle into a tourist trap. Jonathan enlists the aid of the faithful servant Renfield, and the plot spins off in predictably funny directions.
In the second film, Count Dracula (Paul Albert Krumm) needs a

descendant to carry on the family name and attempts to adopt Jonathan (Jurgen Jung). His attempts to show the young man the vampire way are sometimes comedic but more often just dumb. The larger subplot about the revival of the Nazi movement and student unrest was difficult to understand and caused this 1969 production to remain on the shelf for six years.

Neither motion picture was very successful, and they disappeared at the box office shortly after their release. Of the two, *El Jovencito Dracula* is probably the more enjoyable.

1976 *Dracula and Son*

Columbia, 88 min. Director: Edouard Molinaro. Producer: Alan Poire. Starring Christopher Lee, Bernard Menez, Raymond Bussieres, Joe Rignoli, Marie Helene Beillat.

Dracula and Son (1976) is humorless despite the fact that it's a horror comedy. Christopher Lee's talent is completely wasted, and what remains is a shallow caricature of his once great role. (He actually does more with his character in a cameo appearance in *The Magic Christian* [1969] than he does in the entire movie.) The story too is a dismal failure. Apparently, the Communist government which is ruling modern Transylvania exiles Dracula and his son to England because their image is all wrong for the Party. Once in England, they are welcomed by a film company and hired to play cinematic vampires. Directed by Edouard Molinaro, who would later helm *La Cage aux Folles* (1978), the film lacks wit, style, and enthusiasm. (This film marks the last appearance of Christopher Lee as a vampire and is, sadly, not one of his best. In the nineties, Lee began to satirize his roles in Hammer Films by playing a mad scientist in Joe Dante's *Gremlins II* [1990]. It is hoped that he will return to his greatest role one final time.)

1976 *Dracula's Dog* (aka *Zoltan — Hound from Hell*)

Crown International Pictures, 88 min. Director: Albert Brand. Producers: Brand, Frank Ray Perelli. Writer: Perelli. Starring Libbe Chase, Jose Ferrer, Reggie Nalder, Michael Pataki, Jan Shultan.

Similarly, *Dracula's Dog* (aka *Zoltan — Hound from Hell*, 1976) lacks any wit or style, but it does have enthusiasm as it explores new territory. Russian soldiers discover Dracula's crypt and under the direction of Inspector Branco (Jose Ferrer) hastily burn all the coffins. Unwittingly they resurrect the Count's lamia (servant) (Reggie Nalder) and his faithful companion Zoltan. Like Lassie, Rin Tin Tin, and other cinema versions of man's best friend, Zoltan travels to distant Los Angeles (with Nalder) in an effort to locate the Count's only living descendant, Michael Drake (Michael Pataki), who can restore his master. Along the way, Zoltan must fight off other dogs, avoid the dogcatcher, do a Cal-Can commercial, and feed upon the unsuspecting humans he encounters. Finally, on a family camping trip, Drake must choose between his wife (Jan Shutan) and two children and his royal heritage.

Released by Crown International Pictures, this ridiculous film presented some interesting variations on the basic vampire theme. But despite its novelty of subject, *Dracula's Dog* is better left at the pound. The film barely had time to get out and make back its production costs before the dogcatchers chased it away from bigger game.

1977 *Lady Dracula*

German, 86 min. Director: Franz-Joseph Gottlieb. Producers: Guenther Strum, Kurt Kodel. Writer: Redis Read. Starring Evelyne Kraft, Christine Bucheggar, Theo Lingen, Brad Harris, Eddie Arent, Walter Giller.

Lady Dracula (1977) was yet another entry in the series of films about Dracula's fictional wives and offspring. During the precredits sequence, set in 1876, Dracula bites a little girl, who is then staked to her coffin (to prevent her from returning as the undead). One hundred years later, her coffin is unearthed, and she is reborn as a beautiful woman named Barbara (Evelyne Kraft). To maintain a fresh supply of blood, she goes to work in a hospital and begins to feed on the patients and local blood supply. The mysterious deaths are investigated by a detective (Brad Harris), who discovers her secret, then falls madly in love with her. The two lovers join forces and live happily ever after.

The unprecedented success of *Star Wars* in 1977 forever changed the face of fantasy motion pictures and convinced movie magnates that fantasy, whether in the form of space opera or horror, was a surefire moneymaker. American, English, French, and German filmmakers caught the fever and rushed multimillion-dollar exploitations of the theme before the cameras and into general release. In the two years after *Star Wars*, big-budget fantasy productions were plentiful, and there were a number of big-scale vampire films, including *Nosferatu—The Vampire* (1979) and *Dracula* (1979). Unfortunately these early efforts were nothing special. Stripped of their special effects, elaborate sets, and high production values, they were nothing more than previous classics remade. But both were, fortunately, moderate successes and paved the way for future big-budget vampire films. (The real success story, however, was in the low-budget creations of Tobe

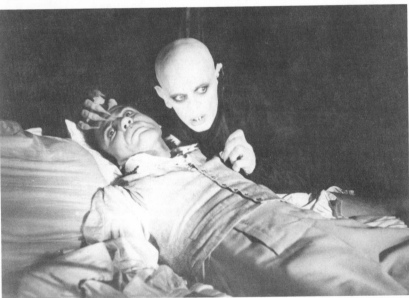

Top: Nosferatu — The Vampire (1979). Klaus Kinski plays Count Dracula in Werner Herzog's remake of Murnau's classic. (Note that the bizarre makeup harkens back to Max Schreck's Orlock in the original.) Photo courtesy of Twentieth Century–Fox. *Bottom:* Count Dracula (Klaus Kinski) hypnotizes the real estate clerk Jonathan (Bruno Ganz) in *Nosferatu — The Vampire* (1979). Photo courtesy of Twentieth Century–Fox.

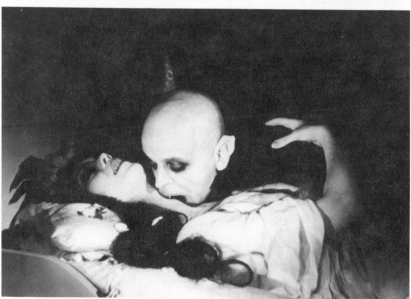

Top: Isabelle Adjani struggles through a trapdoor to reach the Count in Werner Herzog's *Nosferatu—The Vampire* (1979). Photo courtesy of Twentieth Century–Fox. *Bottom:* Lucy (Isabelle Adjani) sacrifices herself to Count Dracula (Klaus Kinski) to rid her town of the pestilence in *Nosferatu—The Vampire* (1979). Photo courtesy of Twentieth Century–Fox.

Count Dracula (Klaus Kinski) sleeps in his coffin in Werner Herzog's *Nosferatu—The Vampire* (1979). Photo courtesy of Twentieth Century-Fox.

Hooper and John Carpenter. Their nightmare visions would have a much longer-range effect on the horror films to come.)

1979 *Nosferatu: Phantom der Nacht* (*Nosferatu—The Vampire,* aka *Nosferatu, Phantom of the Night*)

German, Twentieth Century-Fox, 124 min. Director-Producer-Writer: Werner Herzog, based on the original *Nosferatu—A Symphony of Horror,* by F. W. Murnau. Starring Klaus Kinski, Isabelle Adjani, Bruno Ganz, Roland Topar, Walter Ladengast.

Nosferatu—The Vampire (1979) was Werner Herzog's multimillion-dollar remake of Murnau's classic *Nosferatu—A Symphony of Terror* (1922) and was a further permutation of the Dracula legend. Herzog explained his reasons for a remake in a 1980 interview: "I was lured to horror films because of what you can do with the medium. If you state, as some of my contemporaries do, that cinema is so much dreaming, then horror is one of the best ways of dreaming—in way of a nightmare." For his adaptation, Herzog returned to the basic roots of the vampire film and attempted, like Murnau, Browning, and Dreyer, to convey a true cinematic nightmare.

Poster art for *Nosferatu—The Vampire* (1979). Courtesy of Twentieth Century–Fox.

As in the original, Renfield, the real estate agent and disciple of Dracula, triggers the whole drama by sending his employee to a castle in the Carpathians. Once there, Jonathan (Bruno Ganz) reveals a picture of his fiancée, Lucy (Isabelle Adjani), and the weary centuries-old vampire (Klaus Kinski) falls in love with her. Dracula bites the agent, then travels by boat from his dark and musty lair in Transylvania with a campaign of destruction in hand. Obsessed with Lucy, he moves inexorably toward the town of Weimer, and she begins to experience visions of his coming, symbolized by an almost unbelievable variety of living creatures.

When she refuses the malevolent Count's advances, Dracula takes revenge by releasing thousands of plague-infested rodents into her serenely bourgeois city. The rats (which symbolize the plague of the vampire) roam the streets spreading illness and death. Hundreds of the townspeople die, and the city is quarantined from the rest of Europe, local officials fearing that the Black Death has returned. But Lucy knows the real reason, and no one will believe her.

This nineteenth-century woman transcends the confinement of her bourgeois home and society to take upon herself the destruction of the vampire. In search of Dracula's hideout, she braves the deadly rodents, looking in abandoned buildings and ruins. Dressed only in a luminous costume (which recalls the pre–Raphaelites) and covered with a black shawl, the pale Lucy surrenders herself to the vampire. He makes love to her, but caught in the ecstasy of his passion, Dracula is trapped by the purifying rays of the sun. The malevolent Count is unable to hide himself away and disintegrates into dust in Lucy's arms.

Nosferatu — The Vampire was both compelling and repulsive to audiences. The heavy atmosphere and dreamlike quality, combined with Kinski's demented, misshapen vampire, are to this day still unnerving. But Herzog achieved what he set out to do. This lengthy German film (124 minutes) is surprisingly hypnotic, a true cinematic nightmare. Although hardly in the same class as Murnau, the motion picture does add an interesting dementia to the vampire mythos.

1979 *Dracula*
Universal Pictures, 112 min. Director: John Badham. Producers: Walter Mirisch, Marvin Mirisch, Tom Pevsner. Screenplay: W. D. Richter, based on the novel by Bram Stoker and the stage play by Hamilton Deane and John Balderston. Starring Frank Langella, Laurence Olivier, Kate Nelligan, Donald Pleasence, Trevor Eve.

On the other hand, *Dracula* (1979) is an exercise in futility. Based on the original stage play and starring Frank Langella, the film is a first-class,

In a highly erotic scene from *Dracula* (1979), the famous vampire (Frank Langella) arrives to seduce Mina (Kate Nelligan). Photo courtesy of Universal Pictures.

stylishly atmospheric remake of Stoker's classic, but unfortunately the Count is portrayed as a matinee idol. Langella is much too pretty to be menacing and causes women to swoon rather than cringe in terror. He does not convey any of the innate horror or perversity that Lugosi and Lee radiate. He resembles a latter-day Valentino and brings a romantic elegance to the role. And what remains of the film is a lush, campy, romantic version of a once great horror fantasy.

Top: Dracula (1979). Following the death of his daughter, Professor Van Helsing (Laurence Olivier) confronts the evil Count Dracula with a unique crucifix. Photo courtesy of Universal Pictures. *Bottom:* Count Dracula (Frank Langella) climbs down a castle wall in search of another victim in *Dracula* (1979). Photo courtesy of Universal Pictures.

Dracula (1979). **Frank Langella as the sexy and sensual Count Dracula in the 1979 remake. Photo courtesy of Universal Pictures.**

The story begins after Harker's journey to Transylvania with Dracula's arrival on the doomed clipper ship. The Count soon takes up residence at Carfax Abbey, employs the aid of the local strong man (Renfield), and becomes the talk of polite English society. After midnight, however, his sexual and vampiric needs are satisfied as he seduces both Lucy and Van Helsing's daughter Mina (Kate Nelligan). Eventually, Van Helsing (Laurence

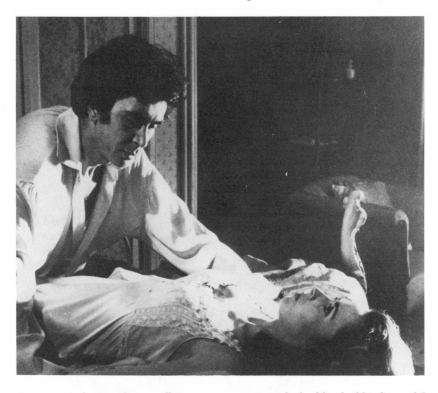

Count Dracula (Frank Langella) prepares to mix with the blood of his beautiful lover (Kate Nelligan) in the 1979 remake of *Dracula*. Photo courtesy of Universal Pictures.

Olivier) and Dr. Seward (Donald Pleasence) learn of his evil and chase him from his home. Dracula flees England on another clipper ship with Mina, and Van Helsing follows in a smaller, faster ship. In the dramatic climax, the evil Count impales Van Helsing to the wall (with the doctor's wooden stake), and he himself is impaled on a large winch hook. Then, with Van Helsing's last dying effort, Dracula is literally run up a flagpole to expire in the sun. But the Count doesn't die; instead (like Barnabas Collins in *House of Dark Shadows*) he changes into a bat and flies off, suggesting a sequel.

Dracula was very successful in its initial release, and it made a star of Frank Langella. The direction of John Badham (who would later make *War Games* and *Blue Thunder*) is first rate, as are the special visual effects of Maurice Binder (who did the titles for the James Bond films). The film also spawned a host of imitators. However, this excellent rendition of the classic story lacks the terror and menace of the original. In spite of the howling wolves, squeaking bats, and murky graveyards, the essence or soul of the vampire was missing, as if the old wine had spilled from the new bottles.

1979 *Dracula Bites the Big Apple*
Independent Films. Starring Peter Lowey.

The first of many spin-offs of Frank Langella's *Dracula* (1979) found Dracula (Peter Lowey) having difficulty coping with life in the Big Apple. Uncredited rip-off of Stan Dragoti's *Love at First Bite* (1979).

1979 *Dracula Blows His Cool (Graf Dracula beistt jetzt in Ober Bayern,* aka *The Diabolic Loves of Nosferatu)*
German, 97 min. Director: Carlo Ombra. Producer: Martin Friedman. Writers: Gruenback, Rosenthal. Starring Gianni Garko, Betty Verges, Giacomo Rizzo, Linda Grondier.

Graf Dracula beistt jetzt in Ober Bayern (1979) was a pornographic imitation of Dragoti's *Love at First Bite.* Fashion photographer Stan (Gianni Garko) returns to his ancestral home where great-grandfather Count Dracula (Garko again) keeps plenty of pretty naked women. Originally entitled *Dracula Sucks,* the film had to be retitled to avoid confusion with the Marshak film.

1979 *Dracula Sucks*
VCX, Media Films. Director: Philip Marshak. Producer: Daryl Marshak. Writers: Philip and Daryl Marshak. Starring Jamie Gillis, John Holmes, Serena, Annette Haven.

Dracula Sucks (1979) was a hard-core pornographic adaptation of Bram Stoker's classic featuring luscious Annette Haven and adult-feature regulars Jamie Gillis and John Holmes. A slightly toned-down version was released several years later.

1979 *Dracula's Last Rites*
New Empire Features, 88 min. Director: Domonic Paris. Producer: Kelly Van Horn. Writers: Ben Donnelly, Paris. Starring Gerald Fielding, Patricia Lee Hammond, Victor Jorge, Michael Lally, Mimi Weddell.

Dracula's Last Rites (1979) was a low-low-budget quickie from New Empire Pictures. In a small town in upstate New York, all the citizens, including a mortician named Alucard, are vampires. They lure unsuspecting motorists from the highway and drink their blood. Combination rip-off of *Dracula* (1979) and Tobe Hooper's *Salem's Lot* (1979). (The film was previewed in select cities in 1979, then released in 1980.)

Eventually, the mistakes, miscalculations, and near misses of the period would lead filmmakers to reexamine their efforts and create a whole new approach to the vampire cinema.

The following films were also released during the period, but no further information beyond the production credits is available:

1973 *Disciple of Death*

AIP. Producers: James Nicholson, Samuel Arkoff. Starring Michael Raven.

1974 *The Nosfératu (Le Nosférat ou les Eaux Glacées du Calcul Egoiste)*

Les Films, Belgium, 100 min. Director: Maurice Rabinowicz. Writers: Rabinowicz, Yvette Michelems. Starring Veronique Peynet, Maite Nahr, Martine Bernard, Guy Pion.

1975 *Bloodsucking Freaks*

Independent Productions. Director-Writer-Producer: Joel Reed. Starring Lynnette Sheldon, Karen Fraser, Michelle Craig, S. O'Brien.

1975 *The Thirsty Dead*

Starring John Considine, Jennifer Billingsley, Judith McConnell.

1976 *Nightmare in Blood*

Independent Productions. Starring Barrie Youngfellow, Hy Pike, Ray Goman, Drew Estelmann, Jerry Walter.

1977 *Blood Relations (Bloedverwanten)*

Jaap Van Rij Productions, French, 97 min. Director: Wim Linder. Producer: Jaap Van Rij. Writer: John Brasom. Starring Maxim

Hamel, Gregorie Aslan, Sophie Deschamps, Robert Dalban, Eddie Constantine.

1978 *Dracula*
Mexican. Starring Enrique Alvarez Felix.

1978 *The Dracula Dynasty (La Dracula Dinastía)*
Mexican. Starring Fabian Forbes.

8

Television Vampires

From "Boris Karloff's Thriller" (1960, NBC)
to "Dark Shadows" (1991, NBC)

Television has produced a number of noteworthy vampire stories during its fifty-year history in forms as varied as the anthology series, the made-for-television movie, the miniseries, the daytime soap, and the weekly program. The early efforts were naive, even bumbling, by today's standards, but some recent appearances have been extraordinarily sophisticated, while others have been mostly ridiculous. Television, like the early cinema, has featured hypnotists, mad scientists, and psychotics who have pretended to be vampires or killer bats. It has also made several exceptional versions of *Dracula*, a ratings-rich *Night Stalker* (1972, ABC), and a town full of vampires in *Salem's Lot* (1979, CBS). Unfortunately, the superior efforts have been few and far between, and the watchword of the three networks has been *caution*.

Horror films (particularly vampire movies) have generally proven moneymakers in the cinema, but the commercial possibilities on television have always been uncertain. Fearing poor ratings from the A. C. Nielsen Company, retribution from network censors, or outright boycotts from special viewer groups, programming executives have been cautious about the use of vampires in prime-time shows other than situation comedies or as gratuitous "monsters" in science-fiction or fantasy shows. Potentially, television, unlike its counterpart, is an ideal medium to bring those "foul things of the night" into the dark living rooms of America, but seldom has it been used to its fullest advantage. The necessity to divide the action between commercials (and at the same time retain viewer interest) has also proven a distinct handicap. Therefore, rather than face such overwhelming difficulties, writers and directors have found it easier to pursue other ventures.

However, the field of television horror is far from undistinguished, and it has produced its share of masterpieces. Apart from appearances in such primitive efforts as "Captain Video" (1949, Dumont), "Tales of Tomorrow" (1951, ABC), and "Superman" (1953, ABC), or the first television broadcasts of Universal's horror films in 1957, little original or imaginative was attempted before the early sixties. Television was too busy experimenting with its form and identity and trying to compete with motion pictures for an audience. The prestigious triumphs of "Studio One," "Playhouse 90," and "The Twilight Zone" earned television its reputation for high-quality drama and paved the way for early diversions into the realm of vampires.

1960 "Boris Karloff's Thriller"
NBC Television, 30 min. Producer: Hubbell Robinson. Host: Boris Karloff. Episode: "Masquerade." Writer: Donald S. Sandford. Director: Herschel Daugherty. Starring Tom Poston, Elizabeth Montgomery, John Carradine.

The first pioneering effort was a segment of Boris Karloff's anthology series "Thriller" (1960, NBC). Skillfully combining the elements of suspense and horror, producer Hubbell Robinson used the medium of television to create a variation of an old traditional theme. Written by Donald S. Sanford, "Masquerade" premiered as "Thriller"'s Halloween offering during its second season. The story tells of a young honeymoon couple (Tom Poston and Elizabeth Montgomery) whose car stalls in a pouring rainstorm. Unable to restart it, they seek shelter in a sinister old house run by vampires. John Carradine appears as the lead vampire. The episode was a successful one, and the interesting plot appeared several years later in the cult classic *The Rocky Horror Picture Show* (1975). (In spite of "Thriller's" success, neither "The Twilight Zone" [1959, CBS] nor the excellent "Outer Limits" [1964, ABC] produced a single vampire in their collective seven years on the air.)

1964 "The Munsters"
CBS Television, Universal Pictures. Creators: Bob Masher, Joe Connelly. Starring: Fred Gwynne, Yvonne De Carlo, Al Lewis, Butch Patrick, Beverly Owen.

"The Munsters" (1964). Al Lewis appears as Grandpa, a hip elderly vampire. Lewis also hosts his own horror show for Ted Turner and runs a New York restaurant named Grandpa's. Photo courtesy of Universal Pictures.

Several years after the "Thriller" segment, both CBS and ABC did produce situational comedies which featured a vampire (or two) in lead roles. "The Munsters" (1964, CBS) was a close-knit family of monsters and ghouls. Herman Munster (Fred Gwynne, in Universal's Frankenstein monster makeup) and his family lived at 1313 Mockingbird Lane in Mockingbird Heights among the other suburbanites. His charming wife, Lily (Yvonne De Carlo), and her 350-year-old father (Al Lewis) are vampires, blood relatives to Dracula, and his son, Eddie (Butch Patrick), is a werewolf. The show was played mostly for laughs, much like *Abbott and Costello Meet Frankenstein* (1948), and left the network after two years on the air.

Munster Go Home! (1966). Television's favorite monster family (Fred Gwynne, Yvonne De Carlo, Al Lewis, and Butch Patrick) inherit a haunted estate in England. Here, Herman Munster (Gwynne) tries on an English monacle as the family looks on. Photo courtesy of Universal Pictures.

Ironically, the series has played continuously in syndication for over twenty years, and Al Lewis appears as a "vampire" host on a local creature-features show. ("The Munsters" was probably inspired by the 1963 *The Horror of It All*, Lippert Associated Pictures, b/w, 75 min. Director: Terence Fisher. Producer: Robert Lippert. Writer: Ray Russell. Starring Pat Boone, Erika Rogers, Dennis Price, Andrea Melly, Valentine Dyall.)

1966 *Munster Go Home!*

Universal, 96 min. Director: Earl Bellamy. Producers: Bob Masher, Joe Connelly. Writers: George Tibbles, Connelly, Masher. Starring Fred Gwynne, Yvonne De Carlo, Al Lewis, Butch Patrick, Debbie Watson, Hermione Gingold, Jeanne Arnold, Terry-Thomas.

Munster Go Home! (1966) was a theatrical expansion of television's favorite family of monsters. Based on the half-hour sitcom "The Munsters" (1964, CBS), the full-length technical feature (originally made for television) was somehow much more satisfying. Herman Munster (Fred Gwynne) and his family (Yvonne De Carlo, Al Lewis, Butch Patrick, and Debbie Watson) learn that they've inherited an estate in England and make arrangements for a visit. Upon arrival, they are greeted by Herman's cousin, Lady Effigie (Herminone Gingold), and her children, Freddie and Grace (Terry-Thomas and Jeanne Arnold), none of whom are pleased to see them. (Apparently, they are using Munster Hall to print counterfeit money.) The English cousins attempt to scare the Munster clan into thinking the castle is haunted, but that only makes the enterprise much more desirable to Herman and Lily. Nicely acted with a fast clip, *Munster Go Home!* is a charming film.

1981 *The Munsters' Revenge*

Universal, 96 min. Director: Don Weis. Producers: Arthur Alsberg, Don Nelson. Writers: Alsberg, Nelson. Starring Fred Gwynne, Yvonne De Carlo, Al Lewis, Butch Patrick, Debbie Watson, Sid Caesar, Howard Morris.

The famous monster family returned several years later in *The Munsters' Revenge*. Originally made for television, the film was released theatrically and on video. The story follows the exploits of Dr. Diablo (Sid Caesar) and his partner (Howard Morris) to create a Frankenstein monster (which happens to have the same features as Herman Munster) to pull off art crimes. Witnesses wrongly identify Herman as the thief, and the chase is on to capture the real criminals. Though not as charming as *Munster Go Home!* (1966), the motion picture was very successful among die-hard fans. (A retooled "Munsters" debuted on cable shortly thereafter with an entirely different cast and crew.)

1964 "The Addams Family"

ABC Television. Creator: Charles Addams, based on his cartoons that appeared in the *New Yorker*. Starring Carolyn Jones, John Astin, Jackie Coogan, Ted Cassidy.

"The Addams Family" (1964, ABC), similar in concept to "The Munsters," was inspired by the cartoons of Charles Addams which appeared in the *New Yorker*. Carolyn Jones played Morticia, a vampire role, which has since inspired horror host Elvira (Cassandra Peterson). John Astin was her husband, Gomez; Jackie Coogan was Uncle Fester (a mad scientist); and the late Ted Cassidy played Lurch, the family butler. The show was stylistically better than "The Munsters" but lasted about the same time. (A big-budget version debuted in 1992 with Angelica Huston as Morticia.)

Jonathan Frid as Barnabas Collins, the 350-year-old vampire from the popular daytime drama "Dark Shadows" (1966–1971). Photo courtesy of MGM and Dan Curtis Productions.

1966 "Dark Shadows"

ABC Television, Dan Curtis Productions. Creator-Producer: Dan Curtis. Starring Jonathan Frid, Joan Bennett, David Selby, Kate Jackson, Jerry Lacy, Thayer David, Roger Davis, Grayson Hall.

Recognizing the potential for horror on television, ABC attempted a daring experiment in its daytime drama. Originally intended as a highly atmospheric gothic romance, "Dark Shadows" (1966, ABC) was in danger of cancellation when producer Dan Curtis introduced a new character, Barnabas Collins. The craggy-faced vampire (brilliantly portrayed by Jonathan Frid) was an immediate success and soon became a cult hero among its younger viewers. The focus of the series was shifted from gothic romance to horror, and through the typical fashion of episodic serials "Dark Shadows" examined not only vampirism but also lycanthropy (with David Selby), witchcraft (with Kate Jackson), spiritualism, and interdimensional travel. Even though the series was canceled in 1971, it produced a handful of novels, two motion pictures (*House of Dark Shadows* [1970] and *Night of Dark Shadows* [1971]), and a cult following which exists to this day. "Dark Shadows" was truly a unique venture into the dark side. (The show is currently being offered on home video by MPI, which plans to issue all 1,225 episodes.)

1966 "Star Trek"

NBC Television. Creator: Gene Roddenberry. Producer: Gene L. Coon. Starring William Shatner, Leonard Nimoy, De Forrest Kelley, James Doohan, and Nichelle Nichols.

Episode 1, "The Man Trap": Writer: George Clayton Johnson. Guest Stars: Jeanne Bal, Francine Pyne, Alfred Ryder, Michael Zaslow.

Episode 2, "Obsession": Writer: Art Wallace. Director: Ralph Senensky. Guest Stars: Stephen Brooks, Jerry Ayres.

Similarly, "Star Trek" (1966, NBC), television's most distinguished science-fiction series, produced two episodes which featured vampires, but these vampires were not the run-of-the-mill bloodsuckers; they were unique. "The Man Trap," written by George Clayton Johnson, introduced a salt vampire who could shape-change at will. The *Enterprise* crew accidentally beams the creature aboard, and through its numerous guises, it drains the salt from each of its victim's bodies. The salt vampire is eventually destroyed by a phaser shot, but not before it has decimated an entire expedition with its suction-cup tentacles. The vampire in "Obsession" is a deadly gaseous cloud creature which craves blood. Written by Art Wallace, the story explains that Captain Kirk has faced the creature once before as a terrified ensign and was unable to prevent it from destroying an entire planet. Now, several years later, he must destroy it before the creature multiplies and threatens the galaxy. Both episodes are brilliantly mounted, and both creatures make fine additions to vampire lore.

1971 *"Night Gallery"*

NBC Television. Producer: Jack Laird. Creator-Host: Rod Serling.

Episode 1, "The Funeral": Writer: Richard Matheson. Director: Jeannot Szwarc. Starring Werner Klemperer, Joe Flynn.

Episode 2, "Miss Lovecraft Sent Me": Writer: Jack Laird. Director: Gene Kearney. Starring Sye Lyon, Joseph Campanella.

Episode 3, "A Midnight Visit to the Blood Bank": Writer: Jack Laird. Director: William Hale. Starring Victor Buono.

Episode 4, "How to Cure the Common Vampire": Writer-Director: Jack Laird. Starring George Carlin, Richard Deacon.

Episode 5, "A Matter of Semantics": Writer: Gene Kearney. Director: Jack Laird. Starring Cesar Romero.

Episode 6, "The Devil Is Not Mocked!": Writer-Director: Gene Kearney. Starring Francis Lederer, Helmut Dantine.

Barnabas Collins (Jonathan Frid) stalks the Collinsport estate searching for victims on the soap opera "Dark Shadows" (1966–1971). Photo courtesy of MGM and Dan Curtis Productions.

Episode 7, "Death on the Barge": Writer: Halsted Welles. Director: Leonard Nimoy. Starring Lesley Anne Warren, Lou Antonio, Brooke Bundy, Robert Pratt.

Rod Serling's "Night Gallery" (1971, NBC) was the finest horror anthology and contained some of the best vampire stories presented on television. The series was produced by Jack Laird; Rod Serling appeared as host and lead writer. Ill-fated and largely misunderstood, the series had a difficult time finding the right audience. It began as a horror trilogy, then became part of NBC's "Four in One," and finally appeared under its own name opposite the popular "Mannix" on Wednesday (and later Sunday) night. But in its brief lifespan "Night Gallery" gave television some of its finest moments, encouraging brand-new directors like Steven Spielberg, Leonard Nimoy, and Jeannot Szwarc, and hot writers like Richard Matheson, Gene Kearney, and Serling to experiment with the medium.

Like all series, "Night Gallery" was variable in quality, although it never in its three-year run descended to the continual reuse of stock formulas. Even though the network insisted on at least one "monster" per segment, the writers always managed to produce top-quality scripts. Probably the finest of the episodes was "Death on the Barge," directed by Leonard Nimoy (Mr. Spock from "Star Trek") and written by Halsted Welles. The vampire tale is a most unusual love story. A lonely, young man (Lou Antonio) falls in love with a mysterious stranger (Lesley Anne Warren) who lives on a barge. He begs her to join him, but her father (Robert Pratt) has imprisoned her on the barge (for a reason) and forbidden her guests. When the young man disobeys her father's wishes, he learns that his true love is really a vampire. This strange drama is played out brilliantly with hauntingly tragic implications.

"The Devil Is Not Mocked!" was another well-made tale. Written and directed by Gene Kearney, the story concerns the occupation of Dracula's castle by German officers in World War II. When the lead general (Helmut Dantine) and his officers confiscate the vampire's home and order his servants to make dinner for them, Dracula (Francis Lederer, reprising his vampiric role from *Return of Dracula*, 1958) makes things difficult for them. Needless to say, the Germans were not only the dinner guests but also the main course. (This episode shares chilling similarities to the recent vampire film *The Keep* [1983]).

Other episodes featured vampires, including "A Midnight Visit to the Blood Bank," "Miss Lovecraft Sent Me," "A Matter of Semantics," "Smile Please," and "How to Cure the Common Vampire," but the most notable was a comedy starring Joe Flynn and Werner Klemperer. Less horrific than the others but probably more compelling, "The Funeral" was written by horror master Richard Matheson and directed by Jeannot Szwarc. Weird and elegant, the episode was shot with great style and panache. A vampire (Klemperer) returns from the dead to stage a more lavish funeral than the one he had. Offered a healthy fortune to stage it, the funeral director (Flynn) is also given a guest list, which includes the wolf man, several witches, vampires, and the phantom of the opera. The funeral is predictably wild with all the famous monsters of filmland in attendance, and the O'Henry-style ending brings the story to a marvelous conclusion.

Rod Serling's "Night Gallery" was not a perfect series, but for consistency of imagination, it had few equals. By the time the series was canceled (in 1973), it had opened many network doors that had previously been closed, and paved the way for many new experiments.

1972 *The Night Stalker*

ABC Telefilms. Director: John Llewellan Moxey. Producer: Dan Curtis. Writer: Richard Matheson, based on an unpublished novel, by Jeff Rice. Starring Darren McGavin, Carol Linley, Simon Oakland, Barry Atwater.

By sharp contrast with the ratings-poor "Night Gallery," *The Night Stalker* (1972, ABC) made ratings history in 1972, becoming the highest-rated television movie of all time. Based on an unpublished novel by journalist Jeff Rice, Dan Curtis (of "Dark Shadows" fame) saw that it had all the ingredients of a good horror story and disregarding the prudish network censors, made this classic vampire film. The sharp camera angles of director John L. Moxey, the crisp, witty writing of Richard Matheson, and the eerie music of Robert Colbert have stayed fresh throughout the years, and even today it is highly regarded among film scholars.

This modern vampire story relates Carl Kolchak's first classic adventure. Kolchak (magnificently played by Darren McGavin) is a middle-aged, down-on-his-luck reporter trying to recapture his glorious past with one last big story. However, his editor, Anthony Vincenzo (Simon Oakland), has other ideas and assigns him to investigate a "two-bit" murder. "Well, in any town," he moralizes, "the size of Las Vegas, the murder of one young girl hardly causes concern." But then there is another, and another. Kolchak's interest is piqued, and he noses around to learn that in each murder there has been an extreme loss of blood. Conning his friend at the Federal Bureau of Investigation (Ralph Meeker), he discovers that a Transylvanian nobleman, Janos Skorzeny (Barry Atwater), is really a vampire. After much tomfoolery with the police, city officials, and his editor, Kolchak decides to face the creature on his own. Armed with Van Helsing's traditional accoutrements, Kolchak destroys the vampire in a hair-raising finale. Unfortu-

The Night Stalker (1972). **Barry Atwater as Janos Skorzeny, the night-stalking vampire, is held at bay by Carl Kolchak (Darren McGavin). Photo courtesy of Dan Curtis Productions.**

nately, the police bury the evidence (that a vampire really existed) and run Carl Kolchak out of town.

The Night Stalker was a most effective, chilling tale. It never attempted to transplant the mythos of the nineteenth-century vampire into modern times. Janos Skorzeny does not resemble Dracula in any way; he has no courtly manner or romantic charms; he is a cold-blooded killer who will stop at nothing. And the strength of the film lies in the possibility that he may indeed be out there stalking the night. (The motion picture was so effective that a real-life psychotic killer who terrorized Los Angeles in the summer of 1985 was named the Night Stalker.) The television movie inspired a sequel (*The Night Strangler*, 1973) and a short-lived ABC series, "Kolchak: The Night Stalker" (1974, ABC).

1974 *"Kolchak: The Night Stalker"*
ABC Television. Creator: Jeff Rice. Producers: Paul Playdon, Darren McGavin. Starring Darren McGavin, Simon Oakland.
Episode: "The Vampire": Writers: David Chase, Bill Stratton, and

Rudolph Bochert. Guest Stars: Kathleen Nolan, William Daniels, Suzanne Chaney.

The series, one step removed from the fast-paced television movie, concerned Kolchak's efforts each week to destroy some new evil monster. Coproduced by Darren McGavin, "Kolchak: The Night Stalker" was certainly a cut above most of the current television offerings. But ABC's new programming executive, Fred Silverman, was concerned with the excessive violence (in the two telefilms) and ordered that scripts be lighter, less horrifying. That in essence took the "bite" out of the series and spelled eventual cancellation. Before its demise in 1975, the show did produce a semisequel—"The Vampire," written by David Chase, Bill Stratton, and Rudolph Bochert, introducing one of Skorzeny's female victims as a prostitute in Los Angeles. Chicago reporter Kolchak learns of the vampire and cons his assignment editor (Oakland as Vincenzo) out of a trip to the West Coast. Once there, he enlists the aid of a realty clerk (Kathleen Nolan) and tracks the vampire to its lair, destroying it. This episode was one of the series's best entries. (Plans for a sequel to the original *Night Stalker* film and television series were announced in 1990 by Dan Curtis. "Kolchak [Darren McGavin] shows up twenty years later in New York City," according to Curtis, "and a series of strange murders take place. It turns out that the body of Janos Skorzeny was never cremated!" Planned for the fall of 1993, the new film could spark interest in a new television series.)

1973 "The Norliss Tapes"
NBC Television. Producer-Director-Creator: Dan Curtis. Writer: William F. Nolan. Starring Roy Thinnes, Angie Dickinson, Claude Akins, Michele Carey, Don Porter.

Dan Curtis, fresh from his two "Dark Shadows" films and the phenomenal success of "The Night Stalker," produced and directed two other vampiric efforts. "The Norliss Tapes" (1973, NBC) was a semiremake of "The Night Stalker" in which author Roy Thinnes and his love interest, Angie Dickinson, uncover a series of vampirelike murders. Predictably, the police refuse to acknowledge the real threat, and Thinnes must dispatch the evil creature.

1973 *Dracula*
CBS Telefilms. Director-Producer: Dan Curtis. Writer: Richard Matheson, based on the novel by Bram Stoker. Starring Jack Palance, Pamela Brown, Simon Ward, Fiona Lewis, Nigel Davenport.

Dracula (1975, CBS) was the small-screen follow-up to the highly successful *Frankenstein — The True Story* (1973, NBC). Written by Richard Matheson, the emphasis was on a sympathetic Dracula — a pitiful human who like Milton's Satan has fallen from God's grace. There were also numerous reference to his early life as Prince Vlad Dracul the Impaler, and to the prince's great love (who resembles Lucy Westenra). The story was basically the same as Stoker's original with Jack Palance playing a tormented, love-starved vampire. The telefilm's epilogue, which explains how this misunderstood nobleman was dubbed "Dracula," or devil, by his countrymen is perhaps heavy-handed, but the movie as a whole was a noble effort. *Dracula* was popular in the nightly ratings, and encouraged other production companies to remake old horror classics, including *The Phantom of Hollywood* (1974, CBS), *Scream of the Wolf* (1974, ABC), *The Picture of Dorian Gray* (1974, ABC), and yet another version of Stoker's classic *Count Dracula*.

1976 *"The Monster Squad"*

NBC Television. Directors: Herman Hoffman, James Sheldon. Producer: Michael McClean. Starring Fred Grandy, Henry Polic II, Buck Kartalian, Michael Lane.

Not to be confused with the 1987 movie, "The Monster Squad" (1976) was also an attempt to revive the famous monsters of filmland. Fred Grandy (who would later turn his talents to "The Love Boat" and politics) plays a criminology student who is forced to moonlight as a night watchman in a wax museum to pay his tuition. Late one night while playing with a unique computer program, he accidentally brings Dracula, the Frankenstein monster, the wolf man, and other wax monsters to life. In an effort to atone for past deeds, the famous monsters agree to join Grandy to fight crime. Predictable sitcom, with the usual situations and laugh track.

1978 *Count Dracula*

PBS, "Great Performances." Director: Philip Seville. Writer: Gerald Savory, based on the novel by Bram Stoker. Starring Louis Jourdan, Frank Finlay, Susan Penhaligon, Mark Burnes.

Count Dracula (1978, PBS) was the first totally faithful adaptation of Bram Stoker's novel. Presented originally as three 60-minute segments of "Great Performances," this prestigious production is veracious in its quest to present an authentic version of the story. The script, by Gerald Savory, even excerpts whole sections of dialogue from the novel. Although the language and situations seem stilted (because they are derived literally from the Victorian mores and sensibilities of the period), the pacing of the drama (thanks to the direction of Philip Seville) and the fine ensemble performances never condescend to the material. Louis Jourdan, the smooth French leading man, brings an unusual charm and grace to Dracula, but underneath the facade, the menace of the vampire still lurks. Frank Finlay portrays Dracula's nemesis, Dr. Van Helsing, and together they make the film a memorable one. This superb PBS production did not attract much of a viewing audience when it was first aired in 1978, but subsequent showings have garnered great critical praise and much stronger ratings.

1979 "Cliffhangers: Curse of Dracula"

NBC Television. Producer-Creator: Fred Silverman. Starring Michael Nouri, Stephen Johnson, Carol Baxter, Antoinette, Louise Sorel.

More than two decades after the last movie serial was produced, NBC tried that format with their own version of *Dracula*. "Curse of Dracula" (1979, NBC) was one of the three shows that aired under the umbrella title "Cliffhangers." Beginning with chapter 4 (as in the old serial tradition), the story told of a contemporary Dracula who was living in San Francisco. The five-hundred-year-old vampire (played by Michael Nouri), a teacher of European history at an evening college, chooses his victims from his unsuspecting attractive female students. Seeking to destroy him, Kurt Van Helsing (Stephen Johnson), grandson of the eminent vampirologist, tracks him at night with the aid of Mary Gibbons (Carol Baxter). Apparently, Mary's mother was made a vampire by Dracula, and she wants to get revenge. By the last chapter, after the series had received its cancellation notice, Mary's mother, Amanda (Louise Sorel), returns to rescue her from the Count, while Kurt kills Dracula with a wooden arrow from a crossbow.

"Curse of Dracula" had tremendous possibilities, but network executive Fred Silverman (who had originated the concept) insisted that suspense replace horror. Instead of allowing Dracula his blood rite, the action always stopped short, and the audience was left unfulfilled. In much the same manner as he had emasculated "Kolchak: The Night Stalker," Silverman condemned this series to an early grave. Fortunately, "Curse of Dracula" was the only show of the "Cliffhangers" series to reach a conclusion, and it has subsequently reappeared as a vastly reedited television movie.

1979 *The Halloween That Almost Wasn't*

Made for Cable/Syndicated Feature, 90 min. Starring Judd Hirsch.

Judd Hirsch (noted for his roles in "Taxi" and "Dear John") appeared as a totally inept Count Dracula in the low-low-budget *The Halloween That Almost Wasn't*. Featuring very little gore, the film was aimed strictly at the kiddie market.

On the other hand, ABC's *Vampire* (1979) and CBS's *Salem's Lot* (1979) took network censors to task and made great strides in the freedom of television movies. Both are very violent and visually explicit, but both are also representative of television at its finest in writing, directing, and acting.

1979 *Vampire*

ABC Telefilms. Director: Earl Swackhammer. Producer-Writer: Stephen Boccho. Starring Richard Lynch, Jason Miller, E. G. Marshall, Kathryn Harold, Jessica Walter.

Vampire, a remarkably effective vampire tale, features the standard formula of a gothic thriller in a fresh new light. An eight-hundred-year-old vampire is unearthed in San Francisco when construction for a new cathedral begins on the site where his mansion once stood. Awakened, he takes revenge on the architect who instigated the project by seducing, then killing his wife. He then begins to terrorize the city, taking victims at will. However, the architect manages to convince an aging detective about the vampire, and the two strike out after him. Richard Lynch is superb as the vampire, with his offbeat blond good looks, and Jason Miller and E. G. Marshall are equally compelling as the vampire stalkers.

Written by Steven Boccho (of "Hill Street Blues" and "L.A. Law" fame) and directed by E. W. Swackhammer, the television movie was left unresolved and intended as a series, but ABC wasn't interested after the poor showing of "Kolchak: The Night Stalker."

1979 *Salem's Lot*

CBS, Warner Television Productions. Director: Tobe Hooper. Producer: Richard Kobritz. Writer: Paul Monash, based on the novel by Stephen King. Starring David Soul, James Mason, Lance Kerwin, Bonnie Bedelia, Lew Ayres, Reggie Nalder.

Salem's Lot (1979, CBS) was similarly destined as a series, but network executives didn't bite. Based on Stephen King's best-selling vampire novel, *Salem's Lot* appeared as a two-part miniseries on CBS in the fall of 1979. (The miniseries has since been reedited into a two-hour movie for release in Europe and on home video.) Horror novelist Ben Mears (David Soul) returns home to the town of Salem's Lot (actually Jerusalem's Lot) to write

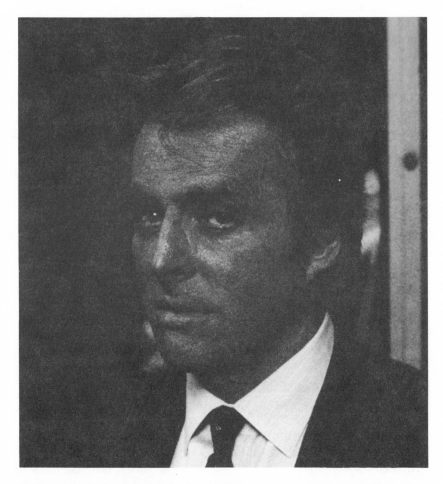

Richard Lynch, the eight-hundred-year-old vampire, appears remarkably modern in *Vampire* (1979). Lynch, with his offbeat blond good looks, makes a memorable character.

a book about the haunted Marsten house. However, when Mr. Barlow (Reggie Nalder) moves into the house, people begin to die, and their deaths are quite gruesome. Mears, his girlfriend, Bonnie (Bonnie Bedelia), and a local youngster Mark (Lance Kerwin) investigate the murders and discover that Barlow (in makeup inspired by Murnau's *Nosferatu*) is a vampire. But it is too late as members of the entire community become vampires. After his girlfriend has been made one, Mears and Mark burn the Marsten house and flee the city. Years later, on the trail of another vampire, Bonnie appears to Mears, and he must also kill her. Graphically violent by television standards, the production values are top rate, and the direction by Tobe Hooper is quite chilling. The miniseries scored very high ratings but not enough to convince CBS to make a series. (Ironically, for one of King's first novels, *Salem's Lot* is also the best adaptation of his work to date.)

1980 "Mr. and Mrs. Dracula"

ABC Television. Director: Doug Rogers. Producer-Creator-Writer: Robert Klane. Starring Dick Shawn, Carol Lawrence, Barry Gordon, Anthony Battaglia, Gail Mayron.

Following the enormous success of Stan Dragoti's *Love at First Bite* (1979), ABC Television attempted to launch its own comedic verson of the time-honored Stoker classic. "Mr. and Mrs. Dracula" debuted as a thirty-minute sitcom (complete with canned laugh track) in the summer of 1980. Starring the talented comedian Dick Shawn (who appeared in the Dragoti film) and singer Carol Lawrence, this one-episode series failed to rise above the tired "Munsters" material. The titular characters live in a decaying South Bronx (New York) brownstone, listen to the rock sounds of the Grateful Dead, and eat living steaks. Get the idea? Well, many faithful viewers did not get the idea, and ABC wisely dumped the show after a single viewing.

1981 *"Darkroom"*

ABC Television (one-hour anthology series hosted by James Coburn). Series format by Christopher Crowe.
Episode, "The Bogeyman Will Get You": Writer: Robert Bloch, based on his short story. Starring Randolph Powell, Helen Hunt, Gloria De Haven.

Vampires also showed up as "monsters" (and stock villains) on "F-Troop" (1967, ABC), "Starsky and Hutch" (1979, ABC), "Buck Rogers in the Twenty-Fifth Century" (1980, NBC), and a half-dozen other shows, followed by guest appearances on "Tales from the Darkside' (1985, Syndicated), "The New Twilight Zone' (1986, CBS), and other horror anthologies. One of those appearances was inspired, two were revisionist fables, and the others were largely forgettable. Probably the most memorable vampire in recent years was on a segment of the anthology series "Darkroom" (1981, ABC, and 1988, USA). "The Bogeyman Will Get You," written by horror great Robert Bloch from his short story, is a suspenseful little chiller. Philip (Randolph Powell) takes advantage of two young girls' (Helen Hunt and Gloria De Haven) fascination with horror movies by telling them that he is a vampire, but they don't believe him.

However, when several of their friends vanish, they begin to suspect the truth. Of course, it is too late. Hosted by James Coburn, "Darkroom" was one of a dozen anthology series inspired by the (original) "Twilight Zone" and "Night Gallery," and was variable in quality, dependent greatly on writing and production values.

Both "Monsters" (1988, Syndicated) and "Friday the 13th — The Series" (1989, Syndicated), two other horror anthologies, featured vampires in individual episodes but chose to tell the story from the other point of view, that of the eminent vampirologist. On "Monsters," Robert Lansing played "The Vampire Hunter," an American Sherlock Holmes-like detective who once hunted vampires for a living. Called out of retirement to save his nephew, he must face the one creature that he fears most. Although the thirty-minute segment was shot on the backlot with a low-low budget, Lansing's performance is superb. Similarly, "Night Prey," an episode of "Friday the 13th — The Series," featured actor Michael Burgress as Kurt Bachman, a vampire hunter. His wife, Michelle (Genevieve Langlois), was abducted by a vampire (Eric Murphy), and he has spent the last twenty years looking for her. Obsessed with revenge, he steals a twelfth-century cross from a local cathedral and uses its "miraculous" powers to destroy all those who get in his way. When he finally finds his wife, Bachman discovers that she has become a vampire and that he must feed her victims to maintain her vitality. The segment was written by Peter Mohan and demonstrated the potential for quality on a syndicated television show. Unfortunately, other serious ventures into the realm have been left unimagined.

1986 *The Midnight Hour*

ABC Circle Telefilms, Vidmark Home Entertainment, 98 min. Director: Jack Bender. Producer: Ervin Zavada. Writer: Bill Bleich. Starring Shari Belafonte-Harper, Lee Montgomery, Joanna Lee, Levar Burton, Jonelle Allen, Peter DeLuise, Kevin McCarthy, Deedee Pfeiffer.

Intended as a holiday treat (rather than a trick), *The Midnight Hour* (1986) was a hodgepodge of horror film clichés. Several local teens (Shari Belafonte-Harper, Lee Montgomery, Joanna Lee, and Levar Burton) break into the historical museum of their sleepy New England town to steal the costumes, cursed ring, and demonic journal of a witchcraft exhibit. Then, gathered at the local cemetery as part of a Halloween prank, they perform an ancient ritual to bring back the vampire witch ancestor of Shari Belafonte-Harper. The ritual works, and suddenly the town is invaded by ghouls, ghosts, zombies, vampires, and even the phantom of the opera. At first the local townspeople think the monsters are simply children dressed in Halloween costumes, but they quickly learn the truth. This made-for-television movie has since become a holiday tradition on most cable stations.

1989 *Dracula—Live from Transylvania*

Syndicated horror documentary featuring host George Hamilton and guests Raymond McNally, Radu Florescu, and Norrine Dresser.

Late in 1989, there was a valiant attempt to revive the genre with three dramatic appearances and a prime-time special. *Dracula—Live from Transylvania* (1989, Syndicated) appeared as a Halloween trick-or-treat special from the struggling cable industry. Although the two-hour documentary attempted to provide information about the historical Dracula (Vlad Tepes) and other real-life vampires (Elizabeth Bathory, Fritz Haarman, John George Haigh, etc.), the linking narrative by George Hamilton is played entirely for laughs. Researchers Raymond McNally and Radu Florescu, who told about the real Dracula in the book and documentary *In Search of Dracula* (1971), and folklorist Norrine Dresser, who wrote *American Vampires*, appear as experts, and discuss the lore and attraction of the most famous vampire. Partly camp and partly informational, *Dracula—Live from Transylvania* offered a mixed bag of treats for Halloween viewers. (This special resembles a 1974 BBC documentary, *The Dracula Business*, which detailed the efforts of the Romania government to cash in on the Dracula craze.)

1989 *Nick Knight*

CBS Telefilms, Universal Productions, 100 min. Starring Rick Springfield, Robert Harper, Laura Johnson, Michael Nalder.

Nick Knight (1989, CBS) was advertised as "a different kind of bat man" in order to capitalize on the sensational Guber-Peters' *Batman* (1989), but it debuted on August 20, 1989, to lukewarm ratings and mixed reviews. The idea for the telefilm (which also served as a pilot for a proposed series) was unique enough, but what it really needed was some of the offbeat style and panache of Tim Burton's direction (in *Batman*). Nick Knight (Rick Springfield) is both a homicide detective for the Los Angeles police department and an ages-old vampire. He has given up his predatory ways in favor of homogenized blood that he keeps refrigerated in his loft apartment. Dr. Butlington (Robert Harper), his friend and the local county coroner, is trying to find a permanent cure so that Nick can watch the sun rise and live a normal life. With the theft of a sacrificial goblet that has left a museum guard dead, drained of blood like three previous victims, Knight realizes that his extraordinary powers may be beneficial in his murder investigation. He suspects Lacroix (Michael Nader), the vampire who made him one. But the body of evidence leads elsewhere. Through the course of his investigation, Knight becomes romantically involved with Alyce Hunter (Laura Johnson), the curator of the museum. He also acquires a new partner (John Kapelos), and travels into a dark world of the vampire. Eventually he uncovers a psychopath whose blood lust is part of a satanic ritual. *Nick Knight* has its moments, particularly in the detective's journey into the subterranean society of vampirism, which recalls the best of Anne Rice and Chelsea Quinn Yarbro. But on the whole, the telefilm was a minor diversion. (In 1992, CBS unveiled a late-night series, entitled *Forever Knight*, with Geraint Wyn Davies replacing Rick Springfield as the vampire detective.)

1989 *Nightlife*

USA Network, Independent Productions, 100 min. Director: Daniel Taplitz. Producer: Robert Skodis. Writers: Taplitz, Anne Beatts, based on her original story and characters inspired by Bram Stoker. Starring Ben Cross, Maryam d'Abo, Keith Szarabajka, Camille Saviola.

Three days after the premiere of *Nick Knight*, *Nightlife* (1989, USA) debuted as a world premiere movie on the USA Cable Network and was much less imaginative with its traditionalist approach to the vampire mythos. Count Vlad Dracula (Ben Cross) has traveled to Mexico City in search of his long-lost love, Angelique (Maryam d'Abo), but she wants nothing to do with him. She has just spent the last hundred years locked in a coffin with bugs crawling over her, and she wants simply to enjoy the "nightlife." Angelique takes a swank modern apartment, hires Rosa Mercedes (Camille Saviola) as her maid, and begins to date an upscale doctor (Keith Szarabajka), who plans to cure her. (She must still be bitten a third time to become a full-fledged vampire.) Jealous, Vlad attempts to win her back, but he is continually frustrated in a series of comic mishaps. The jokes come fast and furious in this lightweight spoof, written by Anne Beatts, which tries its very best to imitate *Love at First Bite* (1979) but never rises above the simplistic plot line of its romantic triangle.

1989 *Carmilla*

Showtime, Nightmare Classics, based on the novel by Joseph Sheridan Le Fanu. Starring Roy Dotrice, Ione Skye, Roddy McDowall, Meg Tilly.

Carmilla (1989, Showtime) fared much better, a very literate adaptation of Joseph Sheridan Le Fanu's classic vampire story. This second

Promotional artwork from USA's *Nightlife* (1989) from *TV Guide*. Excerpt from *TV Guide*.

installment of Showtime's "Nightmare Classics" delightfully contrasts the delirious passion (and sexual energy) of the young women with the anxious puritanism (and entropy) of the older men in the piece. Laura (Ione Skye), the beautiful daughter of a lonely widower (Roy Dotrice), has grown weary of their isolation and wants to have friends with whom to play, but all her contemporaries have become ill or died from a horrible plague. Her father promises that she'll have friends, but he too is powerless to do anything, emotionally crippled by the recent loss of his wife. Suddenly, by happenstance (or is it by design?), a beautiful brunette, the victim of an unfortunate carriate accident, is brought to the house and fulfills not only Laura's desire for a friend but also Father's need for female companionship. Carmilla (Meg Tilly), as they come to know her, is the daughter of wealthy aristocrats, recently deceased; she is also Countess Mircalla Karnstein, an ages-old vampire. Slowly, cunningly, she draws Laura into her power by telling her about the places she's been and the people she's met. When the local witchfinder (Roddy McDowall) arrives, he reveals the truth about Carmilla and allied with her father struggles ineffectively for Laura's salvation.

The made-for-cable movie has none of the nightmare quality of Carl Dreyer's *Vampyr* (1932) nor the erotic sensuality of Hammer's *The Vampire Lovers* (1970) but still manages to be quite entertaining. The setting has been updated to antebellum South to give the story more accessibility for American audiences, and this is one of the production's two masterstrokes. Prior to the Civil War, southerners were somewhat dubious of strangers, and this conceit adds a level of paranoia to the film. The other masterstroke was casting Meg Tilly as Carmilla. She is both seductive and chilling. (Ms. Tilly appeared as the innocent-turned-bad in Tom McLoughlin's vampire tale *One Dark Night*, 1982.) Not too surprisingly, the production was well received by critics and viewers. And unlike its competition (the telefilms *Nick Knight* and *Nightlife*), Showtime's *Carmilla* provides a valuable template and points the direction for future television excursions into the genre.

1990 *Daughter of Darkness*
CBS Television, Lorimar Entertainment, 100 min. Director: Stuart Gordon. Starring Anthony Perkins, Mia Sara, Jack Coleman.

Daughter of Darkness (1990) was yet another made-for-television movie featuring vampires. Directed by horror great Stuart Gordon, the somewhat limited story line followed predictable paths. Mia Sara travels to Romania (during the democratic uprising) to learn more about her family heritage and discovers that her father (Anthony Perkins), who at first pretends simply to be an old member of the family, is a vampire. He has been part of a bloodsucking cult for years (presumably one created by Count Dracula), and his meeting with Sara provides the impetus to resign. But there's only one problem: the other vampires have grown accustomed to his leadership and refuse his request. Better than most of the boob-tube fare, the film unfortunately fails to measure up to the promise of *Salem's Lot* (1979) or *Vampire* (1979).

1990 "Dracula—The Series"

Syndicated, Blair Entertainment Series. Producer-Creator: David Patterson. Starring Georgie Johnson, Bernard Behrens, Jacob Tierney, Joe Roncetti.

"Dracula—The Series" (1990, Syndicated) had the same mix of horror and humor that made the film *Fright Night* (1985) so popular. This modern updating of the classic story finds Dracula a multimillionaire industrialist masquerading under the name Alexander Lucard (Georgie Johnson). Like the Wall Street interests of his American counterpart Donald Trump, business is booming in Europe (particularly with the unification of Germany and the democratization of several Eastern-bloc countries). But when two teens arrive with their mother to take up residence with Lucard's sworn enemy, Professor Van Helsing (their uncle), the classic struggle of good versus evil begins anew. Sometimes amusing but more often predictable, this anemic melodrama, played out in twenty-three minutes like a half-hour sitcom, rarely lives up to the uniqueness of its premise.

1991 "Dark Shadows": The Miniseries and Series

NBC, Dan Curtis Productions. Producer-Director-Writer: Dan Curtis. Starring Ben Cross, Jean Simmons, Roy Thinnes, Jim Fyfe, Barbara Steele, Joanna Going, Rebecca Staab, Michael Cavanaugh, Michael T. Weiss, Stefan Gierasch, Ely Pouget, Barbara Blackburn, Joseph Gordon-Levitt.

During the 1988 writers' strike when the search for old material that could be used again was in full swing, NBC entertainment president Brandon Tartikoff approached producer Dan Curtis with his notion of a revival of the popular daytime soap. Curtis was surprised by the interest in "Dark Shadows" (1966, ABC) but resisted the temptation, having spent the last ten years of his life on *The Winds of War* (1983) and *War and Remembrance* (1988). "I never intended to do it," Curtis said, claiming that he had lost all enthusiasm (and ideas) after four years at the helm of the old show. "When

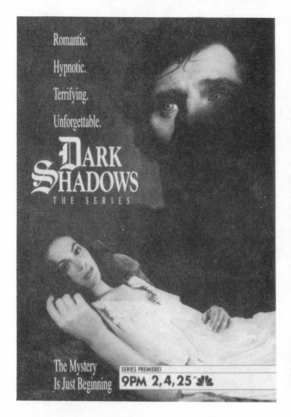

Promotional artwork from NBC's new *Dark Shadows* (1991). Excerpt from *TV Guide*.

I got out of there, I felt like I was let out of jail. I ran to the nearest exit, not walked."

Tartikoff was persistent, and following two years of deliberation, Curtis began reworking the twenty-four-year-old gothic series for an upscale two-hour movie (which was later expanded to a four-hour miniseries and possible weekly prime-time series.) He decided that an all-new cast would be best and signed Ben Cross to portray Barnabas Collins, the reluctant vampire of Collinsport, Maine. Horror B queen Barbara Steele was cast as Dr. Julia Hoffman, Jean Simmons as family matriarch Elizabeth Collins Stoddard, and Roy Thinnes as Roger Collins. The two-hour film finished filming in mid–April (1990) for its fall debut. Two additional hours were added for a January miniseries; then the entertainment president of NBC announced that "Dark Shadows" would debut as a midseason replacement for departing shows.

The story follows the original daytime soap, with Barnabas (Cross)

Ben Cross, as the reluctant vampire Barnabas Collins, puts the moves on Victoria Winters (Joanna Going) in the updated version of "Dark Shadows" (1991). Photo from Dan Curtis Productions.

released from his crypt by the dimwitted Willie (Jim Fyfe) and falling into the arms of the young governess Victoria Winters (Joanna Going), who resembles his lost Josette. Their mutual attraction is offset by the vampire's need for blood, which leads to an attack on his cousin Daphne (Rebecca Staab). Her death, along with several attacks on other women, brings the local sheriff (Michael Cavanaugh) and Julia Hoffman (Barbara Steele) to the Collins estate. At first Barnabas falls under suspicion. But when Daphne returns from the dead and is seen by David (Joseph Gordon-Levitt) and Joe (Michael Weiss), attention is redirected by all except Dr. Hoffman. She knows the truth about Barnabas Collins and attempts to cure him so that he will love her. Subsequent episodes involve the ghost of Sarah Collins (Veronica Lauren), Barnabas's involvement with cousin Carolyn (Barbara

Opposite: Promotional artwork from NBC's new "Dark Shadows" (1991). Excerpt from *TV Guide.*

Ben Cross as the reluctant vampire Barnabas Collins in the big-budget television remake of *Dark Shadows* (1991).

Blackburn), the psychic predictions of Maggie (Ely Pouget), a costume ball, and a flashback to the eighteenth century and witch hunter the Reverend Trask (Roy Thinnes).

Under Curtis's competent direction, the first four hours, which premiered on January 13 and 14, made above-average television viewing, effectively creating the gothic horror atmosphere of the original while telling the familiar story in a sleek and sexy way. "The basic parameters of the story are the same, but the incidents within them have all been replotted," Curtis remarked. "So we have some new ways of getting to some of the same places that we got to before." "Dark Shadows—The Series," which aired opposite the declining "Dallas" on Friday nights, lives up to the promise of the miniseries and delivers some of the finest acting, writing, and special effects seen on network television.

According to the Nielsen ratings, the viewership of twenty-four million people helped make the four-hour miniseries one of the most watched shows of the year. Similar numbers made the series one of the bright spots in an otherwise lackluster television year. In fact, competitors Richard and Esther Shapiro ("Dynasty") were so encouraged by the news that they announced the beginning of production on *Blood Ties*, a multigenerational saga about a family of vampires for the Fox network.

1991 "Tales from the Crypt"

HBO Home Entertainment. Episode: "The Reluctant Vampire." Director: Elliot Silverstein. Producers: Richard Donner, David Giler, Walter Hill, Joel Silver, Robert Zemeckis, Gilbert Adler. Writer: Terry Black, based on an original story from *Vault of Horror* by William Gaines. Starring Malcolm McDowell, Sandra Searles Dickinson, George Wendt, Michael Berryman.

Like *Tales from the Crypt* (1972) and *Vault of Horror* (1973), two anthology films from Amicus Productions inspired by the E. C. horror comics of Al Fedstein and William Gaines, HBO's award-winning cable series offers a weekly dose of "murder, madness, and mayhem." Although most of the episodes of the first three seasons have purposely avoided the subject of vampires, one delightful episode (from the third season) found Malcolm McDowell portraying a hapless reluctant vampire.

"The Reluctant Vampire" disdains the violent activities of his ancestors and seeks a more humane answer to his unusual thirst. Working evenings as a night watchman at a local blood bank, McDowell has access to all the nourishment he needs as a vampire. However, donations have fallen sharply, and boss George Wendt is threatening to fire all his employees if the bank fails to show a profit. Fearing he may lose the security of his position, the vampire decides to take matters into his own hands. He awkwardly attacks several criminals (who are committing crimes) and drains their blood into the little plastic containers the bank uses. Literally overnight, the blood bank becomes successful. Unfortunately, his nocturnal activities draw the attention of a crazed vampire hunter (Michael Berryman), and he must quickly find someone else who is willing to take credit for the blood. Witty and thoroughly engaging, the episode was one of the series's best.

One other episode, "Mournin' Mess," was another retelling of the classic E. C. Comics tale "Midnight Mess" (which had been previously filmed by Amicus for *Vault of Horror*), with a secretive group of subterranean cannibals substituting for vampires. Under the guidance of genre greats Richard (*The Lost Boys*) Donner, David (*Alien*) Giler, Walter (*Alien*)

Hill, Joel (*Predator*) Silver, Robert (*Back to the Future*) Zemeckis, perhaps other excursions into the dark side of vampirism will follow.

1991 *Blood Ties*

Twentieth Century–Fox, 100 min. Producers-Writers: Richard and Esther Shapiro. Starring Harley Venton, Kim Johnston-Ulrich, Salvator Xeureb, Jason London, Grace Zabriskie.

Encouraged by the overnight success of *Dark Shadows*, Richard and Esther Shapiro announced the beginning of production on *Blood Ties*, a multigenerational saga about a family of vampires for the Fox network. Back in the 1980s, the Shapiros (along with Aaron Spelling) created "Dynasty," the popular nighttime drama of glitz and greed that defined the Reagan era. Now, nearly ten years later, the Shapiros have reworked their magic to create a worthy successor for the Carrington clan.

The story opens in Long Beach, California, where a group of dark-complected citizens who call themselves Carpathians resist the increasing pressures for assimilation. They are no ordinary immigrants, however; they are vampires from Transylvania. Harry Martin (Harley Venton), a thirty-something newspaper reporter, keeps telling his fellow Carpathians that "we're Americans and it's time we came out of the coffin." Unfortunately, his plea for peaceful coexistence is interrupted by a war between a group of religious fanatics (called the Southern Coalition Against Vampires) and a violent fringe element of the Carpathians (led by his distant cousin Butch Vlad). Into this conflict, distant cousin Cody (Jason London) wanders looking for a home now that his vampire parents have been murdered.

Various subplots, one revolving around a beautiful prosecuting attorney (Kim Johnston-Ulrich) and another involving Butch's biker gang, further complicate matters in this two-hour television movie. Although the Fox movie does reach a resolution to the central conflict, many plot twists remain unresolved. Only time and the all-powerful television ratings will determine whether American audiences are ready for more weekly excursions into the dark world of the vampire.

9

The Vampire Reconsidered
From *Martin* (1978) to *Fright Night* (1985)

By the late seventies, the vampire film had obtained almost mythic status. For years it had struggled to climb above the B-movie level to reclaim its respectability, and by 1978, it had finally emerged as the predominant standard for horror fantasy. Filmmakers and studio executives had reviewed the form's considerable reputation and eventually revised their opinions of this misunderstood art form. This reevaluation not only strengthened the vampire film's commercial potential in a series of highly atmospheric and imaginative nightmares but also led to a horror renaissance which brought about the last great horror school.

But the triumph of the vampire film was inevitable. From its silent beginnings to its more contemporary forms, the vampire film had survived numerous cycles and horror schools and had continued to advance after other genre favorites (like the Western or the gangster film) had faded away. It had adapted and changed with the varying social and cultural mores. Its total spectrum and unlimited range tended to reflect the cinema's developing sophistication. The form had also demonstrated over the years its ability to make money (in spite of limited budgets and imagination) and maintain an audience. More important, the vampire film had revealed the cinema's potentialities for exploring psychology and psychosexuality, lyricism and violence, and new sensory and visual experiences.

Although many filmmakers attempted to take advantage of the vampire by exploiting its rich heritage or creating hybrids that vastly extended its cinematic horizons, the very nature of the vampire film changed very little throughout its eighty-year history. Each failed attempt—to make it into a Western, a science-fiction opus, or something else—persuaded filmmakers to reevaluate their efforts. Ultimately, certain filmmakers realized that they were diluting the very simplicity that had made the form so popular. The predominance of literary, dramatic, pornographic, and violent traditions were cast aside in favor of a reconsideration of the vampire mystique. This heightened sensibility and awareness (clearly a reflection of the times) restored the evil menace and smooth sensuality of the vampire without the bloody violence or pornography of the previous epochs. It also created some interesting forms that would retain the vampire film's simplicity while expanding its cinematic conventions.

Four predominant forms emerged in the late seventies and eighties because of this reevaluation. One ambitious form attempted to demytholo-gize the traditional vampire story and examine the psychological rationale for vampirism. Films like *Martin* (1978), *The Tenderness of Wolves* (1978), *Fade to Black* (1980), and *One Dark Night* (1982) featured twisted humans who thought they were vampires and scrutinized the psychosis of blood lust. On the other hand, the comic-satiric form attempted to poke fun or parody (rather than investigate) the traditional vampire movie, and films like *Nocturna* (1978), *The Vampire Hookers* (1978), *Love at First Bite* (1978), and *Once Bitten* (1985) tended to produce mixed but generally humorous results. The third form, a novel one which actually dated back to Murnau's *Nosferatu* (1922), evoked the contemporary writings of Anne Rice and Chelsea Quinn Yarbro. In films like *Nightwing* (1979), *The Hunger* (1983), *The Keep* (1983), and *Lifeforce—The Space Vampires* (1985), the vampire was portrayed as a member of a superior race which existed long before human history and was content to feed upon humanity like cattle. And the last form, perhaps the most important one, represented a return to the traditional vampire film. Motion pictures like *Monster Club* (1980), *Mama Dracula* (1981), *The Black Room* (1982), and *Fright Night* (1985) restored the classic Hammer style of horror fantasy and pointed the direction for future vampire movies.

1978 *Martin*

Libra Films, 95 min. Director-Writer: George Romero. Producer: Richard Rubenstein. Starring John Amplas, Lincoln Maazel, Christine Forest, Elayne Nadeau, Fran Middleton, George Romero, Tom Savini.

George Romero's *Martin* (1978) was very much a template for those films which followed, and viewing it today we easily forget that when the film was made, the elements were fresh and controversial. In his fourth film since *Night of the Living Dead* (1968), Romero was anxious to demythologize the vampire film and tell a modern horror story: "I wanted to depict a young man who was a psychotic and not someone wrapped in gothic symbolism." Martin truly believes he is a descendant of Murnau's Nosferatu: he craves human blood and attacks victims in order to obtain it. However, Romero does not cloak his eponymous "hero" in ritual or superstition. He portrays Martin's obsessive need as a type of drug addiction and requires his "vampire" to use a hypodermic to feast on his victim's blood.

After credit titles against the shadowy backdrop of a Pittsburgh train station build ominously, the film opens with Martin (played by John Amplas) stalking his first victim on a train. He murders a young coed, who is glimpsed only briefly reading B. F. Skinner's *Beyond Freedom and Dignity*. He then slashes her wrists and injects himself with the blood that is still pulsating from her body. For a moment his vampiric craving is satisfied, and he too is relieved, masturbating over the girl's dead body. Martin cannot have a normal sexual relationship and substitutes blood lust and necrophilia for his adolescent passions.

When he returns home, he is greeted warmly by his cousin (Christine Forrest) and his grandfather Cuda (Lincoln Maazel), but Martin is incapable of expressing affection even with his own family and runs from their tenderness. He retreats to his darkroom and dreams about his vampire heritage in self-indulgent fantasies. Once he is sufficiently aroused, Martin goes in search of other victims. At one point Martin is seduced by a housewife (Elayne Nadeau) whom he sought to victimize, and he is momentarily freed from his pathological desires. However, when she commits suicide, Martin discovers her bloodied body, and his vampiric passions return.

News of the housewife's death convinces Cuda that his grandson is a vampire. Fearing for his life and the life of his granddaughter, he surrounds his household with mirrors, crosses, and garlic. Martin not only laughs off the old man's foolishness but also rips away the garlic and hides the crucifix. The old talismans don't work anymore, for the young man has become a different kind of vampire. Martin continues to poke fun at the movie-vampire lore, dressing up in a black cape and fangs, and at exorcism, seeking out the services of a Catholic priest (in a satiric send-up of *The Exorcist*, 1973). After more deaths, however, and overwhelming evidence that Martin is a vampire, Cuda produces a wooden stake and plots to rid suburban Pittsburgh of the menace. In the climactic finale, Martin is killed by his grandfather while dreaming of vampires!

Martin (1978) is a disturbing yet visionary examination of the psychosis of vampirism. Produced with funds that Romero earned from industrial commercials, the film never reveals its low-low budget, maintaining high

production values and quality acting. John Amplas is totally believable as
the young psychotic, and Maazel, Forrest, Nadeau, and Tom Savini are first
rate in their supporting functions. But the true genius of the film is George
Romero. Rejecting all the trappings that had made vampire films passé,
Romero reconsidered what had made the classics like *Nosferatu* (1922),
Vampyr (1932), and *The Vampire Bat* (1933) so popular and restored the terror and menace of the vampire which had been missing from so many contemporary films. *Martin* may not be a classic film, but it is certainly a
superior effort.

1978 *The Tenderness of Wolves (Zärtlichkeit der Wölfe)*

Tango Films, German. 87 min. Director: Uli Lommel. Producer:
Rainer Werner. Writer: Kurt Raab. Starring Jeff Roden, Margit
Carstenden, Kurt Raab, Wolfgang Schreck, Rainer Werner.

Following closely on the success of *Martin, The Tenderness of Wolves*
(1978) was concerned with another psychotic vampire, the real-life
murderer Fritz Haarman of Hanover, Germany. Directed by the award-
winning German filmmaker Uli Lommel, this film was not as oppressive as
Romero's and was told in an avant-garde symbolic fashion (owing much in
style to Vadim and Buñuel). But once again the real menace of the film is
a twisted human who believes that he is a vampire.

Set in pre–Hitler Germany (1925), the motion picture focuses on the
Hanover vampire. Fritz Haarman (Kurt Raab), a onetime soldier and police
informer, believes himself to be descended from Transylvanian vampires
and derives both nourishment and sexual fulfillment from young boys. Day
after day, he picks up refugee boys near the local railway and takes them
back to his apartment. Once there, Haarman first rapes them, then tears out
his victim's throats, draining their blood. After several bodies are
discovered, a local police inspector (Jeff Roden) traces the murders to Haarman. The Hanover vampire is arrested, and it is revealed at his trial that he
has killed more than forty young men between the ages of twelve and eighteen. This revelation causes a great commotion that rocks the very foundation of polite German society. The people demand his execution, and this
pedophiliac, homosexual rapist is beheaded (one of the traditional ways to
dispose of a vampire) in the closing minutes of the film.

The Tenderness of Wolves is a bizarre, flawed film which works better
as a historical document than as entertaining cinema. The details of his exploits are painfully recorded in frame after frame of dramatic symbolism.
Lommel's variation of the basic vampire themes is audacious, but it suffers
from the most basic flaw of avant-garde moviemaking: It is boring. The risk
of pushing his imagination so far and testing the receptivity of his audience

goes too far, and what remains is a diatribe of symbols and historical facts. Raab's performance—bald head and pointed ears—is downright scary, evoking both Schreck from Murnau's *Nosferatu* and Peter Lorre from Fritz Lang's *M* (1931), but it is simply not strong enough to carry the film. The public never took to the film, and Lommel soon gave up his attempts to copy Buñuel and Vadim, and produced a series of successful shockers, including *The Boogey Man* (1980).

1980 *Fade to Black*
American Cinema, 102 min. Director-Writer: Vernon Zimmerman. Producers: George Braunstein, Ron Hamady. Starring Dennis Christopher, Linda Kerridge, Tim Rhamerson, Gwynne Gilford, Norman Burton, Morgan Paul, James Luisi, John Steadman.

Greater maturity of thought and cinematic entertainment were apparent in *Fade to Black* (1980), Vernon Zimmerman's compelling study of a lonely, misunderstood youth who becomes a psychotic killer. Zimmerman makes skilled use of classic cinema's signs and conventions, and produces a tightly wound thriller that is also a people story. Unlike Romero's *Martin,* the focus on the young man, who has retreated from the world to his own make-believe fantasy land, is more sympathetic and evokes great pity and pathos. The story is simple enough but is sensitively written (by Zimmerman) and sensitively portrayed by Dennis Christopher, who earned much critical attention.

Eric Binford (Christopher) is an obsessive movie buff who watches and memorizes films in nightly rituals when he's not working for a video store. Because he is slightly odd, he has no friends, and he is often ridiculed for his fascination with old movies. But it is more than fascination. The old movies are his friends and represent a type of release from a cold, unfeeling world. However, his perceptions of reality and fantasy collapse when he delivers a cassette to a Marilyn Monroe look-alike (Linda Kerridge). He falls head over heels for her, but she rejects his love. Suddenly he assumes the guises of famous movie monsters, such as the mummy, Norman Bates (of *Psycho* fame), and his favorite, Dracula, and murders those who have abused him throughout the years. The killings are cleverly conceived, based entirely on Binford's favorite movie-murder scenes. Unfortunately, the police track the deaths to him, and in an exciting climax above Mann's (Grauman's) Chinese Theatre, Binford is gunned down.

Fade to Black (1980) is rich in cinematic images and conventions, and represents an intelligent approach to the psychosis of vampirism. Christopher commits the murders not to satisfy a particular blood lust but to pay tribute to a ritualistic tradition (that of the vampire film, with Dracula sucking the blood of his victims) which is at the core of his loneliness and mental illness. He is unable to separate the fantasy world of the movies from reality and becomes lost in a netherworld of cinematic nightmares. When he attends a showing of Romero's *Night of the Living Dead* (1968), he dresses up like Dracula, in part as a tribute, in part as his own identity. Although *Fade to Black* is not a perfect film, it is a wonderful examination of the cinema's role in its audience's perception of reality.

1982 *One Dark Night*
Independent. Director-Writer: Tom McLoughlin. Starring Meg Tilly, Robin Evans, Adam West.

Superficially similar to *Fade to Black*, Tom McLoughlin's *One Dark Night* (1982), based on his original story, offered a far more atmospheric story and setting but failed to tell as compelling a tale. McLoughlin, the veteran director of other scene chillers, chose as his central focus a lonely young college girl who is the victim of sorority pranks and allies herself with a "psychic vampire." He cast Meg Tilly (Academy Award nominee for *Agnes of God*, 1985) in the role of the sensitive misfit and surrounded her with a fine array of character actors, including (the original *Batman*) Adam West. But this film is not up to the originality of Zimmerman's effort.

The film opens (much like Brian De Palma's *Carrie*, 1976, with which it shares many similarities) with Tilly attempting to adjust to the rigors and social climate of college life. She is not very successful and quickly becomes the brunt of numerous practical jokes. Meanwhile, psychopath Karl Raymar has developed the power to rob young girls of their bioenergy and becomes a "psychic" vampire, striking at will. His seemingly "dead" corpse is placed in a mausoleum, and Tilly, who deperately wants to fit in, must spend the night locked inside the vault as part of a sorority initiation pledge. Her "sisters" have no intention of letting her join, and as the "one dark night" progresses, she begins to realize that. She joins forces with the vampire, and together they set about to kill each of the sorority girls. In the film's climactic conclusion, 154 corpses (designed by Tom Burman) are brought to life (in a scene reminiscent of *Night of the Living Dead*) and turned loose on the campus, literally smothering the principals to death.

Horror elements are plentiful and harsh in *One Dark Night:* an eerie, mist-laden mausoleum; a sinister vampire; the walking dead; wicked yet vulnerable stepsisters; and a sensitive heroine turned evil. The phony backlot town is cleverly used with the right elaborate camera movement and editing styles. Yet despite its many trappings and cinematic conventions, the film lacks the vision of Romero's *Martin* or the soul of Zimmerman's *Fade to Black*. McLoughlin's film is an exercise in horror fantasy rather than a study of the psychosis of the vampire and never rises to the same level as the others.

By sharp contrast to the psychotic vampire, the comic efforts sought to poke fun or parody the conventions of the vampire film. The enormous and totally unsuspected success of *The Rocky Horror Picture Show* (1975) (in limited midnight showings) set in motion this new cycle of films. Some, like *Love at First Bite* (1979) and *Once Bitten* (1985), were particularly good; others, like *Nocturna* (1978), *Vampire Hookers* (1978), *A Polish Vampire in Burbank* (1984), and *Transylvania 6-5000* (1985), were quite forgettable. But while such diverse entries shed considerable light on (what they perceived were) the worn-out traditions of the vampire film, the patterns were ones of feedback rather than genuine originality. *The Rocky Horror Picture Show* had seized audiences with imaginative delight, daring to tread on the hallowed conventions with true parody (as well as a bizarre mixture of sex and rock); whereas these films approached their subject with an unstated reverence that seemed to nullify any attacks on the vampire film's sacred heritage. The period would witness a number of comic vampire movies, but none with the biting satire of their predecessor.

1978 *Nocturna*
Media Films/AIP, 89 min. Director: Harvey Tampa. Starring John Carradine, Yvonne De Carlo, Brother Theodore, Nai Bonet.

Both *Nocturna* (1978) and *Vampire Hookers* (aka *Sensuous Vampires,* 1978) were played for laughs rather than parody, but they both suffered from a general lack of imagination. While the films attempt to substitute soft-core pornography and silly one-liners in place of originality, the stock characterization, rough editing, low-low production values, and comic-strip form make concentration difficult if not impossible. Dracula (portrayed by John Carradine in both efforts) is depicted as a decrepit, denture-wearing old man, and his once sinister castle in old Transylvania has been converted for guests. In fact, the points of similarity between the two films are so obvious that the plot lines seems to merge together interchangeably.

In *Nocturna*, Dracula's castle has been transformed into a hotel, complete with a rock group for entertaining guests. Servants provide guests with every imaginable comfort, and when they are sufficiently satisfied, the guests are drained of blood for the old Count. (With dentures, he can no longer do it for himself.) Nocturna (Nai Bonet), Dracula's hip granddaughter, falls in love with one of the rock musicians and runs away to New York with him. She proves herself a very contemporary vampire, dancing at discos and taking bubble baths in witches' cauldrons. When Dracula learns that his granddaughter has flown the coop, he rushes to the States to save her from the evil world. The film's redeeming factors are few. Comic Brother Theodore plays Nocturna's voyeuristic manservant with great flair, and Yvonne De Carlo recreates her role from *The Munsters* as Nocturna's chaperone.

1978 *Vampire Hookers* (aka *The Sensuous Vampires*)
Filipino, AIP. 86 min. Director: Sirio H. Santiago. Producer: Robert Waters. Starring John Carradine, Karen Stride, Lenka Novak, Katie Dolan.

In *Vampire Hookers* there are no redeeming factors. Here Dracula's castle has been converted into a bordello where navy sailors are lured by shapely, negligeed vampires working for Dracula. Once there, all of the men's desires are satisfied by these "vampire hookers," and they become the victims of the old Count. (He no longer has the energy to bite victims and must be fed the blood in alcoholic cocktails.) During the course of the film, however, the girls become attracted to one young stud they pick up, and Dracula's swank, comfortable setup is threatened.

Both films were box-office failures, lacking wit, imagination, and humor, and represent a low point for the period. In fact, the pattern might have ended prematurely if it hadn't been for the unprecedented success of what some critics term "the funniest vampire film ever made"—*Love at First Bite* (1978).

1979 *Love at First Bite*
AIP, 96 min. Director: Stan Dragoti. Producer: Joel Freeman. Writer: Robert Kaufman. Starring George Hamilton, Susan St. James, Arte Johnson, Dick Shawn, Richard Benjamin.

Like *Young Frankenstein* (1974) and *The Rocky Horror Picture Show* (1975), *Love at First Bite* is composed of nearly every joke and witticism about horror movies, but this time performed as broadly as the classic burlesque skits of the 1930s. Irritated by howling wolves outside his castle, Dracula exclaims: "Children of the night—shut up!" It is also full of sight gags and sexual innuendo, at the same time poking fun at the vampire mythos and modern society. Count Dracula not only raids the local blood bank but gets drunk, draining the blood of a street wino. When Susan St. James is swept off her feet by the vampire (during the taping of her television commercial), her concern is not with her safety but reaching her orgasm as a fulfilled, sexually liberated woman of the eighties.

Love at First Bite (1979). George Hamilton played Count Dracula with tongue firmly planted in cheek in this comic parody of the classic vampire story. Photo courtesy of American International Pictures.

The film opens (predictably) in Transylvania. As with *Dracula and Son* (1976) and *Dracula's Dog* (1976), the Communists have sold Dracula's castle for back taxes, and he, along with his servant Renfield (Arte Johnson), decides to go to New York to claim a fashion model (St. James) whose face he's seen on the cover of a magazine. However, his coffin is accidentally sent to a Harlem chapel, and after interrupting a soulful black funeral, his visit to the Big Apple goes downhill. He gets mugged, wanders into a nightly disco, and becomes intoxicated on the wrong blood type. When he finally meets the fashion model, he must contend not only with her liberated outlook but also her psychiatrist boyfriend (Richard Benjamin), who is coincidentally the descendant of his former nemesis, Dr. Van Helsing. Dracula handles each of these problems with great style and panache but each time ends up on the short end of the stake. Eventually he decides to leave New York for warmer climates and succeeds in making St. James his vampire bride. As the two fly off to South America (as bats), Van Helsing is put in a straitjacket and confined to the booby hatch.

George Hamilton is funny and engaging as Dracula, his comedic style more Rodney Dangerfield than Abbott and Costello. He is the most foul creature of the night, feasting on human blood at will, yet his Count gets no respect. Arte Johnson is similarly memorable in his imitation-parody of Dwight Frye's Renfield. The wisecracks come fast and furious, and the cumulative effect forces laughter even when you are too exhausted to laugh. But there is also a higher wit to *Love at First Bite*, in throwaway references to vampire traditions and clichés, particularly Van Helsing's scrambling of monster lore. Out of all the comic patterns, this film comes the closest in satire of the vampire film.

1985 *Once Bitten*
Samuel Goldwyn Company, 93 min. Director: Howard Storm. Producer-Writer: Dimitri Villard, based on his original story. Starring Clevon Little, Karen Kopins, Jim Carrey, Skip Lackey, Tom Ballatore, Lauren Hutton.

Howard Storm was obviously influenced by *Love at First Bite* in making *Once Bitten* (1985), a clever diversion that rises above the commonplace. Dismissed at the time of its release as another teenage sex comedy and virtually forgotten today, the movie is an imaginative send-up of the vampire film. Storm, a former stand-up comedian and television sit-com writer, extracts comedy from the familiar rituals and traditions of horror fantasy with enough clever gags and high camp that it takes more than one viewing to catch them all. Coupled with a fine supporting cast, including Lauren Hutton and Cleavon Little, *Once Bitten* is a delightful surprise for vampire filmgoers and anticipates a whole subgenre of teen vampire movies, including *Vamp* (1986), *Dracula's Widow* (1988), *My Best Friend Is a Vampire* (1988), and *Teen Vamp* (1988).

Set in the kinky confines of contemporary Los Angeles, the film focuses on the "countess" (Hutton), a four-hundred-year-old vampire who needs the virgin blood of an eighteen-year-old male every generation or so. (She must bite the inner thigh of the virgin three times to perpetuate her beautiful persona.) Sebastian (Little), her flamboyant gay servant, has a number of fine prospects in mind for her; but she has her sights set on Mark (Jim Carrey), a young high school boy whom she has picked up at a bar. Mark has been

Lauren Hutton plays the mysterious Countess in Howard Storm's wonderfully funny *Once Bitten* (1985). Photo courtesy of the Samuel Goldwyn Company.

anxious, like most boys his age, to lose his virginity, but his girlfriend Robin (Karen Kopins, a former Miss America candidate) wants to wait. She's not a prude; she just needs time to think and doesn't want to appear "easy." Unfortunately, with the encouragement of his buddies Russ (Skip Lackey) and Jamie (Tom Ballatore), Mark succumbs to his temptations and goes home with the countess. After Mark is bitten twice, he begins to act and dress like a vampire, and his nihilistic attitudes scare Robin. The comic climax occurs at the countess's castle mansion where Robin learns of the vampire's scheme and makes the supreme sacrifice of her virginity to rescue her boyfriend.

1984 *A Polish Vampire in Burbank*

Vistar International Productions, 88 min. Starring Mark Pierro, High O'Fields, Barry Atwater.

Poster art from *Once Bitten* (1985). Poster art courtesy of the Samuel Goldwyn Company.

Reporters Jeff Goldblum and Ed Begley, Jr., set out to prove that vampires, werewolves, and mad scientists really exist in New World Pictures' horror-spoof comedy *Transylvania 6-5000*. Courtesy of Trans Atlantic Entertainment.

1985 *Transylvania 6-5000*

New World Pictures, 90 min. Director: Rudy DeLuca. Starring Jeff Goldblum, Geena Davis, Ed Begley, Jr., Carol Kane, Joseph Bologna, John Byner, Norman Fell.

Anxious to capitalize on the success of *Love at First Bite* and *Once Bitten, A Polish Vampire in Burbank* (1984) and *Transylvania 6-5000* (1985) were rushed into production. These films were cheap in production values and cinematic techniques and lack any skill, imagination, or wit. (In fact, Brian De Palma's framing movie for *Body Double* [1985] about the punk-rock vampire is better staged and more humorous.) The concepts for the two films are ludicrous. In *A Polish Vampire in Burbank*, Count Dracula kicks his nerdy son out of their posh Burbank home and forces him to fend for himself. Predictably, he becomes involved with hookers, gangsters, and the swinging singles scene. In *Transylvania 6-5000*, Jeff Goldblum and Ed Begley, Jr., are reporters who write sensational stories for a tabloid newspaper (like the *National Enquirer*). They become involved with all sorts of monsters, including the mummy, the werewolf, the Frankenstein monster, and a vampire (sexy Geena Davis). Neither film succeeded, and both have been happily forgotten.

In spite of the many failures, the comic-satiric form remains a very vital

Mad scientist Joseph Bologna roughs up two servants (John Byner and Carol Kane) after failing to create the perfect vampire in New World Pictures' *Transylvania 6-5000*. Courtesy of Trans Atlantic Entertainment.

part of horror fantasy. Without films like *The Rocky Horror Picture Show*, *Love at First Bite*, and *Once Bitten* to keep the genre in check, the vampire film would become a stuffy, self-important form, without its traditional rituals and symbols, never growing beyond a set pattern.

A third group of films—more vital, ambitious, and cinematically important—sprang from current literary trends and a new-wave approach to the vampire. George R. R. Martin's *Fevre Dream*, Fred Saberhagen's *An Old Friend of the Family*, S. P. Somtow's *Vampire Junction*, Michael Talbot's *Delicate Dependency*, Chelsea Quinn Yarbro's St. Germain series, and Anne Rice's *Vampire Chronicles* (as well as the bestselling precursors to *The Keep* and *The Hunger*) were all fascinated with the origins of the vampire species and its mythology. Like Murnau's *Nosferatu* (1922), these books expressed a theory that the vampire existed long before human history and that a consideration of the vampire's origins would provide renewed interest in the genre. In *The Hunger* (1983) and *Lifeforce—The Space Vampires* (1985), this preoccupation had its most general and commercial expression, though it is also apparent as background material in *Nightwing* (1979) and *The Keep* (1983).

By any standards, all four films represent a noble experiment with the traditional concepts of the vampire film, presenting material that is both new and thought-provoking.

1979 *Nightwing*

United Artists, 105 min. Director: Arthur Hiller. Producer: Martin Ransohoff. Writers: Steve Shagan, Bud Shraka, based on the book by Martin Cruz Smith. Starring Nick Mancuso, David Warner, Kathryn Harold, Ben Piazza, Stephen Macht.

In *Nightwing*, Steve Shagan's adaptation of the Martin Cruz Smith novel, the vampire is mystically rooted in American-Indian folklore and manifests itself in a colony of vampire bats. Although the vampire never appears in human form, the ages-old creature is said to have evolved into a higher existence (requiring human blood to maintain its immortality). And when thousands of plague-invested vampire bats invade a Hopi-Navajo reservation in southwest Arizona, the local Indian sheriff (Nick Mancuso) calls upon a maddened Van Helsing (David Warner), with his truckload of scientific tracking equipment, to rid their settlement of the menace. The story, with its mysterious deaths, bat attacks, and search for the bat cave, becomes a traditional vampire tale, provided that we accept its revisionist assumption of the vampire's origin. Unfortunately, though the plotting is tense and the special effects are first rate, the audience was unable to grasp its cerebral premise, and the film failed miserably at the box office.

1983 *The Hunger*

MGM, 99 min. Director: Tony Scott. Producer: Richard Shepherd. Writers: James Costigan, Ivan Davis, Michael Thomas, based on the novel by Whitney Strieber. Starring Catherine Deneuve, David Bowie, Susan Sarandon, Cliff De Young, Dan Hedaya, James Aubrey.

The Hunger (1983) was less cerebral and more a commercial thriller but was also unable to make back even its initial costs of production. (The film barely lasted a week in the theaters during the summer of 1983.) Nevertheless, this adaptation of Whitney Strieber's novel is stunning, impressive, and visually dazzling, and in years to come it will be recognized as a minor masterpiece of horror fantasy. Directed by former television commercial maker Tony Scott, the film examines in great detail the history and contemporary lifestyle of a modern vampire. "The word 'vampire' never occurs in our screenplay," stated producer Richard Shepherd about his offbeat production. "There are no fangs or bats or capes or people who sleep while the sun is up. They are someone you might meet. They are beings like us, just beyond our reality."

Miriam Blaylock (Catherine Deneuve) is an immortal (as long as she has a constant supply of human blood to sustain her). She has existed almost from the beginning of human history, from ancient Egypt and imperial Rome through the Dark Ages to modern times, feeding upon mankind. Throughout the centuries, as her kind has died from wars, pestilence, or other causes, she has been forced to convert humans to her unique body chemistry to have love and companionship. Yet while she lives forever, her human lovers survive for only a few hundred years, and she is forced to recruit again. When the film opens, John Blaylock (David Bowie) suddenly ages and dies (literally) overnight, and Miriam needs a new companion.

She turns her attentions to Sarah Roberts (Susan Sarandon), a young pathologist and researcher in the field of longevity who is on the verge of discovering a special blood chemistry. When Sarah accidentally wanders into the vampire's lair while researching a criminal case, Miriam seduces her and begins the conversion process. However, Roberts's boyfriend (Cliff De Young) learns the truth behind John Blaylock's death and takes steps to destroy the vampire. He fails when Sarah, protecting her new lover, feels the hunger for blood and kills him. Later, sickened by what she has done, she plots Miriam's demise. In the chilling climax, all of Miriam's lovers return from the grave (at Sarah's bidding) and strip away her immortality, draining her lifeforce.

Intriguing though one may find the historical perspective of the vampire in *The Hunger,* the stylish acting and superb makeup contribute much to this cinematic triumph. Deneuve, who had played the innocent in Bunuel's surreal *Tristana* (1970), is very much in control of the film, with a masklike beauty that reminds one of Helen of Troy. Bowie is both sensitive and eloquent as the rapidly aging lover, and Sarandon rises above her empty-headed role as Janet in *The Rocky Horror Picture* (1975) to a fascinating portrayal as the guileless pathologist. But the real stars of the film are Dick Smith and Carl Fullerton for their flawless "make-up illusions." Smith had created the makeup for Barnabas Collins's vampire in *House of Dark Shadows* (1970) in his early days, but his transformation of Bowie is the supreme achievement of a master. (One year later, Dick Smith won an Academy Award for his makeup of Saleri in *Amadeus* [1984].)

The Hunger is a rich, intelligent approach to the vampire mythos which never condescends to the traditions or clichés of the genre. The current influence of literary form and revisionist thinking is predominant and helps to enhance and raise this production to the level of a fine art form. Though unsuccessful at the box office, the film deserves a second viewing.

The Hunger (1983). Catherine Deneuve and David Bowie appear in the film version of Whitney Strieber's revisionist vampire story. Courtesy of MGM.

1983 *The Keep*

Paramount Pictures, 101 min. Director: Michael Mann. Producer: Gene Kirkwood. Writer: Michael Mann, based on the novel by F. Paul Wilson. Starring Scott Glenn, Alberta Watson, Robert Prosky, Jurgen Prochnow.

The pattern's influence is also noticeable in *The Keep* (1983), one of the more bizarre films of the last great horror school. Borrowing equally from Murnau, Browning, Dreyer, and contemporary forms, the film asks its audience to accept two revisionist speculations about the vampire, then develops swiftly into a classic struggle of good versus evil. The first contention is that the vampire draws its strength not only from blood but also from human pain, misery, and madness. And the second contention, strangely reminiscent of H. P. Lovecraft's Cthulu mythos, is that the vampire descended from the evil gods of the first mystical age. Once these assumptions are made, the pacing picks up, and the audience is plunged into a gothic horror fantasy.

The film opens in World War II Romania. A unit of German soldiers has been dispatched to occupy a medieval fortress in the Transylvanian Alps. When they arrive, they discover thousands of crosses embedded in the wall of the "keep." They can find no reason for the peculiar arrangement of crosses, and the SS orders the crosses removed in spite of warnings from the German commandant (Jurgen Prochnow). He does not know their significance but suspects they have some hidden purpose. His suspicions prove correct. With the removal of one cross, the evil, imprisoned there for centuries, escapes from his cell and murders several of the German soldiers. The fortress is sealed off, and word of the evil menace is sent to Berlin.

Meanwhile, Glaeken (Scott Glenn), the immortal being who first imprisoned the evil, receives word that the keep has been opened and hurries through Allied and German lines to seal the crypt once again. However, dubious of Glaeken's power, the SS bring in Dr. Theodore Cuza (Robert Prosky), a Jewish scholar, and his daughter (Alberta Watson) to solve the problem. Cuza confronts the evil, which transforms itself into a being named Molasar. Molasar reveals that he is a vampire, a survivor from the mystical First Age, and that he has been revived by the human pain and misery of the Nazi death camps. He offers to destroy the Germans if the Jewish scholar will free him. Tempted, Cuza allows him access to the fortress, and Molasar consumes the life force of everyone (including Cuza) to regain his strength. But Glaeken arrives before the evil can escape, and in a climactic struggle, he seals Molasar in the keep forever.

Written and directed by Michael Mann (who created the stylish, revisionist police drama "Miami Vice," 1984, NBC), the film is an honorable attempt to bring F. Paul Wilson's cerebral vision to the screen. The high production values, outstanding set and costume designs, and state-of-the-art special effects are brilliant, as are the acting and directing, but unfortunately *The Keep* is never able to transcend its highbrow, literary heritage. There are too many questions left unanswered at the film's conclusion, and this is a pity because the movie opens with such great possibilities. Perhaps when *The Keep* is released on home video or reedited for television, those ambiguities will be eliminated. (The film's plot bears a striking resemblance to the "Night Gallery" episode "The Devil Is Not Mocked.")

1985 *Lifeforce—The Space Vampires*

MGM/United Artists, Cannon Films, 100 min. Director: Tobe Hooper. Writers: Dan O'Bannon, Don Jakoby, based on the novel *The Space Vampires*, by Colin Wilson. Starring Steve Railsback, Frank Finlay, Peter Firth, Michael Gothard, Nicholas Ball, Patrick Stewart, Mathilda May.

Lifeforce—The Space Vampires (1985), on the other hand, frees itself from its literary bond and most familiar traditions and clichés of the vampire film without abandoning its attitudes and visual conventions. The vampire is shown as something alien threatening human existence, certainly not an ordinary force (as portrayed in hundreds of other movies) with which

tional values for more contemporary ones. The successful appearance of two remakes, *Dracula* and *Nosferatu,* in 1979 signaled that the audience was anxious for a return to that simplicity. The reemergence of the traditional vampire film in the eighties benefited not only from a rich heritage but also from the modern visual techniques of the field, producing one poor film, two somewhat average, and one superior.

1980 *Monster Club*

Sword and Sorcery Productions, 100 min. Director: Roy Ward Baker. Producer: Milton Subotsky. Writers: Edward Abrahams, Valerie Abrahams, based on material by Ronald Chetwynd-Hayes. Starring Vincent Price, John Carradine, Donald Pleasance, Stuart Whitman, Britt Ekland, Simon Ward, James Laurenson, Richard Johnson.

The Monster Club (1980), while an absolute failure, was an ambitious attempt to revive Hammer Films and restore its conventions of horror fantasy to the cinema. Directed by Hammer veteran Roy Ward Baker, this British anthology of stories by writer Ronald Chetwynd-Hayes was a short compendium of horror types, three short stories offering a sample of the most common themes of Hammer horror. It starred an excellent cast—including Vincent Price, Donald Pleasance, John Carradine, Stuart Whitman, Richard Johnson, Britt Ekland, Simon Ward, and Patrick Magee—and the movie featured some of the finest British technical talent. However, its grandiose, almost epic scale is too overpowering for the film's simple-minded story treatments. The second segment purports to be an autobiographical piece by film producer "Lintom Busotsky" (Anthony Steel playing real-life producer Milton Subotsky) involving his vampire father (Carradine) and a policeman (Pleasance) on whom he turns the tables. If it had been done as a parody, the story would have worked, but unfortunately the story is meant as a straight out-of-the-coffin and go-for-the-jugular thriller. *The Monster Club* was never released in the United States (except on videocassette), and the effort to resuscitate Hammer Films (as Sword and Sorcery Productions) failed miserably.

1981 *Mama Dracula*

French/Belgian, 90 min. Director-Producer-Writer: Boris Szulzinger, based on material by Marc-Henri Wajnberg and Pierre Sterckx. Starring Louise Fletcher, Marc-Henri and Alexandre Wajnberg, Maria Schneider, Suzy Falk, Michael Israel, Pierre Sterckx.

Mama Dracula (1981) was considerably less pretentious and far more satisfactory, with an excellent performance by Academy-Award-winner

Louise Fletcher. Derivative in parts of *Countess Dracula* (1972) and a half-dozen other Elizabeth Bathory tales, the movie nevertheless had some chilling moments, and Boris Szulzinger made imaginative use of some well-worn but still effective vampiric conventions.

The film focuses on a contemporary vampire who must periodically bathe in the blood of virgins. The countess (Fletcher), a descendant of the famous Transylvanian Count, hunts victims with her twin vampire sons (Marc-Henri and Alexandre Wajnberg) from her castle, which is nestled in the Carpathian Mountains. When she abducts brilliant young Professor Van Bloed (Jimmy Shuman) by accident, she quickly realizes that his research on artificial blood might free her of her vampiric dependence. However, Nancy Hawaii (Maria Schneider), a female Van Helsing, follows the trail of death to the countess's castle and attempts to put an end to the family of vampires. But Mama Dracula pleads for her life, explaining that all she wants is life and eternal beauty. In the end, Hawaii sympathizes with her plight and joins forces to search for her own immortality.

This French-Belgian effort was far from being a perfect film, but it did put the traditional vampire film back on track after the failure of *The Monster Club*. The images and conventions, though brought into a contemporary setting, are most refreshing, particularly after years of graphic violence, pornography, and psychoanalysis. *Mama Dracula* is an old-fashioned horror fantasy with just the right amount of comedy and wit to prevent the movie from becoming too melodramatic, and it is a welcome addition to the vampire's long cinematic history.

1981 *The Sleep of the Dead* (*Ondskans Värdshus*, aka *The Inn of the Flying Dragon*)

Irish/Swedish, National Film Studios of Ireland, 93 min. Director: Calvin Floyd. Producer: Rudolf Hertzog. Writers: Yvonne and Calvin Floyd, based on a story by Joseph Sheridan Le Fanu. Starring Per Oscarsson, Patrick Magee, Marilu Tolo, Brendan Price, Curt Jürgens.

The Sleep of the Dead (1981) was a cinematic adaptation of Joseph Sheridan Le Fanu's other vampire tale, *The Room in the Dragon Volant*. Set in France in 1815, the story recounts the strange adventure of a young nobleman (Brendan Price) at the equally strange Inn of the Flying Dragon. While traveling through Europe, he becomes entranced with a beautiful but mysterious woman (Marilu Tolo), who is always in the company of a demonic old man (Curt Jürgens). Upon arrival at the French inn, he finds the courage to talk with her and falls for her seductive charms. Several vampiric deaths occur, and he eventually discovers that she must drink blood to stay young. Without it, she resorts back to an ugly old countess (and paramour of Jürgens). Told mostly through suggestion, the tale is hypnotic and surreal, and resembles Dreyer's *Vampyr* (1932).

1982 *The Black Room*
Directors-Writers: Elly Kenner, Norman Thaddeus Vane. Starring Stephen Knight, Cassandra Gaviola, Jimmy Stathis, Clara Perryman.

The Black Room (1982) has also been highly regarded in some critical quarters as the best contemporary vampire film. Admittedly, the epic sense of grandeur and doom may be missing, and the story reverts to the common images of traditional vampire movies, but the tale is treated with great seriousness and imagination. Although hampered by limited resources, the film makes great use of its small budget and produces an effectively scary, highly atmospheric adult vampire tale.

The story, though it may appear simple, is chilling and sophisticated in its exploration of the emotional dimension of its characters. A sexually dissatisfied husband (Jimmy Stathis) rents a swank apartment to enact his sexual fantasies with strangers and hopefully rekindle the passion he still has for his wife. After several weeks of enjoyment, his wife (Clara Perryman) learns of her husband's secret hideaway and rents the room next door to even the score. What they don't realize is that they are caught in a destructive net which their landlords have set. Their two landlords are an attractive, kinky, brother-sister couple (Stephen Knight and Cassandra Gaviola) who kidnap their tenants' lovers and drain them of blood. Eventually the husband and wife learn the truth, but it is much too late as the vampires close in.

The film is full of subtleties, and director Norman Thaddeus Vane's handling of the subtle scenes reveals the social and cultural decay that the vampires have brought into this contemporary setting. *The Black Room* never attempts to psychoanalyze the emotional dimensions of its characters, but it does juxtapose the conventional images of the vampire couple with the adulterous actions of the man and wife to suggest a higher meaning. The film succeeds, then, on a multitude of levels.

1985 *Fright Night*
Columbia, 100 min. Director-Writer: Tom Holland. Producer: Herb Jaffe. Starring Chris Sarandon, William Ragsdale, Amanda Bearce, Stephen Geoffreys, Roddy McDowall.

Skillfully crafted, *Fright Night* (1985) is the apotheosis of the vampire film to date and represents a high point of the last horror school. In the

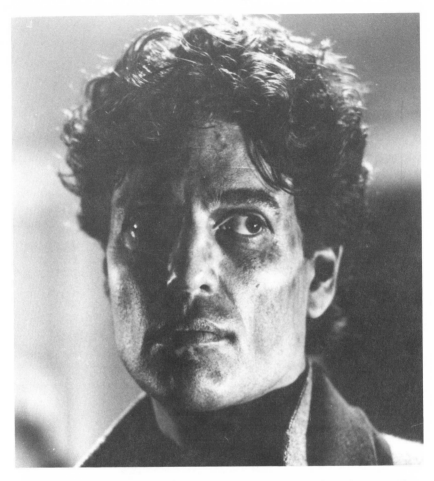

Fright Night (1985). Seductive, sinister vampire Jerry Dandridge (Chris Sarandon).
Photo courtesy of Columbia Pictures.

history of the vampire film, there has been a definite progression from
naivete to sophistication, as witnessed in the earliest productions of Méliès,
Fevillade, and Murnau to the revisionist work of Romero and Hooper. This
has been partially due to changing social and cultural attitudes and the in-
tellectual growth of its potential audience. Coupled with the technological
advances in film and cinematic techniques, the vampire film has attempted
to keep pace with the evolution of the cinema. Yet throughout this progression, there have been few films that have integrated the technologies of today with the legacy of the past as successfully as *Fright Night*.

Fright Night is a modern telling of the time-honored vampire tale.
Written and directed by first-timer Tom Holland, the film returns full cycle

Fright Night (1985). Peter Vincent (Roddy McDowall) comes face-to-face with a neighborhood vampire in this Columbia Pictures release. Photo courtesy of Columbia Pictures.

to the early traditions of Universal's *Dracula* (1931) and Hammer's vampire series. "I love vampires," Holland revealed in a recent interview. "And I have a lot of affection for the old, sometimes corny, vampire movies and all the Hammer horror films. So when I decided to make a vampire movie myself, I chose to stick to the established traditions and to play all the conventions fairly to my audience." Holland's pastiche is sometimes corny but more often chilling and frightening. His imaginative use of visuals is engaging but never overpowering, and he brilliantly intercuts humor when a scene becomes threatened by melodrama.

The movie begins with the traditional howl of a wolf against a full moon. As the camera pans down, we realize that we are not in Transylvania but a suburb of Los Angeles and that the wolf's howl was merely an echo from the late-night horror film that Charley Brewster (William Ragsdale) and his girlfriend Amy (Amanda Bearse) are "watching" in his bedroom. Charley is a vampire-film aficionado, and beyond the prospect of getting laid by his girlfriend, he is devoted to "Fright Night Theatre" and its cinematic nightmares.

When the attractive but mysterious Jerry Dandridge (Chris Sarandon) takes up residence in Charley's peaceful neighborhood, unearthly things begin to happen. Several mangled corpses, their throats torn out and their heads removed, turn up around town, and one night Charley witnesses Dandridge put the bite on a beautiful young hooker. However, he is unable to convince his mother, friends, or the local police that Dandridge is a vampire. They think that his affinity for horror films has contributed to an overactive imagination. With nowhere else to go, he approaches the host of "Fright Night Theatre," Peter Vincent (Roddy McDowall), who has just been fired. Vincent, the aging star and "vampire killer" of numerous B movies, thinks that Charley is crazy and refuses to lend him assistance.

Eventually Charley's friends hire Vincent to pacify the vampire-film aficionado with a few bogus rituals. Vincent gives the vampire holy water to drink, and Dandridge swallows it whole with no side effects. But (in a scene that recalls Van Helsing's discovery of Dracula in the 1931 version) the "vampire killer" discovers that Dandridge casts no reflection in a pocket mirror. He is terrified because he has faced only cinematic vampires and tries to leave town. However, when the vampire turns Evil Ed (Stephen Geoffreys) into a werewolf and transforms Amy into a mindless servant, Vincent must join forces with Charley to destroy the undead creature. In the climactic confrontation, they force Dandridge into his basement lair, and after failing to drive a stake into his heart, they smash all the opaque basement windows. The vampire explodes into flames with the first rays of dawn. Peter Vincent has found the courage he pretended to have in all those films, and Amy and Charley are reunited. But what happened to Evil Ed? The film closes as the camera pans back to the Dandridge house to reveal a pair of glowing vampire eyes.

Fright Night was Columbia Picture's big box-office winner for the summer of 1985, remaining on *Variety*'s top-ten list for seven consecutive weeks. And though it was clearly no more than an updating of *Dracula* and other horror classics, the film's well-rooted, traditional approach to the vampire mythos (in an era of parody and reevaluation) proved a major selling point for contemporary audiences. *Fright Night* also demonstrated that the vampire film was still one of the cinema's most viable and commercial art forms. In fact, soon after *Fright Night* was released, Warner Brothers and Universal announced the start of two large-budget vampire films. Other television and motion-picture projects followed, leading to a major rebirth of the form. And if *Fright Night* was to vampire movies what *Star Wars* (1977) had been to science-fiction films, the efforts of the next few years would pay deference to a truly original cinematic nightmare.

The following films were also released during the period, but no further information beyond the production credits is available.

1980 *Lust at First Bite*
VCX/Media Films. Starring Kay Parker, Michael Ranger, John Holmes, Seka.

1981 *Frightmare*
Heritage Ltd. Films. Director-Writer: Norman Thaddeus Vane. Starring Ferdinand Mayne, Lucia Bercovici, Conrad Radzoff, Nita Talbot.

1982 *Dracula Rises from His Coffin*
Korean, 92 min. Director: Lee Hyoung Pyo. Producer: Lim Wom Sik. Writer: Lee Hee Woo. Starring Kang Young Suk, Park Yang Rae.

1983 *Dracula Tan Exarchia*
Greek, 84 min. Director: Nikos Zervous. Writers: Yannis Panousis, Vangelis Cotronis. Starring Kostas Joumas, Yannis Panousis, Vangelis Cotronis.

1984 *Pure Blood (Pura Sangue)*
Luis Ospina Films, Columbian, 98 min. Director-Producer: Luis Ospina. Writers: Ospina, Rodrigo Castana. Starring Florina Lamaitre, Carlos Mayola, Humberto Arango, Luis Alberto.

Our Old Friend of the Family, the Ageless Vampire

From *Vamp* (1986) to *Fright Night II* (1989),
Rockula (1990), *Bram Stoker's Dracula*
(1992), and Beyond!

"I wonder if—one hundred years from now—anybody would believe that there were once vampires." These prophetic words from the conclusion of Larry Cohen's *Return to Salem's Lot* (1986) pose a profound question and echo our deepest sentiments and fears as we ponder the fate of that unique art form. As the vampire film approached its hundredth anniversary, it had come full cycle, returning to its humble origins, having explored (and exhausted) many new directions, visual styles, and unique characterizations. The mythic theme of good versus evil, deeply rooted in established ritual and convention, remained unchanged, and the struggle of the outcast romantic *anti*-hero (to maintain an eternal life of sensation) was strangely familiar and fresh. Although *Fright Night* (1985) represented the culmination of ninety years of cinematic nightmares with its evocative richness, its use of common elements and set symbols, and its technological achievements in special effects and makeup, there were many avenues still unexplored. Many critics still believed that the definitive vampire film had yet to be made.

Throughout the late eighties and into the early nineties, numerous

268

studios and independent filmmakers produced interpretations of the vampire mythos. Most of the motion pictures came and went with very little fanfare and even less box-office appeal, but there were a number of notable exceptions that lured a younger hip (and often punk) audience to the theater and still received critical and commercial approval. To some, our old friend of the family, the ageless vampire, was after all a popular draw. And while many—like *Vamp* (1986), *Return to Salem's Lot* (1986), *The Monster Squad* (1987), *Beverly Hills Vampire* (1988), *My Best Friend Is a Vampire* (1988), and *Teen Vamp* (1988)—attempted merely to imitate the successful formula of *Fright Night*, a few—particularly *Graveyard Shift* (1986), *The Lost Boys* (1987), and *Near Dark* (1987)—managed to strike out in distinctive, provocative directions of their own.

1986 *Vamp*

New World Pictures, 91 min. Director: Richard Wenk. Producer: Donald P. Borchers. Writers: Wenk, Borchers. Starring Grace Jones, Chris Makepeace, Sandy Baron, Robert Rusler, Deedee Pfeiffer, Billy Drago, Gedde Watanabe.

Vamp (1986) was the first vampire movie to follow in the wake of *Fright Night's* enormous popularity. Directed by Richard Wenk (from his own script), the film is foolish and unintentionally funny when it should be scary and is a veritable hodgepodge of worn-out clichés and stereotypic characters from any number of horror films. *Vamp* debuted in the same summer crop of movies which featured *Top Gun, Aliens,* and *The Fly,* and disappeared a mere seven days after it had opened.

The story focuses on three nerdy college students who want to win the favor of a campus fraternity as they set out to capture the sexiest stripper to entertain their buddies. Keith (Chris Makepeace), A. J. (Robert Rusler), and Duncan (Gedde Watanabe) wander into the After Dark Club, a sleazy burlesque joint in downtown Los Angeles, and discover that the manager (played with great camp style by Sandy Baron), the employees, and the star attraction (Grace Jones) are all vampires. But before they can make good an escape, A. J. and Duncan are seduced and made into vampires, and Keith, along with his childhood sweetheart Amaretto (Deedee Pfeiffer), who coincidentally works there, must spend the balance of the movie fighting off the undead creatures.

Technically, the film is brilliantly done. The special effects are first rate, and Greg Cannom's makeup transforms Grace Jones's Katrina flawlessly from exotic dancer-seductress to queen of the vampires. But the plot similarities to *Fright Night* and *Once Bitten,* as well as the silliness of the unexplained preposterous events, make this film largely forgettable. It was

Poster art from New World Pictures' *Vamp*. Courtesy of Trans Atlantic Entertainment.

Katrina (Grace Jones), queen of the vampires, performs a mysteriously erotic dance at the After Dark Club in New World Pictures' *Vamp*. Courtesy of Trans Atlantic Entertainment.

pity that Greg Cannom wasted his efforts on a commercial trifle such as this when his talents would produce work of a much more lasting quality, as in the case of Joel Schumacher's *The Lost Boys*.

1986 *Return to Salem's Lot*
Warner Brothers, 90 min. Director-Writer-Producer: Larry Cohen. Starring Michael Moriarity, Andrew Duggan, Sam Fuller.

Left: Strippers at the After Dark Club are more than simply undressed—they're vampires! *Right:* Keith (Chris Makepeace) and his frat brothers from Emma Dipsa Phi nearly fall victim to the vampiric strippers at the After Dark Club. Both photographs from *Vamp.* Courtesy of Trans Atlantic Entertainment.

Return to Salem's Lot (1986) was also a major disappointment, but for very different reasons. Originally produced for the video-cable market, the movie was a low-budget follow-up (if you can call it that) to the two-part CBS miniseries. "Creating sequels to hit pictures for the video market is a good idea," Larry Cohen, writer and director, stated in a recent interview, "and I believe that it makes no difference whether a film is geared to theatres or video. If the quality is there, as in *Return to Salem's Lot,* the audience will enjoy it!" Creator of *The Invaders* (1967, ABC) and fantasy *auteur* of *It's Alive* (1975) and *God Told Me To* (1980), Cohen had been intimately involved with the original. He had written a treatment of Stephen King's vampire novel for Warner Brothers in 1977, but Warner felt that his adaptation was too expensive to make as a theatrical film and turned the writing assignment to Paul Monash, who eventually wrote the miniseries. Cohen was not pleased with their decision, but he leaped at the opportunity to make the sequel.

The sequel opens in the sleepy New England village of Salem's Lot. Anthropologist Michael Moriarity and his delinquent son arrive for the summer to work out problems in their relationship. Not long after their arrival, they learn that most of the townspeople are vampires, including some of

Left: Recently hired stripper Amaretto (Deedee Pfeiffer) enlists Keith (Chris Makepeace) to help her expose the vampires of the After Dark Club. *Right:* Katrina (Grace Jones) is about to put the bite on another victim in New World Pictures' *Vamp.* Courtesy of Trans Atlantic Entertainment.

their relatives. Judge Axel (Andrew Duggan), the town leader and head vampire, explains that they have existed apart from the rest of the country for hundreds of years. Many of them came to America with the Pilgrims because they were hounded and persecuted in Europe, and they sought peace and freedom in the New World. They have even developed their own culture and lifestyle, and they are very protective of their home, particularly when outside strangers threaten to upset the natural order. But before Moriarity and his son are overcome by the vampires, they join forces with Nazi hunter Dr. Van Meer (played by action-adventure director Sam Fuller) and put an end to the nightmare of Salem's Lot once and for all.

Beyond the title and setting, *Return to Salem's Lot* bears little resemblance to Stephen King's book or the original chiller by Tobe Hooper. In fact, Cohen's story line actually ignores (and often contradicts) details of the novel and miniseries. Rather than cover the same ground twice, Larry Cohen strikes out boldly on his own, with mixed results. His opening sequences are remarkable for creating a usually convincing atmosphere of evil, and the final staking and disintegration of Judge Axel, though derivative of recent vampire-movie climaxes, is exciting and well done. However, the film offers little advance of the vampire mythos and pales greatly in comparison to the original.

**Grace Jones in two seductive poses as exotic, erotic Katrina in *Vamp* (1986).
Courtesy of New World Pictures.**

1986 *Graveyard Shift* (aka *Central Park Driver*)

Shapiro Entertainment/Lightshow Communications, 88 min.
Director-Writer: Gerard Ciccoritti. Producers: Arnold Bruck,
Stephen R. Flaks. Starring Silvio Oliviero, Helen Papas.

Only one 1986 film offered anything that was genuinely new and imaginative, and this, though flawed by poor theatrical distribution, was made
by an independent in Toronto, Canada. Written and directed by Gerald
Ciccoritti, *Graveyard Shift* (which bears no relationship to the Stephen
King story) cleverly entangles the myth of Dionysius (the god of rejuvena-
tion who was continually killed to be reborn and live forever) with the vampire mystique. This hybrid produces a vampire that is more ancient and
mythic than Dracula and can relate more to the common man. Instead of
virgins for nourishment, the vampire seeks women who are dying and afraid
of death, and the union he forms is a symbiotic one which restores them
to health (as vampires). The concept is a unique one to the vampire lore and
helps tell a sexy, avant-garde tale of social and philosophical relevance. Unfortunately, the film was too nouveau for some censors and had to be
reedited to avoid an X rating (for its excessive sex and violence).

The 350-year-old vampire Stephen Tsepes (Silvio Oliviero) is not
wealthy, does not own a castle in Transylvania, and does not employ a servant named Igor. He is a common working stiff, a cabdriver who works the

"graveyard shift" for the Black Cat cab company. He picks up fares and victims nightly while traveling the dark streets of New York City. Things move along smoothly for Tsepes until one night he bites Michelle (Helen Papas), a hot television director who is dying of an incurable disease. She is repulsed at first by the prospect of becoming an undead bloodsucker, but later she welcomes the chance at immortality. As he passionately restores Michelle to her former beauty, a romance develops between them. However, the woman's estranged husband learns of her fate and hires a Stephen King–like vampire killer to dispatch the cabdriver. A battle between good and evil ensues, and in the end, Michelle, now a vampire who cannot die, takes over other drivers of the cab company in preparation for the sequel.

Graveyard Shift is a chilling but elegant variation that challenges the conventions of the vampire film. "Horror films," according to Ciccoritti, "are the closest things we have to Greek tragedies," and his production, built upon a foundation of recognition, reversal, and catharsis, works on several levels, like classical theater. On one level it is a fast-paced, stylish thriller; on another, it is an imaginative and thought-provoking examination of the human condition. The movie was charged with tension and terror and proved to be more satisfying than many of the current studio offerings.

1988 *Graveyard Shift II: The Understudy*

Shapiro Entertainment/Lightshow Communications, 88 min. Director-Writer: Gerard Ciccoritti. Producers: Arnold Bruck, Stephen R. Flaks. Starring Silvio Oliviero.

Graveyard Shift II: The Understudy went into production late in 1987 and was released in 1988 through Canadian-based Shapiro Entertainment/ Lightshow Communications. The story line details the return of Silvio Oliviero's vampire and his efforts to teach the director of a low-budget horror film the real meaning of terror.

1987 *The Monster Squad*

Tri-Star, Taft/Barish Productions, 88 min. Director: Fred Dekker. Producer: Peter Hyams. Writers: Shane Black, Dekker. Starring Duncan Regehr, Michael MacKay, Carl Thibault, Stephen Macht, Tom Noonan, Tom Woodruff, Ryan Lambert, Brent Chalem, Ashley Bank, Andre Gower.

Lacking any common sense or insight into the genre, *The Monster Squad* (1987) was supposed to have been a loving tribute to the Universal horror spoofs and the *Our Gang* comedies, sort of a "What if the Little

Rascals took on the famous monsters of filmland." However, the film succeeds only in setting the form back nearly forty years. *Abbott and Costello
Meet Frankenstein* (1948) had been the worst of Universal's series and was
single-handedly responsible for the decline of the horror film in the United
States. And though Steven Spielberg's formula of teaming children with
monsters (as in *E.T.—The Extraterrestrial* [1982], *Gremlins* [1984], *The
Goonies* [1985], and *Harry and the Hendersons* [1987]) had proven successful
to eighties audiences, the subject matter of *The Monster Squad* was much
too tame and far from inspired. In fact, the motion picture is weak, juvenile,
and downright embarrassing. (Universal Pictures refused to be involved in
the project because the studio executives did not want "their" monsters
treated ridiculously on film.)

The overly complicated plot concerns the struggle for possession of an
ancient amulet which controls the balance between good and evil. Count
Dracula (Duncan Regehr) owned the icon back in 1888, but Dr. Van Helsing (Jack Gwillim) stole the amulet and hid it in a small southern town in
the United States. Now, one hundred years later, the balance has become
unstable, and Dracula intends, along with the Frankenstein monster (Tom
Noonan), the wolf man (Carl Thibault), gill man (aka the creature from the
Black Lagoon) (Tom Woodruff), and the mummy (Michael MacKay), to use
the icon to unleash evil forever onto the world. Meanwhile, Sean (Andre
Gower), Phoebe (Ashley Bank), and three other children (ages 5–15, Ryan
Lambert, Brent Chalem, and Robby Kiger)—known as the "Monster
Squad" because of their interest in horror films—discover they have only
forty-eight hours to stop the unholy scheme. Their parents, of course, don't
believe them, so they enlist the aid of the Frankenstein monster (who has
been charmed by Phoebe) and boldly challenge Dracula's plans for world
domination. During the climactic battle, which resembles more an episode
of "Pee-Wee Herman's Playhouse" than a horror film, the five children
deftly dispatch the monsters one by one with wooden stakes, silver bullets,
and other occult paraphernalia.

The Monster Squad clearly follows the same disappointing path as
Vamp and *Return to Salem's Lot* and makes many of the same mistakes. The
plot fails to make up its mind to be a comedy-spoof or a horror film.
Whereas comedy actually enhances *Fright Night* with its satiric edge, the
strong language and graphic violence is inconsistent with *The Monster
Squad's* lighter tone. The characters, with the possible exception of
Dracula, are played as stereotypes, and it is somewhat irritating that the
children are infinitely more intelligent than the adults or the monsters. The

Opposite: Dracula (Duncan Regehr), gill man (Tom Woodruff, Jr.), the Frankenstein monster (Tom Noonan), mummy (Michael MacKay), and the wolf man (Carl
Thibault) battle a gang of youngsters known as *The Monster Squad* (1987).

script is overly complicated and relies on wild coincidences to bind its loose ends, and the direction by Fred Dekker (whose *Night of the Creeps* [1984] is a cult classic) is at best pedestrian. The film has only two saving graves: Richard Edlund's superior special effects and Duncan Regehr's Dracula. (Fresh from appearances on *Wizards and Warriors* [1983, CBS] and *V: The Series* [1984: NBC], and a starring role as Errol Flynn in *My Wicked, Wicked Ways* [1985, NBC], Regehr creates a wonderfully sinister and charismatic Dracula.) Otherwise, the production pales in comparison with the effort mounted by Warner Brothers, which was released, coincidentally, one week later.

1987 *The Lost Boys*
Warner Brothers, 99 min. Director: Joel Schumacher. Producers: Richard Donner, Harvey Bernhard. Writers: Janice Fischer, James Jeremias, Jeffrey Boam. Starring Dianne Wiest, Edward Herrmann, Barnard Hughes, Kiefer Sutherland, Jami Gertz, Jason Patric, Corey Haim, Corey Feldman, Jason Newlander.

Greater maturity of thought was apparent in *The Lost Boys* (1987), Joel Schumacher and Richard Donner's imaginative excursion into the dark nightmare world of punk vampires. Ostensibly made for the teenage market, this tale of ageless adolescents who prey upon a California beach community skillfully combines the classic children's tale of Peter Pan with the vampire mythos. This unique mixture produces a vampire that is surprisingly contemporary and real. Instead of the traditional image of the wealthy, dignified aristocrat of European extraction in a black dinner suit, these bloodsuckers dress in punk fashions, drive motorcycles, and hibernate like actual bats in the never-never land of a beach cave. And the conflicts implicit in the confrontation between the fantasy world of the boy who never grew up and the reality of vampirism result in a stylish, provocative film that is rich in black comedy and bloody terror—a true cinematic nightmare.

The story begins when Lucy Emerson (Dianne Wiest, fresh from her Academy-Award-winning performance in *Hannah and Her Sisters*, 1986), a recently divorced mother, moves her family to Santa Carla, the murder capital of the world, to begin a new life with her father (Barnard Hughes). She goes to work at a video store and falls for her mysterious boss (Edward Herrmann). Meanwhile, her two sons, Michael (Jason Patric) and Sam (Corey Haim), as the innocent new kids in town, wander into an amusement park on the boardwalk and become involved in a nightmare. Patric, the elder son, falls for enigmatic Jami Gertz and tangles with Kiefer Sutherland, the charismatic vampire leader, and his group of "lost boys" (Brooke

The Lost Boys (1987). Sex, drugs, and rock. The "lost boys" (Kiefer Sutherland, Brooke McCarter, Billy Wirth, Alex Winter, and Chance Corbitt) and friend (Jami Gertz) in the punk, new-wave vampire film. Photo courtesy of Warner Brothers.

McCarter, Billy Wirth, Alex Winter, and Chance Corbitt). Haim seeks out the innocence of the local SF-comic shop and learns about local vampires from the Frog brothers, Edgar (Corey Feldman) and Allan (Jason Newlander). At first he doesn't believe them and dismisses their story as an attempt to scare the new kid in town. But as soon as Patric falls prey to the teenage bloodsuckers and his mother begins dating a man who is never seen in the daylight, Haim must enlist the aid of the Frog brothers, teenage Van Helsings, to save his family.

Schumacher's unraveling of this crisp thriller is tough and involving, as he cleverly weaves moments of pure terror (like the discovery of the vampire's lair) with satiric irony (loading the boys' squirt guns with holy water).

The Lost Boys also functions on several thematic levels. On one level the film explores the paradoxical nature (vitality vs. apathy) of the punk counterculture. On another, it is an apt symbol of the period, a parable, like Stanley Kubrick's *A Clockwork Orange* (1971) that reveals something innately wrong in our culture.

The Lost Boys can hardly be considered a masterpiece, but like many flawed films, it rises occasionally to a special brilliance that outshines any other vampire film since *Fright Night.* The special makeup by Greg Cannom (particularly on Kiefer Sutherland) is stunning, and the superb rock score (by Lou Gramm, Roger Daltrey, the Inks, the Doors, and other rock groups) contributes much to the constructive scheme and style of the film. But perhaps the most remarkable quality of *The Lost Boys* is the honest portrayal of teenagers. Whereas the children in *The Monster Squad* are portrayed as one-dimensional stereotypes, the adolescents here are multifaceted and convincingly authentic in their actions and dialogue. Credit must go to both Richard Donner, who had worked so effectively with children in *The Goonies,* and Joel Shumacher, who had demonstrated his knowledge of teenage customs and mores in *St. Elmo's Fire* (1985). Even though the film falls short in other areas, it remains an interesting chronicle of one subculture.

1987 *Near Dark*

DEG Group, 87 min. Director: Kathryn Bigelow. Producers: Edward Feldman, Charles Meeker. Writers: Eric Red, Bigelow. Starring Adrian Pasdar, Jenny Wright, Lance Henrickson, Bill Paxton, Jeanette Goldstein, Joshua Miller, Tim Thomerson, Marcie Leeds.

Like *The Lost Boys,* though cinematically an entirely different film, *Near Dark* (1987) was a valiant attempt to breathe new life into the traditional vampire story. Whereas *The Lost Boys* derived its plot and thematic structure from J. M. Barrie's children's tale, *Near Dark* borrows elements from Peckinpah's *The Wild Bunch* (1969) and Miller's *Mad Max* films to create a nihilistic vampire Western. But this film is much more than a cross-pollination of classic genres. That concept was tried twenty-five years before in such films as *Curse of the Undead* (1959) and *Billy the Kid Versus Dracula* (1965), and recently in *Sundown: The Vampire in Retreat* (1989) and proved both unpopular and unsuccessful. However, *Near Dark* succeeds in the same thematic vein in which the others failed because it consciously adopts the structure of the Western while purposely discarding the trappings. The film is also laced heavily with dark humor and satire, and never takes itself too seriously.

The story begins when Caleb (Adrian Pasdar), a spirited but naive

In one hot hungry kiss
He gave her
everlasting love.
She gave him
everlasting life.

NEAR DARK

A FELDMAN/MEEKER PRODUCTION A KATHRYN BIGELOW FILM "NEAR DARK"
Written by ERIC RED & KATHRYN BIGELOW Director of Photography ADAM GREENBERG
Executive Producer STEVEN-CHARLES JAFFE Co-Producer ERIC RED
Produced by EDWARD S. FELDMAN and CHARLES R. MEEKER
Directed by KATHRYN BIGELOW © 1986 F/M ENTERTAINMENT, INC. ALL RIGHTS RESERVED AN FM ENTERTAINMENT RELEASE

Poster art from Kathryn Bigelow's nihilistic vision *Near Dark* (1987). The word *vampire* is never used in this film. Courtesy of FM Entertainment.

young man, glimpses Mae (Jenny Wright) for the first time. He is immediately attracted by her innocence and sensuality, and allows himself to be lured into a secret clan of savage vampires who prowl the night seeking victims. The leader, a veteran of the Civil War named Jesse Hooker (played superbly by chameleon Lance Henrickson), overrules the protests of the others—Severn (Bill Paxton), Diamondback (Jeanette Goldstein), and Homer (Joshua Miller)—and declares that the newcomer can join the group as long as he makes his first kill. Soon Caleb's worst nightmares unfold against the setting of the dark and desolate highways of America's heartland as the vampires coldly eliminate travelers in the night, brutally murder customers of a redneck bar, and violently shoot it out with the police. They kill without shame or mercy, and they seem unstoppable. Meanwhile, Caleb's father, Loy (Tim Thomerson), and his sister, Sarah (Marcie Leeds), dissatisfied with the efforts of the local sheriff to find him, begin their own search for Caleb. The film reaches its climax when Loy and Sarah are captured by the vampire clan and Caleb must make a choice between his biological family and his new extended family of bloodsuckers.

Thirty-five-year-old director Kathryn Bigelow, who cowrote the screenplay with Eric Red, had very definite ideas of what a modern vampire movie should be. "I call the film a vampire-Western," she said in a recent interview. "We wanted the vampires to be this group of outlaws that were sort of like modern-day gunslingers. In an effort to sort of modernize the material, we got rid of all the gothic aspects—the teeth, the bats, holy water, crosses, mirrors, all of that. We kept the most salient aspects—the burn up in sunshine, bullets don't hurt them, and they're very strong. Then we set them in the mid-west and used aspects of a Western—shootouts, showdowns at high noon, only in this case it's high midnight." The result is a film that is both chilling and fast-paced with a great deal of wit and kinetic energy behind it. (The MPAA wanted to give it an X rating for excessive violence, particularly in the barroom massacre, and Bigelow was forced to do some major reediting for its R rating.)

Unfortunately, the company which was set to release the film (before it was picked up by DEG for home video) refused to identify the immortal bloodsucking nomads as "vampires" because it didn't want the film called a "horror" movie; not once is the word *vampire* used in the film. As a result, *Near Dark* could not find the right audience and became a box-office failure. The motion picture opened in September 1987, and by year's end, had taken in (according to *Variety*) only $1,068,327 in grosses. *Near Dark* was sold immediately to home video to make up its losses and has been received by the public with lukewarm results.

Home video has given new life to several other vampire films which ordinarily would never have been released. Whereas the early seventies witnessed a decline of the horror film, the VCR and cable explosion of the eighties has opened the market wide for low-budget films, independents, or those that were simply too soft for theatrical distribution. Patrons across America, Japan, and a dozen other countries generally rent at least one film per night (from the local video store) and tape more than ten movies a week (from cable television). Since the number of A titles is limited, B (and even the lower grade Z) movies are in the greatest demand. For example, *The Toxic Avenger* (1984), produced through independent Troma films, played in only a handful of movie theatres and would have disappeared entirely had it not been for home video. The motion picture has since become the most successful independent film ever released on videocassette and has inspired a sequel, which was released theatrically as *The Toxic Avenger II* (1988). Vampire films with wildly camp titles like *Vampire of Bikini Beach* (1987), *Beverly Hills Vampire* (1988), *Dracula's Widow* (1988), *My Best Friend Is a Vampire* (1988), and *Vampire's Kiss* (1989) have followed, with mixed results.

1988 *Dracula's Widow*

DEG Group/HBO Home Video, 92 min. Director: Christopher Coppola. Writer: Tom Bloomquist. Starring Sylvia Kristel, Josef Sommer, Lenny von Dohlen, George Stover, Marc Coppola, Stefan Schnabel, Rachel Jones.

Two films which failed commercially at the box office but have become moderate successes on home video were *Dracula's Widow* (1988) and *Not of This Earth* (1988). Although the films have completely different story lines, they do share a number of striking similarities. Both were made on a limited budget; both were shot in and around Los Angeles using many of the same locations in a relatively short timespan; and both feature a former porn queen in a starring role. Neither, however, offered anything new to the vampire mythos, and had they not been released on videocassette, they would have been largely forgotten.

Dracula's Widow (1988) is derivative in parts of Hammer's *Countess Dracula* (1972) and Howard Storm's *Once Bitten* (1985) but fails to generate the interest those efforts did. Sylvia Kristel, the French porn star of *Emmanuelle* (1974) and others, plays Vanessa, Count Dracula's raven-haired widow. She relocates to California when her coffin is accidentally delivered to the Hollywood Wax Museum instead of her quiet Eastern European repose. Once there, she renews her bloodsucking ways and attracts the attention of the museum curator (Lenny von Dohlen). Victor Helsing (Stefan Schnabel), grandson of Dr. Abraham Van Helsing, uncovers evidence of Vanessa's existence and tracks her to Los Angeles to put an end to Dracula's curse once and forever. First-time director Christopher Coppola (nephew of Francis Ford Coppola) tried to make many of the formulas look fresh. "The horror film is the only genre where you can be extremely artistic and stylized, just as long as you keep it scary," he said in a recent interview. But unfortunately his film-school approach is little more than a rehash of material that had been done before—and much better.

1988 *Not of This Earth*

Concorde Release, 87 min. Director: Jim Wynorski. Producers: Wynorski, Roger Corman, Murray Miller. Writers: Wynorski, R. J. Robertson, based on a story by Charles B. Griffith and Mark Hanna. Starring Traci Lords, Arthur Roberts, Michael Delano, Monique Gabrielle.

Not of This Earth (1988) was considerably less pretentious and only slightly more satisfying than *Dracula's Widow* because it never claimed to be anything more than a remake of a 1950s B sci-fi movie. Traci Lords, the porn queen who had caused a major scandal several years before when it was revealed that she lied about her age to adult film producers, plays a nurse to an intergalactic vampire, identified as Mr. Johnson (Arthur Roberts). Johnson has come to Earth looking for isotopically pure human blood and has sought out the services of Dr. Rocelle (Michael Delano) and his pretty assistant, Nadine Story (Lords). The blood in his veins is drying up (just like the blood in the veins of his people) because of a devastating nuclear war that has turned his home world Davanna into a radioactive hell. Johnson quickly discovers that a simple transfusion will arrest the problem only temporarily and that human hosts, bred specifically for the Davannans, will be needed for a more permanent solution.

Made in twelve days on a budget that would barely pay for an hour episode of "Star Trek: The Next Generation," *Not of This Earth* is a spoofy-goofy send-up of the original 1957 Corman film. The directing by Jim Wynorski, who wrote articles for *Fangoria* magazine, is pedestrian; the acting is embarrassing (with perhaps the exception of *Penthouse* centerfold Monique Gabrielle); the makeup and special effects are laughable; and the screenplay is unintentionally funny where it should be serious. Scenes which make little sense have been cut in from *Humanoids of the Deep* (1980) to pad its length. The film also looks like a pale copy of *Horror of the Blood Creatures* (1971) and *Lifeforce—The Space Vampires* (1985), as well as its black-and-white original. However, *Not of This Earth* found renewed life on the video shelves with the curious patrons who rent Z movies like *Surf Nazis Must Die* (1987), *Sorority Babes of the Slime Bowlarama* (1988), *Galactic Gigolo* (1988), and a hundred other titles.

Several other motion pictures were not as well received, theatrically or otherwise, and are probably gathering dust (rightly so) at your local video store. The problem wasn't that the pictures were made on such a low budget, that they featured unknowns in the lead, or that they didn't take themselves too seriously, but that they were shameless copies of other films, which themselves had been problematic.

1988 *Beverly Hills Vampire*

Euphoria Productions. Director-Producer-Writer: Fred Olen Ray. Starring Britt Ekland.

1988 *Vampire of Bikini Beach*

No additional information available.

Beverly Hills Vampire (1988), from Euphoria Productions, was also strictly run-of-the-mill, with a plot and characters that closely parallel *A Polish Vampire in Burbank* (1984) and *Once Bitten* (1985). What the film needed was a humorously clever black comedian (like Eddie Murphy) in the lead. Like *Beverly Hills Vampire, Vampire of Bikini Beach* (1988) was another in the year's overabundance of "youthful" vampire films, following *The Lost Boys* and *Monster Squad*, but this one was a real low-budgeter. The vampire of Bikini Beach is an ex-surfer–ex-biker who seeks vengeance upon fellow surfers, a rival biker gang, and several bikini-clad maidens. If the acting or plot had been as campy as the title, this might have been fun to watch. But the film is not *Annette and Frankie Meet Dracula*, as it should have been, and its underlying mean spirit betrays the most ardent fan of vampire movies.

1988 *Lair of the White Witch*

Russo Productions, 89 min. Director-Producer: Ken Russell. Writer: Ken Russell, based on the novel by Bram Stoker. Starring Amanda Donohoe, Hugh Grant, Catherine Oxenberg, Peter Capaldi, Sammi Davis.

Based on a largely unknown (and unread) novel by Bram Stoker, *Lair of the White Witch* (1988) was a strange combination of paganism, witchcraft, and vampirism. In a remote corner of England's lavish Peak district, young archeologist Angus Flint (Hugh Grant) discovers a mysterious skull while digging for fossils. Some time later, when Flint escorts Eve (Amanda Donohoe) and Mary (Catherine Oxenberg) to holiday festivities at Lord

James's castle, Lady Silvia Marsh, a sensuous snake woman, steals the skull from him. She takes the skull into the castle dungeon to bring the White Worm, a pagan god, back to life. Once resurrected, he hungers for virginal blood, demanding that Eve and her friend be brought before him as human sacrifices. Throughout the film, Russell indulges his distorted view of reality in camp images which recall the best of Bava and Vadim, so much so that any attempt at storytelling has been lost to the notion of "art." *Lair of the White Witch* is less horrifying than its contemporarires, and less satisfying.

1988 *My Best Friend Is a Vampire*

HBO Home Entertainment, 90 min. Director: Jimmy Huston. Producer: Dennis Murphy. Writer: Tab Murphy. Starring Robert Sean Leonard, David Warner, Fannie Flagg, Rene Auberjonois, Cheryl Pollack.

My Best Friend Is a Vampire (1988), *Teen Vamp* (1988), *Vampire at Midnight* (1988), and *Vampire's Kiss* (1989) were also unintentional (?) remakes of earlier motion pictures. The commercial slogan for *My Best Friend*—"Vampires and teenagers are a lot alike. They're both misunderstood" was catchy, and the coffin-shaped locker used in all the promotional ads was certainly inspired. However, by the close of the opening credits, most audiences knew exactly where this film was heading. When Jeremy Capello (Robert Sean Leonard) goes to deliver groceries to the owner of a dilapidated mansion, the innocent high school student is seduced by Darla (Cheryl Pollack), the lady of the house. He falls head over heels for the older woman, not knowing she is a vampire, and her love bites turn him slowly, somewhat comically, into a vampire. At first, the transition from grocery clerk to bloodsucker is difficult, but with the help of his guardian vampire (Rene Auberjonois), Jeremy adjust to being a member of the undead. Coincidentally, Professor McCarthy (David Warner), a Dr. Van Helsing clone, and his bumbling assistant show up at Jeremy's high school looking for Darla and her vampiric friends, and of course the chase is on. Several critics were generous enough to call the film "pleasingly offbeat" when in fact *My Best Friend* is a rehash of a dozen (or so) other teen comedies, including *Once Bitten*.

1988 *Teen Vamp* (aka *Murphy Gilcrease: Teenage Vampire*)

New World Pictures.

Teen Vamp (1988) followed in a similar vein. Despite a few atmospheric shots and two (count them — *two*) suspenseful moments, it's the same old story. "Once bitten" by a vampire, the class nerd (Murphy Gilcrease) begins a transition to nocturnal bloodsucker and campus stud. This film copies not only Howard Storm's 1985 comedy but also Michael J. Fox's *Teen Wolf* (1985) and the mildly amusing *Can't Buy Me Love* (1987). For a couple of million dollars, you'd think that they could at least come up with a new slant to tell that familiar story.

1988 *Vampire at Midnight*

Independent, 100 min. Director: Gregory McCletchy. Producers: Jason Williams, Tom Friedman. Writer: Dulany Ross Clements, based on a story by Williams and Friedman. Starring Williams, Gustav Vintas, Leslie Milne, Esther Alise, Jeannie Moore, Ted Hamaguchi, Robert Random, Shendt.

Like *My Best Friend, Vampire at Midnight* (1988) also used an innovative advertising campaign. The print ads read: "He's dead . . . until dark." Producers Jason Williams and Tom Friedman were convinced that their vampire movie would be unique and ground breaking. Set against the (now quite familiar) backdrop of contemporary Los Angeles, the story concerns the efforts of Dr. Victor Radkoff (Gustav Vintas), hypnotherapist and vampire, to drain the creative energies of a community of artists. When several unexplained deaths occur, detective Jason Williams follows the trail of blood to the mad doctor. Regrettably, the same thematic ground had been covered much more successfully before in the *Count Yorga* films and the Hammer release *Theatre of Death* (1966).

1989 *Vampire's Kiss*

Hemdale Films/Tri-Star Pictures, 98 min. Director: Robert Bierman. Producers: Barbara Zitwer, Barry Shils. Writer: Joe Minion. Starring Nicholas Cage, Maria Conchita Alonso, Elizabeth Ashley, Jennifer Beals.

Vampire's Kiss (1989) was another offbeat comedy about a young man who is bitten by a female vampire. Peter Loew (Nicholas Cage), a New York literary agent, is your typical young urban professional (yuppie); he works hard and plays hard, especially with the women he picks up at Manhattan night spots. That is, until the night he picks up a hungry vampire (Jennifer Beals). She bites him on the neck in the heat of passion, and Loew begins to fantasize that he is turning into a vampire. Like Dracula's twisted servant

Nicholas Cage as Peter Loew, a demented book editor who thinks he's becoming a vampire in *Vampire's Kiss* (1989). Courtesy of Hemdale Pictures.

Renfield, he hungers after rats, pigeons, and even a roach (which Cage apparently consumes for real) to satisfy his craving for blood. Still hungry, he purchases a $3 pair of plastic novelty fangs and chases women through Greenwich Village, shouting, "I'm a vampire! I'm a vampire!" There's very little question about the outcome of the film, particularly since the crazier Loew gets, the more he begins to mimic Max Schreck's Count Orlock from *Nosferatu* (1922). (Nicholas Cage played a demented vampire in one scene of Francis Ford Coppola's *Peggy Sue Got Married* [1986].) Unfortunately, Robert Bierman's motion picture (from a script by Joe Minion) never rises above the one-joke premise, and viewers are left hungering for George Romero's much superior effort, *Martin* (1978). Even the movie's title is derivative: *Vampire's Kiss* was the title of the sleazy horror film within Brian De Palma's *Body Double* (1985), and those few scenes looked much more interesting than this entire Hemdale release.

Two films — one a low-budget Western and the other a sequel to the 1985 hit *Fright Night* — had yet to make a theatrical appearance (except to a select number of preview audiences) by the end of 1989, and their potential for success was still unmeasured.

1989 *Sundown: The Vampire in Retreat*

Vestron Entertainment, 100 min. Director: Anthony Hickox. Writers: Hickox, John Burgess. Starring David Carradine, John Ireland, Maxwell Caulfield, Bruce Campbell.

Sundown: The Vampire in Retreat (1989), from Vestron, follows in the same tradition as *Curse of the Undead* (1959) and *Billy the Kid Versus Dracula* (1966). The desert town of Purgatory, Arizona, is populated by vampires trying to kick the blood habit. Their leader, Count Mardulak (David Carradine, whose father played Dracula in the 1966 vampire Western) believes in a peaceful coexistence with humans and has devised a technological alternative to the vampire's predatory ways. However, Jefferson (John Ireland), his servant Shane (Maxwell Caulfield), and other local bullies want to return to their normal feeding habits and oppose Mardulak's plans. The two factions reach a Mexican standoff until the grandson of Dr. Van Helsing (Bruce Campbell) arrives and Purgatory's hemotechnics plant is destroyed. Then all hell breaks loose. Directed by Anthony Hickox and cowritten by Hickox and John Burgess, this film is definitely a revisionist vampire tale in keeping with the works of Anne Rice and Chelsea Quinn Yarbro. But is *Sundown* original enough to transcend the legacy of those other lackluster productions? Cowboys and vampires have made for a strange mixture in the past, and part of the motion picture's success will be contingent on whether the two clichés can work for contemporary audiences.

1989 *Fright Night II*

Vista Pictures, 96 min. Director: Tommy Lee Wallace. Producer: Herb Jaffe. Based on material by Tom Holland. Starring William Ragsdale, Jonathan Gries, Brian Thompson, Traci Lyn, Julie Carmen, Russell Clark, Merritt Buttrick, Roddy McDowall.

Fright Night II (1989), on the other hand, is the big-budget follow-up to the most successful vampire film in recent history. Although some of the novelty and charm of the original had worn off, this sequel is still quite chilling and enjoyable. This motion picture, however, almost didn't get made. Following a shake-up in the management at Columbia Pictures, the proposed sequel was shelved permanently, and Tom Holland left to direct *Fatal Beauty* (1987) and *Childsplay* (1988). But Herb Jaffe, the original film's producer, believed that he had a valuable property and moved the production to Vista Pictures. As a result, *Fright Night II* had the best box-office potential of any horror film in 1989, with theatrical prebookings well in advance of the original film.

The story picks up three years after the events in *Fright Night* (1985). Charley Brewster (William Ragsdale) is now in college and lives a relatively normal life. He is romantically involved with Alex (Traci Lyn), a beautiful psychology student, and he has been seeing a psychiatrist, who has convinced him everything that happened in the first film was a dream. Suddenly the undead sister of Jerry Dandridge appears in the guise of Regine (Julie Carmen), seeking revenge on the person who murdered her brother. She mistakenly seduces Charley's best friend, Richie (Merritt Buttrick), into the vampire life (à la *Once Bitten*), then sets a trap for the youthful vampire hunter. After a series of near misses, which includes Alex's fending off the amorous advances of Regine's "lost boys" (played by Jonathan Gries, Brian Thompson, and Russell Clark), Charley enlists the aid of horror host Peter Vincent (Roddy McDowall), who again has been fired from the television station, to battle the sexy vampiress and her personal ghouls and nasties. The climactic confrontation takes place in the gloomy basement and narrow elevator shaft of a deserted building.

The formula of horrific thrills laced with humor that made *Fright Night* a box-office champion is developed skillfully in this impressive sequel. Directed by Tommy Lee Wallace (who made his directoral debut with the disappointing *Halloween III*, 1984), *Fright Night II* is well staged and moves along at a chilling, breakneck pace. There is also a punk, new-wave element in the film (which seems to have been influenced by *The Lost Boys*), but it seems to contribute to the characterization and 1980s feel rather than detract. Another quality that makes this motion picture memorable is the first-rate makeup by Greg Cannom and his assistants, Bart Mixon and Brian Wade. When asked about *Fright Night II* and the enduring popularity of vampire films, Wallace replied: "I think that people just like to be scared, and vampire legends have been around a long time. The latest rebirth of the vampire craze is simply due to a handful of very good pictures." *Fright Night II* is more than just a very good film; it is the latest in a long legacy of cinematic nightmares that can trace their ancestry back to *The Devil's Castle* (1896).

1990 *Dracula: The Love Story* (aka *To Die For*)

Skouras Pictures, 94 min. Director: Deran Sarafian. Producers: Greg Sims, Basin Kumar. Writer: Leslie King, based on an original story by Sims. Starring Brendan Hughes, Sidney Walsh, Amanda Wyss, Duane Jones, Scott Jacoby.

Greg Sims's *Dracula: The Love Story* (released on home video as *To Die For*) was perhaps the strangest entry in the lucrative vampire film market. Touted as an updating of Bram Stoker's classic by way of *Romeo and Juliet*, the screen story focused on a young, virile Vlad Tepes (Brendan Hughes) and his attempts to win Kate (Amanda Wyss), the love of his life, from his rival. For two hundred years they had stalked each other in the far corners of the world, and the final showdown occurs when Vlad resurfaces in Los Angeles with a new look and lifestyle. The *Los Angeles Times* called the motion picture "gripping," but it was far more than that. The romantic tale, though not written for fans of old horror movies, raises this effort above the ordinary. Unfortunately, the blood and gore of the final confrontation between vampiric rivals overshadows what could have been a superior entry.

1990 *Red-Blooded American Girl*

Canadian, Paramount Pictures, 89 min. Director: David Blyth. Producer: Nicolas Stiliadis. Writer: Allan Moyle. Starring Christopher Plummer, Andrew Stevens, Heather Thomas.

Although the concept of a scientifically created vampire dates back to Bogart's *Return of Dr. X* (1939), the first half of *Red-Blooded American Girl* (1990) was still very interesting to watch. Mad scientist John Alcore (Christopher Plummer) has been conducting a genetics experiment in life extension. On the verge of a major breakthrough, something goes wrong (doesn't it always?) with the formula and transforms his volunteer subject, Paula (Heather Thomas), into a vampire. Predictably, she fails to deal with her blood lust and seeks out male victims to satisfy her unholy cravings. Owen Urban (Andrew Stevens), a young pharmaceutical wiz, is brought in to help and falls madly in love with Paula. The rest of the picture follows a familiar path that even a five-year-old could guess. This Canadian-American coproduction was so poorly received that it went straight to the home video market.

1990 *Rockula*

Cannon Entertainment Group, 90 min. Director: Luca Bercovici. Producer: Jeffrey Levy. Writers: Bercovici, Levy, Christopher Verwiel. Starring Dean Cameron, Tawny Fere, Susan Tyrrell, Bo Diddley, Thomas Dolby.

Rockula (1990) was a dumb low-budget movie that lasted about a week in the theaters before being banished to the home video shelves. Every few decades, three-hundred-year-old vampire, rocker, virgin Ralph (Dean Cameron) is doomed to watch his would-be girlfriend Mona get clubbed to death by a crazy pirate with a large hambone. This decade, he decides to take matters into his own hands and stop his evil rival before it's too late.

From the director of *Ghoulies*, this vampire film is better left buried at the video store.

1992 *Bram Stoker's Dracula* (aka *Dracula: The Untold Story*)

Columbia Pictures/American Zoetrope, 120 min. Director-Producer: Francis Ford Coppola. Writer: James Hart, based on the original novel by Bram Stoker. Starring Gary Oldman, Anthony Hopkins, Keanu Reeves, Winona Ryder, Richard E. Grant, Sadie Frost, Cary Elwes, Bill Campbell, Tom Waits.

Bram Stoker's Dracula (1992) provides an erotic spin on time-honored classic vampire tale by casting the Transylvanian Count as a lovesick nobleman. The object of his desire is Mina Murray, the living embodiment of his long dead wife. Estimated to cost $35–40 million, Francis Ford Coppola's remake may well go down as the most expensive vampire film to date. At this writing, the production was scheduled to begin shooting in late August 1991, but the start date was pushed back to October 14, 1991, when production designer Dante Ferretti's grandly gothic sets would finally be completed at the Culver City lot. Anthony Hopkins, fresh from his role as Hannibal the Cannibal in *The Silence of the Lambs*, plays an obsessed Dr. Van Helsing; Winona Ryder, who had to withdraw from Coppola's third *Godfather* film, plays Mina; Keanu Reeves is a youthful Jonathan Harker; and Gary Oldman (seen recently as Lee Harvey Oswald in Oliver Stone's *JFK*) is a virile Count Dracula.

Based on the original source material by Bram Stoker, the new film follows a familiar outline. Count Dracula, a lonely but charismatic vampire, journeys from his homeland in Transylvania to London, drawn by an innocent young woman who is the miraculous double image of the love he lost four centuries earlier. But that is where the familiarity to the previous Dracula films (which were all based on a 1920s play by Hamilton Deane) ends.

"The original novel is written as a fragment of diaries . . . a Victorian horror story," Coppola explained. "Stoker's innovation was to use a real historical figure — a great king, the founder of Bucharest — but all the same a fourteenth-century man who impaled people on spikes. At the same time, we are aware that many elements commonly used in Victorian storytelling are perceived by modern audiences as camp, so we will be taking a more modern approach to what is shocking. This film will be scary."

Michael Ballhaus, the Oscar-nominated cinematographer for *Broadcast News,* has photographed the film with a visual style that suggests Victorian London, and internationally renowned designer Eiko Ishioka has created costumes that are museum quality. But regardless of how the film looks visually, the production ultimately falls upon the shoulders of the title character — Dracula.

"Women always tells us that Dracula is all buildup but never does anything." Coppola revealed the shortcomings of previous adaptations, and promised more from his film. "This Dracula does something! The story also explores the motivations of this creature who has traits we all carry at least to some degree . . . the essence of the vampire: the psychological hunger."

Seventy years ago, a midnight train first left the Transylvania station (with F. W. Murnau's classic *Nosferatu*, 1922). Francis Ford Coppola's new film follows that long tradition of motion pictures inspired by Bram Stoker's *Dracula*.

1992 *Buffy, the Vampire Slayer*
20th Century–Fox/Sandollar/Kuzui Enterprises, 93 min. Director: Fran Rubel Kuzui. Producers: Kaz Kuzui and Howard Rosenman. Writer: Joss Whedon. Starring Kristy Swanson, Don Sutherland, Paul Reubens, Rutger Hauer, Luke Perry.

Derivative of *Captain Kronos — Vampire Hunter, Heathers, Bill and Ted's Excellent Adventure*, and *The Lost Boys*, Fran Rubel Kuzui's *Buffy, the Vampire Slayer* finds the titular character (played by Kristy Swanson) posing as a Valley Girl by day and a vampire hunter at night in this 1992 teen spoof. Buffy is, at first, hesitant to accept her lethal role, but soon learns that she has been slaying vampires for centuries in a variety of guises. She is joined in her quest to rid a Los Angeles suburb of the Romanian vampires (Rutger Hauer and Paul Reubens) by the town bad boy ("Beverly Hills, 90210"'s brooding Luke Perry) and a batty character named the Watcher (Donald Sutherland). "In a subversive way, it's really the story of a woman accepting responsibility and leadership," explained Sandollar's Howard Rosenman, who co-produces the comic romp with the director's husband, Kaz Kuzui.

1992 *Innocent Blood*
Warner Brothers/Lee Rich Productions. Director: John Landis. Producer: John Sheinberg. Executive Producer: Lee Rich. Writer: Michael Wolk, based on his original story. Starring Anne Parillaud, Anthony LaPaglia, Robert Loggia, Don Rickles.

Innocent Blood, written by Michael Wolk, is a black comedy about a sexy female vampire with a conscience who feeds only on killers. One of her most ruthless victims, a mob chieftain, survives her vampiric attack only to be transformed into an even more powerful vampire. Realizing that the mob boss is now killing innocent victims to satisfy his blood lust, the female vampire enlists the help of a disbelieving cop to help destroy him.

Purchased by Lee Rich Productions for the exorbitant price of $500,000 for release through Warner Brothers, *Innocent Blood* may well be the most expensive independent production in the works for 1992 release. "We didn't buy this script because we thought vampire scripts were hot (which they are)," said Lee Rich. "We bought it because it was a great script that we liked a lot."

Despite the preponderance of other vampire films currently in production, Jon Sheinberg, president of motion pictures at Lee Rich Productions, remains hopeful that their project will find its audience. "I don't know that vampire movies are appealing," Sheinberg explained in a recent interview, "but you see a trend in the industry where films with archetypal characters with a twist look promising and profitable."

Only time will tell if this film, which promises to be different from other cinematic nightmares because of its stylistic approach, can survive the competition of these few films and the fifteen others in production.

"There will always be vampire movies until a stake is driven through the heart of every producer in Hollywood." This old adage may well be true as long as the film studios continue to make cinematic nightmares. Clearly, *Graveyard Shift*, *The Lost Boys*, and *Near Dark* were the most serious attempts by filmmakers to impose contemporary ideas on the vampire film, and although the three films showed skill and intellect, not one of them was a serious competitor for box-office revenue. They succeed as cinematic nightmares to the degree they fail as successors to *Fright Night*'s large commercial audience. (*The Lost Boys* was moderately successful as a late summer entry, but business dropped off dramatically by early September and the beginning of school.) The three films were in fact squarely opposed to the traditions of previous vampire movies while attempting to advance a style and spirit of their own.

On the other hand, *Vamp*, *Return to Salem's Lot*, *The Monster Squad*, *My Best Friend Is a Vampire*, and *Dracula's Widow* were closer to the traditions and substance of *Fright Night*, but they were even less successful. The only successor to that tradition (and box-office revenue) was the sequel *Fright Night II*. Future productions will have to chart an uncertain course between the two extremes to satisfy the audience and be commercially viable. Of the many films currently in production, only a few have the chance to cash in on that market. Fangoria Film's *Children of the Night* will probably be the first of those new releases. Touted as a unique horror film, the story chronicles the takeover of a small town by vampiric children.

Following closely on its heels, both Lamberto Bava's *Dinner with a Vampire* and *Heartstopper* (with Tom Savino) are scheduled to debut in the spring of 1993. *Demon Prince: Genesis of the Vampire* and *The Lost Platoon* had limited releases in 1991 and were slated for wider distribution both theatrically and on home video later.

Others, like Rosco Pollenberg's new version of *I Am Legend*, John Russo's Civil War vampire tale *The Awakening*, Anne Rice's *The Vampire Trilogy*, George Hamilton's *Love at Second Bite: Dracula Goes to Las Vegas* (written by Robert Kaufman, directed by Stan Dragoti, and produced by George Schlatter), Warner Brother's sequel to *The Lost Boys*, New World's *They Thirst* (written by Robert McCammon), *Sherlock Holmes Versus Dracula* (with Tony Randall and Sid Caesar), *Dance of the Damned*, *Pale Blood*, and *Subspecies*, were (at this writing) in various stages of production. Some of the films will undoubtedly adhere to the traditional concepts and approaches of the vampire movie, while others may discard the irrelevant patterns of the past and adopt a new distinctive and provocative style in quest of the cinematic nightmare.

Appendix A
Vampire Films in 1993

1993 *Nightland*

Paramount Pictures. Director: Andrew Birkin. Producers: Steve Meerson, Peter Krikes. Executive Producer: Bernie Brillstein. Writers: John Ries, Cory Tynan. (Cast to be decided.)

When Paramount Pictures let the option to Anne Rice's vampire trilogy fall to Lorimar (and finally to Warner Brothers), former studio chairman Frank Mancuso may have lost one of the most high-profile projects in decades. Thus, when another hot vampire tale became available, Paramount outbid Touchstone, Geffen, and others by paying a reported $500,000 to John Ries and Cory Tynan for their *Nightland*. The story concerns the night world of the vampire community in a modern city and the struggle of two feuding groups (one good, one evil) to control a rare substance.

"I'm the last person in the world you think would do a vampire film — although I work with them every day," said executive producer Bernie Brillstein in a recent interview. "We brought the Anne Rice trilogy to Lorimar, before it became a best-seller, but that will be a film on a very different level than this one. *Nightland* is a reality-based action film with a special twist and features a brand new kind of hero. You must take people to a place where they have never been before in order to have a hit and the world of the vampire has not been examined correctly. It's always B or C exploitation movies—other than the classics—and you wouldn't expect a movie dealing with a vampire to be an A movie from a major."

Producer Steve Meerson said he was drawn to the project not because it was a vampire film but "because it was a story that could happen to anyone." He further stated that in *Nightland* the problems are not necessarily about being a vampire but about being human, "with the vampires becoming a metaphor for the human condition."

The film is currently in preproduction stages at Paramount Pictures and should debut in the winter of 1993.

1993 *Red Sleep*
Silver Pictures/Warner Brothers. Producers: Michael Levy, George Jackson, Doug McHenry. Writers: Mick Garris, Richard Christian Matheson, based on their original story. Cast and other crew to be decided.

Red Sleep, from the creative team who made *Bill and Ted's Excellent Adventure* and *Bill and Ted's Bogus Journey* into box-office bonanzas, is a hard-hitting thriller about bloodsuckers who threaten visitors to a contemporary American city. The story details the efforts of a recovering alcoholic to beat a much more deadly addiction to vampirism. When the alcoholic visits Las Vegas for an important business conference, he is bitten by a beautiful vampire and slowly drawn into a vampire subculture of the city that plays all night.

Michael Levy, chief executive for fledgling Silver Pictures, described *Red Sleep* as "an action/adventure vampire film." He further stated in a recent interview that the film would "have credibility and a reality base and do for vampires what *Rosemary's Baby* did for witchcraft and what *The Exorcist* did for demonic possession. We often equate Las Vegas with vampirism, and *Red Sleep* will be a commentary on contemporary America with vampirism and Vegas representing greed, addiction and compulsion in this decade—and how we can be victimized by it."

Though comparisons to *The* (original) *Night Stalker* may seem appropriate, Levy is quick to point out that Silver Pictures intends to make a top-notch film that is "seductive, sexy, and deals with a lot of myth and lore that hasn't been focused on in recent cinematic entries. We will do it with great special effects and opticals in a way that it hasn't been done before—coupled with a lot of resonance, irony, and humor as well as a commentary on this society."

Because Mick Garris and Richard Christian Matheson had just recently completed the final draft of the screenplay, *Red Sleep* was ready to begin filming late in 1991, with possible release in 1993.

1993 *Blue Blood*

Largo Entertainment/Robert Lawrence Productions. Producer: Robert Lawrence. Writer: John Fasano, based on his original story. Cast and other crew to be decided.

Nick Knight (1989) may not have been the final word about police officials who turn into creatures of the night. John Fasano, the young scenarist who contributed the script for *Another 48 Hours*, has written a compelling story about a Seattle cop who (while working on a homicide case) is bitten by a vampire and slowly becomes one. Ultimately the transformation makes him a better policeman and lover.

"It's a unique combination of law enforcement and vampirism," said Robert Lawrence of his new action thriller *Blue Blood*, forgetting the made-for-television movie which featured Rick Springfield. The traditional appeal of the vampire, continued the producer, is that he is "the personification of man's most primal forces — sexuality, death, and rebirth — and vampire films are an obvious exploration of our dark side."

Blue Blood promises to be an action police thriller, like *Another 48 Hours*, with a single supernational element added for depth. "The traditional gothic portrayals have become quaint and lost their currency," Lawrence explained with modest enthusiasm. "Thus, putting vampires in action films places them in a genre that is immediately accessible to a contemporary audience. We are simply taking away his cape and giving him a cop uniform."

Robert Lawrence believes the new resurgence of vampire films has much to do with the type of society in which we live. "I think there is a strong sociological connection between vampirism and the new conservatism, traditionalism, and a concern about AIDS. The vampire is a subversive character, literally an underground character, who is sexually promiscuous and associated with death. Maybe there is also some unconscious association with Victorian times and the emergence of traditional values on one hand and the vampire's behavior becoming the romanticization of what we can no longer do (on the other)."

Currently in development, *Blue Blood* should be ready for release in 1993.

1993 *Dracula Rising* and *To Sleep with a Vampire*

Roger Corman Productions. Producer: Roger Corman. Cast and other crew to be decided.

Roger Corman, the legendary producer of *Little Shop of Horrors* and *The Tomb of Ligeia*, jumps on the vampire bandwagon with not one but two new features. *Dracula Rising* tells the story of a medical researcher who time travels to 19th century Transylvania in order to seek out the advice of Count Dracula. *To Sleep with a Vampire* is about a vampire who coerces a strip-tease artist to exchange bodies with him so that he can experience the sunlight. Both films are scheduled for a 1993 release.

1993 *Dressed for Dark*

Director-Writer: Dave DeCoteau. Cast and other crew to be decided.

Dressed for Dark promises to be a sexy thriller about several Transylvania models who moonlight as "vampire call girls" in Los Angeles. Written and directed by Dave DeCoteau, who made the infamous *Dr. Alien*, the $3 million production has already engaged some of the talent responsible for the early Hammer Films. DeCoteau is also searching for "the quintessential *femme fatales*" to play his three vampires in what is heralded as "the most sexually bold horror film of the year."

1993 *The Reluctant Vampire*

Director-Writer: Malcolm Marmorstein. Screenplay adapted from his original stage play. Starring Adam Ant.

As *The Reluctant Vampire*, rock musician Adam Ant tries to make the woman he loves happy by reforming and becoming a young, urban professional. Malcolm Marmorstein, the film's director and writer, based the script on his Off-Off Broadway comedy from the seventies.

1993 *Valerie*

Director-Writer: Jay Lind. Based on Joseph Sheridan Le Fanu's *Carmilla*. Cast and other crew to be decided.

Described as a cross between *The Vampire Lovers* and *Lemora, Lady Dracula*, Jay Lind's *Valerie* examines the life of a trouble teen, obsessed with horror films, who believes she's becoming a vampire. She is, in fact, the victim of an ages-old bloodsucker who wishes to take her as a lesbian lover.

Appendix B
The Ten Best and Worst

During the summer of 1988, an independent survey of film students, critics, moviegoers, and several horror writers was taken to determine the ten all-time great vampire films. At the same time, a survey to determine the ten worst vampire films was taken, independently of the first. The results of that survey, along with the single best comment, were tabulated, and compiled into the following list. The films are shown in chronological order.

The Ten Best Vampire Films

1. *Nosferatu* (1922): "The first adaptation of Bram Stoker's classic!"
2. *London After Midnight* (1927): "Lon Chaney's last great movie monster — a vampire."
3. *Dracula* (1931): "The one (and only) Bela Lugosi as Dracula."
4. *Vampyr* (1932): "The textbook on cinematic nightmares."
5. *Horror of Dracula* (1958): "The first full-color vampire movie Hammer-style, with winning performances from Lee and Cushing."
6. *The Fearless Vampire Killers* (1967): "The best parody of Hammer-horror and vampires."
7. *The Night Stalker* (1972): "The highest-rated and most terrifying made-for-television movie."

8. *Martin* (1978): "George Romero's dark vision of human psychosis."
9. *The Hunger* (1983): "Chic, new wave approach to vampirism."
10. *Fright Night* (1985): "At last, a return to the traditional vampire story."

The Ten Worst Vampire Movies

1. *Abbott and Costello Meet Frankenstein* (1948): "The one film singularly responsible for the degradation and decline of the horror film."
2. *Old Mother Riley Meets the Vampire* (1952): "Lugosi and a drag queen — how the mighty have fallen."
3. *Plan Nine from Outer Space* (1959): "Probably one of the worst movies ever made."
4. *Billy the Kid Versus Dracula* (1965): "A vampire-Western? You've got to be kidding!"
5. *Orgy of the Damned* (1966): "Cheap, exploitative Edward D. Wood crap!"
6. *Blood for Dracula* (1974): "Pretentious dribble (disguised as art) aimed at the sadomasochistic freak market."
7. *The Legend of the Seven Golden Vampires* (1974): "Kung fu and vampires — the worst of Hammer's films."
8. *Dracula's Dog* (1976): "Better left at the dog pound."
9. *Vampire Hookers* (1978): "Sexploitation!"
10. *The Monster Squad* (1987): "The film succeeds in setting the form back nearly forty years."

Appendix C
Proposed Films Never Made

During my extensive research, I discovered three vampire film projects that for one reason or another were never made. On all three, the script had been finished, an announcement of casting and production had appeared in *Variety*, and filming was set to commense on a particular date, but they were simply not made. The projects are listed below in chronological order.

1975 *Dracula Walks the Night*

Warner Brothers/Hammer Films. Director: Terence Fisher. Producers: Anthony Hinds, Anthony Nelson Keyes. Writers: Jimmy Sangster, Richard Matheson. Starring Christopher Lee, Peter Cushing, Barbara Shelley, Michael Gough, Ronald Lewis, Ferdy Mayne, Andrew Kier, Jack McGowran, Michael Gwyn, James Donald, Michael Ripper, and Jack Palance as Macatta, Dracula's slave and disciple.

The film proposed to remake the original *Dracula* by Bram Stoker, using historical material to trace the vampire's origin to the Hungarian Prince Vlad Dracul, the infamous impaler. The story would then shift to 1895 when Dr. Van Helsing (Cushing, of course) enlists the aid of Sherlock Holmes

(James Donald) and Dr. Watson (Michael Ripper) to fight the evil of Dracula. The shooting was to take place at the MGM/EMI studios in Great Britain and was to have been the ultimate Dracula story. But apparently Christopher Lee had hung up his vampire cape for the last time in favor of more serious roles, and Hammer Films, on its last financial legs, was unable to put the project together. What a shame! Sherlock Holmes versus Dracula would have been a novel addition to the Hammer *Dracula* series.

1979 *Interview with the Vampire*
Paramount Pictures. Director: Nicholas Roeg. Producer: Richard Sylbert. Writers: Frank De Felitta, Anne Rice, based on her novel. Starring Mick Jagger, David Bowie, Jon Voight, Peter O'Toole.

Based on the popular revisionist vampire novel by Anne Rice, the film would have told the story of a vampire family living through the ages. The focus would have been to examine the sexual, Freudian, and emotional trama involved in accepting immortality. Interesting concept, but Paramount was unable to sign either Bowie or Jagger (or both) to play lead roles, and vampire films were becoming less important in the public eye. Several years later, however, Paramount did manage to produce a vampirelike story (*The Keep*), and Bowie did play John Blaylock, the victim-servant-lover of a vampire in *The Hunger*. Renewed interest in vampires has made the Anne Rice series popular subjects again for the cinema.

1981 *Divorce, Vampire Style*
AIP. Director-Writer: Stan Dragoti. Starring George Hamilton, Susan St. James, Arte Johnson.

The film was to have been a sequel to the popular *Love at First Bite* (1979), picking up the action in Rio de Janeiro. Dracula (George Hamilton) and his new bride (Susan St. James) find after a number of vampire arguments that they are ill-suited for each other. They file for divorce, vampire style. Like its predecessor, the film would have been a campy send-up of both vampire films and sex comedies. However, the stars became unavailable, and the project fell through. A new sequel has recently been announced, so it is possible that George Hamilton's campy Count Dracula will return again.

Appendix D
Dracula, the Stage Play

Bram Stoker's *Dracula* (published in 1897) was not made into a stage play until 1924 when actor-manager Hamilton Deane adapted it. (Stoker, in his capacity as a second-rate actor and theatrical manager, had written a version in 1898 which he hoped to produce prior to his death, but he was unable to raise the funds.) Deane had read the book a number of years before and thought that it would make an excellent play. However, the rights had fallen to Stoker's widow, and after the debacle over Murnau's *Nosferatu* (1922), she was hesitant to lend her support to any projects. Deane remained persistent and finally convinced her with a sample scene.

Following a successful test run at the Little Theatre in Scotland, the play opened in London at the Prince of Wales Theatre. It was an instant success, and played for more than 250 performances. Deane then revised his play for New York, collaborating with American playwright John L. Balderston. The newly revised version opened on Broadway in October 1927 and starred a Hungarian immigrant (Bela Lugosi) in the title role. The play received rave reviews and broke all existing box office records during its initial run.

The play *Dracula* has since played successfully on Broadway three times, featuring Frank Langella, Martin Landau, and others in the title role, and it has inspired two screen adaptations, one in 1931 and one in 1979. Although the book has been filmed often, the play remains a special classic.

LITTLE THEATRE

JOHN STREET, ADELPHI, STRAND

Licensed by the Lord Chamberlain to JOSÉ G. LEVY   Lessee: JOSÉ G. LEVY

MONDAY, FEBRUARY 14th, at 8.30

By arrangement with JOSÉ G. LEVY and HENRY MILLAR

HAMILTON DEANE and H. L. WARBURTON

PRESENT

THE VAMPIRE PLAY

"DRACULA"

By

HAMILTON DEANE

Adapted from BRAM STOKER'S Famous Novel

PROGRAMME

Top: Bram Stoker, the author of *Dracula*. *Bottom:* Program from the original play.

ACT I.	..	The Study of Jonathan Harker's House on Hampstead Heath (Evening)
ACT II.	..	Mrs. Harker's Boudoir (Night)
ACT III.	..	The Study of Jonathan Harker's House (Afternoon)
EPILOGUE	..	The Coach House at Carfax (6 p.m.)

There will be an Interval of ten minutes after Act I, twelve minutes after Act II, and no interval
between Act III and the Epilogue.

Play produced by HAMILTON DEANE

Furniture by LYON & Co.

General Manager	..		..	ALBERT KAVANAGH
Stage Director ..	..	For Hamilton Deane and	.. ..	LODGE PERCY
Stage Manager ..	..	H. L. Warburton	.. ..	JACK HOWARTH
Assistant Stage Manager			.. ..	BERNARD GUEST

ISABEL HIRSTFIELD, of the Albert Hall and Queen's Hall Concerts,
will play selections from the following during the intervals :

1.	Prelude C Minor ...	...	...	...	.. *Glière*
2.	Sonata Tragica ...	...	...	...	*Macdowell*
3.	Preludes ...	...	...	...	... *Chopin*
4.	Rhapsody	...	...	...	*Dohnanyi*
5.	Scherzo E flat Minor	...	...	...	*Brahms*
6.	Fantasie-Impromptu	...	...	...	... *Chopin*
7.	Danse Rituelle du Feu	...	...	...	*de Falla*
	(pour chasser les mauvais esprits)				
8.	Hungarian Rhapsody No. 8	...	...	... *Liszt*
9.	Au Printemps	...	...	...	*Grieg*
10.	Slovakia ...	...	...	...	... *Novak.*

ERARD GRAND PIANO.

A Bell will ring in the Lounge Two Minutes before the curtain rises.

| Manager | .. | (For José G. Levy & Henry Millar) | .. | Miss MARY GROVES |

EXTRACTS FROM THE RULES MADE BY THE LORD CHAMBERLAIN.—The name of
the actual and responsible Manager of the Theatre must be printed on every play
bill. The Public can leave the Theatre at the end of the Performance by all exit
and entrance doors, which must open outwards.

Where there is a fireproof screen to the proscenium opening, it must be lowered
at least once during every Performance to ensure its being in proper working order.
Smoking is not permitted in the auditorium. All gangways, passages and staircases
must be kept free from chairs or any other obstructions, whether permanent or
temporary.

| Box Office | .. | .. | .. | (Open 10 to 10) | .. | .. | .. | E. G. NORMAN |

Summary of Acts 1, 2, 3, and epilogue makes the stage play appear like a "drawing-room mystery."

A new version of the Dracula story written by horror fan and first-time playwright Ron Magid recently opened in Los Angeles at the Globe Theatre. *Dracula Tyrannus: The Tragical History of Vlad the Impaler* examines (as you might expect from the title) the fifteenth-century historical figure rather than the vampire envisioned by Bram Stoker. Vlad Tepes was said to have killed 100,000 of his countrymen (by impaling them on large stakes) during his brutal reign of terror in Wallachia, and that horrific story is ambitiously retold in some forty-two separate scenes. Featuring Chris Nixon in the lead, the play received rave reviews when it was mounted for a two-week pre–Halloween run in 1988 and seems destined for the silver screen. Other vampiric plays, like Justin Tanner's *Red Tide* (about a vampire who contracts AIDS), the comedic *Lesbian Vampires of Sodom,* and Goodman-Ashman's musical adaptation of *Little Shop of Horrors,* have played off–Broadway to mixed reviews but strong box-office returns.

Appendix E
Vampire Film Trivia

Questions

1. What actor has portrayed Dracula, or a vampire, most often for the silver screen?

2. Excluding the spoofs, sequels, and X-rated films, how many times has Bram Stoker's classic novel *Dracula* been made into a film (motion picture or television)?

3. What other classic vampire novel has been adapted the most often for the screen?

4. How many times, between 1896 and 1991, has the word *vampire* been used in a film title? *Dracula*? *Blood*?

5. What famous actor was actually buried in his vampire cloak and costume?

6. Peter Cushing has played the intrepid Dr. Van Helsing or a similar vampire hunter in at least seven films. Can you name two other actors who have played the eminent vampirologist?

309

7. Name two other famous vampire hunters.

8. Which film company has produced the most vampire films?

9. Has horror great Vincent Price ever played a vampire?

10. Have any films been made about the historical Dracula?

Answers

1. Christopher Lee, fourteen times (to date), in *Horror of Dracula* (1958), *Uncle Was a Vampire* (1960), *Dracula — Prince of Darkness* (1966), *The Magic Christian* (1967, parodying his role as Dracula), *Dracula Has Risen from the Grave* (1968), *One More Time* (1969, parodying his role as Dracula), *Taste the Blood of Dracula* (1969), *Scars of Dracula* (1970), *In Search of Dracula* (1971), *Count Dracula* (1972), *Dracula A.D. 1972* (1972), *The Satanic Rites of Dracula* (1973), *Tendre Dracula* (1974), and *Dracula and Son* (1976). John Carradine, nine times. Bela Lugosi, six times (including his last screen appearance in *Plan Nine from Outer Space*, 1959).

2. Eleven times (to date), in *Nosferatu* (1922), *Dracula* (1931), *Dracula* (Spanish-language version, 1931), *Horror of Dracula* (1958), *Ahkea Kkots* (1961), *Count Dracula* (1972, *El Conde Dracula*), *Dracula* (1973, CBS), *Count Dracula* (1978, PBS), *Dracula* (1979), *Nosferatu* (1979), and *Bram Stoker's Dracula* (1992).

3. *Carmilla*, by Joseph Sheridan Le Fanu, six times, in *Vampyr* (1932), *Blood and Roses* (1961), *Crypt of the Incubus* (1963), *Blood and Black Lace* (1964), *The Vampire Lovers* (1970), and *Carmilla* (1989, Showtime). (Plus a 1976 opera and three others which are considered loose adaptations: *Vampyros Lesbos* [1970], *The Blood-Spattered Bride* [1972], and *Daughter of Dracula* [1971].)

Alraune by Hanns Heinz Ewers was adapted for the screen five times — twice in 1918, once in 1928, 1930, and 1952. *I Am Legend* by Richard Matheson is a distant third — two times, in *The Last Man on Earth* (1964) and *The Omega Man* (1971) (with a third adaptation in preproduction stages and an inspiration credit to Romero's *Night of the Living Dead*, 1968).

4. Vampire: 1046 times. Dracula: 62 times. Blood: 32 times.

5. Bela Lugosi.

6. Edward Van Sloan, in *Dracula* (1931) and *Dracula's Daughter* (1936) (as well as the first theatrical production in the United States).

Andrew Kier, in *Dracula, Prince of Darkness* (1966).
Herbert Lom, in *Count Dracula* (1972).
Nigel Davenport, in *Dracula* (1973, CBS).
Frank Finlay, in *Count Dracula* (1978, PBS) and a similar role in *Lifeforce — The Space Vampires* (1985).
Richard Benjamin, in *Love at First Bite* (1979).
Sir Laurence Olivier, in *Dracula* (1979).

7. Carl Kolchak (Darren McGavin), in *The Night Stalker* (1972, ABC) and "Kolchak: The Night Stalker" (1974, ABC).
Captain Kronos (Horst Janson), in *Captain Kronos, Vampire Hunter* (1972).
David Gray (Julien West), in *Vampyr* (1932).
And many, many others!

8. Hammer Films: sixteen (to date).

9. No. He played the "last man on earth" trying to survive in a world of vampires in *The Last Man on Earth* (1964) and the lonely lover awaiting his vampiric wife in *Tomb of Ligeia* (1964). On television, he had a cameo appearance on "F-Troop" (1965, CBS) as a vampire, but never in the movies.

10. One film. Vlad Tepes was portrayed by Christopher Lee in the documentary *In Search of Dracula* (1971) (although many recent Dracula movies feature references to the Romanian despot).

Selected Bibliography

Andrews, Nigel. *Horror Films.* New York: Gallery Books, 1985.
Ashley, Mike. *Who's Who in Horror and Fantasy Fiction.* New York: Taplinger, 1978.
Aylesworth, Thomas G. *Monsters from the Movies.* New York: Bantam Skylark Books, 1972.
Butler, Ivan. *Horror in the Cinema.* New York: Paperback Library, 1971.
Clarens, Carlos. *Horror Movies.* London: Secker and Warburg, 1968.
Cohen, Daniel. *Horror in the Movies.* New York: Houghton Mifflin, 1982.
Di Franco, J. Philip, ed. *The Movie World of Roger Corman.* New York: Chelsea House, 1979.
Edelson, Edward. *Great Monsters of the Movies.* New York: Doubleday, 1973.
Everson, William Keith. *Classics of the Horror Film.* New York: Citadel Press, 1974.
Famous Monsters of Filmland magazine. Forrest J Ackerman, ed. Philadelphia: Warren Publishing, 1958.
Franklin, Joe. *Classics of the Silent Screen.* New York: Citadel Press, 1959.
Glut, Donald. *The Dracula Book.* Metuchen, N.J.: Scarecrow Press, 1975.
Haining, Peter, ed. *The Dracula Scrapbook.* New York: Bramhall House, 1976.
Halliwell, Leslie. *Halliwell's Film Guide.* New York: Scribner's, 1984.
Huss, Roy Gerard. *Focus on the Horror Film.* New York: Prentice-Hall, 1972.
King, Stephen. *Dance Macabre.* New York: Berkeley, 1982.
Kraucauer, Sigfried. *From Caligari to Hitler.* Princeton, N.J.: Princeton University Press, 1964.
Kyrou, Ado. *Le Surréalisme au cinéma.* Paris: 1964.
Laclos, Michael. *Le Fantastique au cinéma.* Paris: 1958.
Lee, Walt. *Reference Guide to Fantastic Films.* Los Angeles: Chelsea-Lee Books, 1978.
Ludlum, Harry. *A Biography of Dracula — The Life Story of Bram Stoker.* London: Fireside Press, 1962.

Monsterland magazine, nos. 1–6. Forrest J Ackerman, ed. Los Angeles: New Media
    Publishing.
Neergaard, Ebbe. *Carl Dreyer.* London: British Film Institute, 1950.
Sadoul, Georges. *Georges Méliès.* Paris: 1961.
Settel, Irving. *A Pictorial History of Television.* New York: Frederick Ungar, 1983.
Stanley, John. *The Creature Features Movie Guide.* New York: Warner Books, 1981.
Terrace, Vincent. *Complete Encyclopedia of Television Programs.* New York: A. S.
    Barnes, 1979.
Thorne, Ian. *Monsters Series: Dracula.* Mankato, Minn.: Crestwood House, 1977.

Index of Films

Alternate titles follow date.